IMAGES
of Rail

East Broad Top Railroad

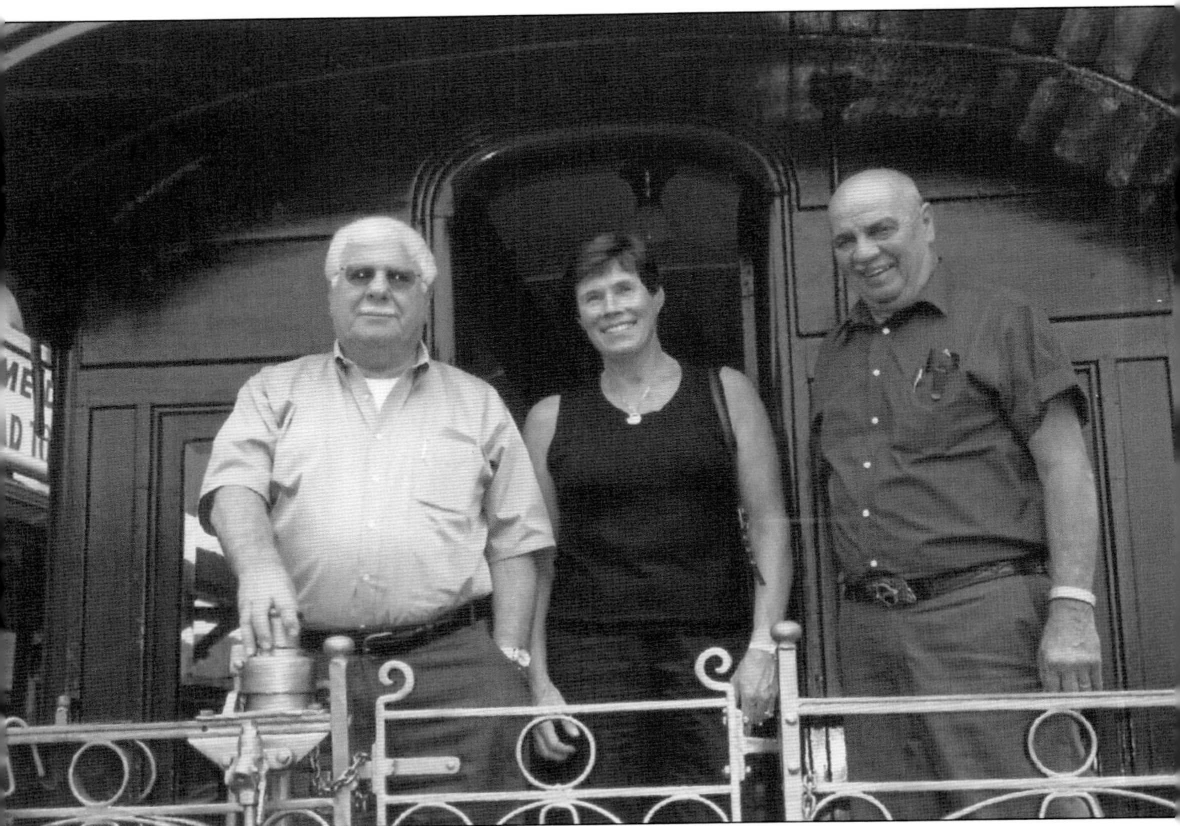

From left to right, Joseph Kovalchick, president of the East Broad Top Railroad; Judy Kovalchick, vice president of the East Broad Top Railroad; and Stanley G. Hall, general manager of the East Broad Top Railroad, are on parlor car No. 20 on August 5, 2007. Since 1960, the Kovalchick family has operated excursion service and maintained the historical integrity of the East Broad Top Railroad. (Photograph by Kenneth C. Springirth.)

On the cover: On May 3, 1936, locomotive No. 12 is coming out of the north end of the Sideling Hill Tunnel for a photograph run for the passengers on the Lancaster Chapter of the National Railway Historical Society excursion. This was the first of six Mikado-type locomotives built by the Baldwin Locomotive Works for the East Broad Top Railroad. (Photograph by Robert G. Lewis.)

IMAGES
of Rail

EAST BROAD TOP RAILROAD

Kenneth C. Springirth

ARCADIA
PUBLISHING

ISBN 978-0-7385-5754-0

Published by Arcadia Publishing
Charleston, South Carolina

Printed in the United States of America

Library of Congress Catalog Card Number: 2007934699

For all general information contact Arcadia Publishing at:
Telephone 843-853-2070
Fax 843-853-0044
E-mail sales@arcadiapublishing.com
For customer service and orders:
Toll-Free 1-888-313-2665

Visit us on the Internet at www.arcadiapublishing.com

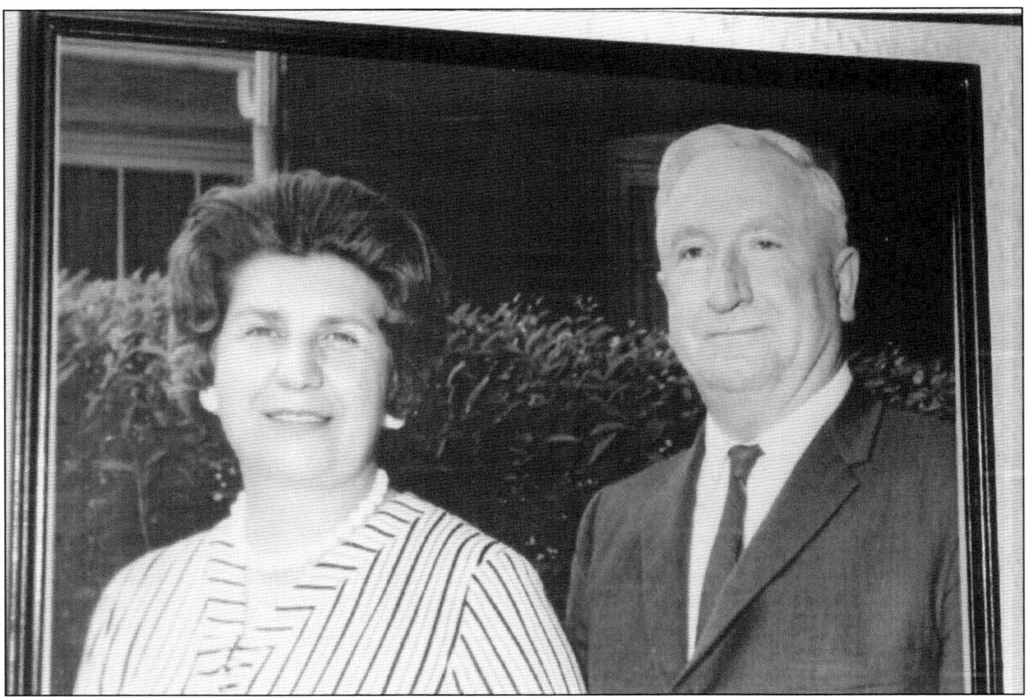

This book is dedicated to Nick Kovalchick and his wife, Fanny Kovalchick. When the East Broad Top Railroad ended operation in 1956, Nick Kovalchick, president of Kovalchick Salvage Company of Indiana, Pennsylvania, purchased the line and reopened a portion of it in 1960. The Kovalchick family has kept the railroad in place. Today it is the most original preserved railroad site in the United States.

CONTENTS

ACKNOWLEDGMENTS

The East Broad Top Railroad is the most complete and original historic railroad site in the United States. When the railroad closed in 1956, Nick Kovalchick, president of the Kovalchick Salvage Company of Indiana, Pennsylvania, purchased the line and began operation on a portion of it in 1960. Following his death in 1977, his son Joseph Kovalchick became president of the East Broad Top Railroad. The Kovalchick family kept the railroad in place and carefully operated a five-mile section. General manager Stanley G. Hall and his dedicated staff have done a magnificent job in maintaining service. Hall made a number of East Broad Top Railroad pictures available for use in this book. Joel Salomon, president of the Rockhill Trolley Museum, provided pictures and text. Matthew W. Nawn, first vice president and maintenance department cochairman of the Rockhill Trolley Museum, provided information. James A. Gillin and Robert G. Lewis provided photographs. Oliver J. Ogden of the Museum of Bus Transportation provided pictures and information on the East Broad Top Transit Company. Susan Yosten had a collection of Pennsylvania Railroad material that provided an insight into the railroad, and her father, Herbert Wildman, was a source of information. Brian Young of the Huntingdon County Planning and Development Department provided a map of the current operating section of the railroad. John C. Corson provided bus schedule information. The Huntingdon County Library was an excellent information center. The Juniata College library had on microfilm the *Mount Union Times*, the *Huntingdon and Mount Union Daily News*, and the *Huntingdon Journal*, which provided historical details on the railroad. *American Narrow Gauge Railroads* by George W. Hilton, published in 1990 by Stanford University Press, was an excellent source of background information. *Poor's Manual of Railroads* 1907 and 1908 published by Poor's Manual Company and the *1924 Coal Catalog* published by Keystone Consolidated Publishing Company provided historical data. Public tours of the Rockhill shops conducted by volunteers of the Friends of the East Broad Top made history come alive. Thanks goes to the East Broad Top Railroad employees whose hard work and ingenuity created an amazing railroad.

INTRODUCTION

About 112 miles east of Pittsburgh is the East Broad Top Railroad, which is the last authentic, original narrow-gauge steam railroad east of the Rocky Mountains. As a three-foot narrow-gauge line, it was 20.5 inches smaller then the four-foot-eight-and-a-half-inch standard railroad gauge. On April 16, 1856, the East Broad Top Railroad and Coal Company (commonly known as the East Broad Top Railroad) was chartered to mine and transport coal from Broad Top Mountain in Huntingdon County, which is in south-central Pennsylvania. However, lack of funding prevented construction of the railroad. A group of Philadelphia businessmen incorporated the Rockhill Iron and Coal Company and purchased a controlling interest in the East Broad Top Railroad. Construction of the narrow-gauge railroad began on September 16, 1872, at the borough of Mount Union. The line was completed from the borough of Mount Union to the borough of Rockhill Furnace on August 30, 1873. As noted in the *Huntingdon Journal* newspaper for Wednesday, October 1, 1873, the East Broad Top Railroad schedule, effective August 30, 1873, showed two passenger trains leaving Orbisonia at 8:30 a.m. and 3:20 p.m., arriving at Mount Union at 9:35 a.m. and 4:25 p.m., respectively. Two trains left Mount Union at 11:50 a.m. and 5:30 p.m., arriving at Orbisonia at 12:55 p.m. and 6:35 p.m., respectively. The railroad was completed to Robertsdale with freight service beginning on September 23, 1874. Mount Union was a transfer point on the Pennsylvania Railroad's Philadelphia-to-Pittsburgh main line. The *Mount Union Times* newspaper for Thursday, September 26, 1889, showed the May 13, 1889, schedule, which listed three passenger trains leaving Robertsdale at 6:00 a.m., 9:00 a.m., and 1:00 p.m., arriving at Mount Union at 8:25 a.m., 11:05 a.m., and 3:39 p.m., respectively. Three passenger trains left Mount Union at 9:25 a.m., 2:05 p.m., and 3:54 p.m., arriving at Robertsdale at 12:09 p.m., 4:21 p.m., and 6:42 p.m., respectively. There were two round-trips on the Shade Gap branch between the borough of Rockhill Furnace and Goshorn, the location of an iron mine on Shade Mountain. During 1891, the railroad was completed to a new mine at Woodvale and reached the mine at Alvan in 1916. An economic recession resulted in a decline in revenues and deferred maintenance by 1898. However, prosperity returned with trackage and bridges rebuilt during the early 1900s. The railroad's passenger service provided accessibility to residents of this remote area. Madeira, Hill and Company purchased the East Broad Top Railroad in 1919.

According to the *1924 Coal Catalog*, bituminous coal tonnage from Rockhill Coal and Iron Company mines at Robertsdale, served by the East Broad Top Railroad, during 1922 by mine were as follows: No. 1 Mine, 33,712 tons; No. 5 Mine, 88,394 tons; No. 6 Mine, 42,706 tons; No. 7 Mine, 11,796 tons; No. 8 Mine, 23,035 tons; and No. 9 Mine, 35,986 tons. In 1921, United States railroads shipped 371,327,642 tons of coal of which 92,254,343 tons came from Pennsylvania with the East Broad Top Railroad handling 267,985 tons. *Poor's 1926* (manual) railroad and banking section for 1925 listed mileage for the East Broad Railroad and Coal Company as of December 31, 1925, as follows: Mount Union to Alvan 32.54 miles; Shade Gap branch, Orbisonia to Neelyton, 9.60 miles; Rocky Ridge branch, Rocky Ridge to Evanston, 4.90 miles; Coles Valley branch, Coles to Joller, 2.49 miles; and Stanton Rock spur, Neelyton to Stanton, 1.53 miles, making the total 51.06 miles. There were 20.02 miles of sidings and 2.16 miles of industrial tracks. For the years 1920 to 1925 ending December 31, net income (revenues minus expenses equals profit) was as follows: 1920, $119,654 profit; 1921, $26,794 deficit; 1922, $12,207 deficit; 1923, $75,150 profit; 1924, $91,670 profit; and 1925, $93,286 profit.

Wood was transferred from narrow-gauge freight cars to standard-gauge freight cars from the McKelvey Brothers Lumber Company in what became known as the timber transfer. In 1933, McKelvey Brothers Lumber Company went out of business, and its timber transfer crane became idle. The railroad was losing general merchandise to trucks because of the cost and time involved in transferring freight from one gauge car to another. East Broad Top vice president and general manager C. D. Jones decided to use the timber transfer to change the trucks under a standard-gauge freight car to narrow-gauge trucks so that a standard-gauge freight car could travel on East Broad Top Railroad trackage. The crane lifted one end of the freight car and its standard-gauge truck was rolled out from under the car and through a switch to a side track. A narrow-gauge truck was then rolled under the car. The process was repeated for the other end of the car. Upon return of the standard-gauge car back to the yard, the process was reversed with narrow-gauge trucks replaced with the standard-gauge trucks. According to the *Railway Age* magazine of October 7, 1933, page 501, the first standard-gauge freight car transferred to narrow-gauge trucks was a Barber Asphalt Company tank car carrying 88,000 pounds of road tar. Special designed narrow-gauge trucks were used to reduce the motion of the standard-gauge cars. The results were successful.

Continuous heavy rains and melting snowdrifts late Tuesday night, March 17, 1936, and Wednesday morning, March 18, 1936, resulted in the Juniata River sweeping through Mount Union. The Pennsylvania Railroad suffered heavy damage between Huntingdon and Altoona. The *Mount Union Times* for Thursday, March 19, 1936, reported that "although the East Broad Top had three washouts at Aughwick, Three Springs, and Martins Meadow, they resumed normal service several days later." Madeira, Hill and Company went bankrupt in 1938, and the company reorganized as the Rockhill Coal Company.

The years after World War II were difficult for the East Broad Top Railroad with rising labor costs, labor strikes, declining coal deposits, and a diminishing market. Passenger service ended on August 15, 1954. In a September 2, 1954, letter, C. Roy Wilburn (operating vice president of the East Broad Top Railroad) notified C. W. Jeffries (superintendent of the Pennsylvania Railroad eastern region, middle division Altoona) and Lory D. Brandt (superintendent of the Pennsylvania Electric Company Huntingdon) that they were no longer leasing the Mount Union passenger station and requested discontinuance of electric service to the station. With a decline in freight traffic, which was primarily coal, the railroad started the abandonment process on November 18, 1955. The Rockhill Coal Company shipped its last coal on the East Broad Top Railroad on March 31, 1956. The Pennsylvania Public Utility Commission approved the abandonment request on April 3, 1956. North American Refractories Company received its last load of ganister rock from the East Broad Top Railroad on April 6, 1956. "Unique East Broad Top Railroad Makes Quiet Run into Oblivion" was the headline in the *Mount Union Times* newspaper of Friday, April 20, 1956, which reported that on Friday April 13, 1956, shortly after 3:00 p.m. service ended, noting that "no flags were flying, no bands playing and no people waving a last farewell as engine No. 3 made its last clean-up run manned by a veteran crew of the East Broad Top Railroad. Making the last run with No. 3 were engineer Otis Scott, with nearly 40 years of service on his record; James M. App, brakeman for 32 years; Drue Colyer, fireman for 33 years; Gene Ulsh, brakeman for 20 years; and John Hooper, conductor for nearly 43 years." The newspaper reported that the last regular run was made with engine No. 17 on Friday, April 6, 1956, noting that "engine No. 17, a 90 ton Baldwin locomotive built in 1921 made its last trip to the station at Orbisonia manned by James Pheasant, fireman for 31 years; H.A. Steninger, brakeman since 1911; Charles Hooper, conductor since 1908; Steve Painter, brakeman since 1912 and Drue Colyer." The article reported, "In 1947 and 1948 the East Broad Top shipped 500,000 tons of coal. The amount dropped in 1954 to 185,000 and in the first 10 months of 1955 to 134,000. In 1950 revenue from passenger fares, a secondary service of the railroad, totaled $3,764; in 1954 that total had dropped to $144.29 and passenger traffic was permanently discontinued." Kovalchick Salvage Company of Indiana, Pennsylvania, purchased the railroad on May 1, 1956. The Narco and Shade Gap branch lines were dismantled in 1957, but everything else was left intact. The yards, shops, buildings, and rolling stock of the East Broad Railroad were antiques when the line shut down in 1956. In 2007, the East Broad Top Railroad provides a picture of how steam railroads functioned.

The *Huntingdon and Mount Union Daily News* of Friday, August 12, 1960, reported that "excitement is mounting hourly in the Orbisonia-Rockhill area as the opening of the Bi-Centennial, Aug. 13-20 nears. The 200th anniversary event, plus the opening of the East Broad Top Railroad as a stellar tourist attraction, has received publicity far and wide." As reported by the *Daily News* for Saturday, August 13, 1960, "The honor of reopening the 100 year old East Broad Top Railroad as a Central Pennsylvania tourist attraction went to Dr. Maurice K. Goddard, secretary of the Pennsylvania Department of Forests and Waters, who represented the commonwealth at this morning's ceremonies. Dr. Goddard spoke briefly and then opened the throttle on Old No. 12 so that the 49 year old Baldwin built locomotive might cut the ribbon marking the return of steam railroading on the EBT, the last narrow gauge railroad east of the Mississippi." Judge Swirles L. Himes of Huntingdon, a native of nearby Shade Gap, was the main speaker and in his address, titled "More than a Million Whistles Ago," commented that he thrilled to the East Broad Top's whistle in the Shade Gap narrows declaring, "Old Eastie was no ordinary railroad—she was a personal part of us—the very warp and wool of our lives." The *Daily News* for Monday, August 15, 1960, noted that the "opening of the East Broad Top Railroad as a tourist attraction for the area was called a tremendous success by C. Roy Wilburn, operating vice president of the EBT. The 100 year old narrow gauge line made nine trips on Saturday and 10 yesterday, hauling nearly 4,000 rail fans during the two days." Nick Kovalchick, head of Kovalchick Salvage Company and owner of the East Broad Top Railroad, "urged every person present to give his support so that the railroad could be a success." East Broad Top Railroad operating vice president C. Roy Wilburn explained that the name *Millie* on the Baldwin engine No. 12 that made the first run on Saturday was named by Kovalchick after his youngest daughter when he inspected the railroad after he purchased it in September 1956. Young Millie Kovalchick had the honor of christening the locomotive with a bottle of ginger ale. The train was filled to capacity for the first trip up the Aughwick Valley, plus many spectators watched and photographed the train along the route. "EBT Is Cited as Historic Line" was the headline in the *Daily News* newspaper for Monday, August 17, 1964, which noted that "the sun was shining, flags flying, the band playing, train whistles blowing and a gay crowd cheering at Rockhill Furnace on Saturday afternoon, August 15, when the East Broad Top Railroad became a national historic landmark." Kittridge A. Wing, superintendent of the Gettysburg National Military Park, presented the citation certificate to Nick Kovalchick, president of the East Broad Top Railroad. The certificate stated, "The East Broad Top Railroad is hereby designated a registered national historic landmark under the provisions of the Historic Sites Act of August 21, 1935. This site possesses exceptional value in commemorating and illustrating the history of the United States." The newspaper article noted that in accepting the certificate, Kovalchick asked the support of those present commenting, "Tell your friends what you see today. This project takes a lot of money. Your help is needed." It is to the credit of the Kovalchick family that the East Broad Top Railroad has survived. When East Broad Top Railroad president Nick Kovalchick died on April 20, 1977, his son Joseph and daughter-in-law Judy took over the property. Continuing excursion service, Joseph Kovalchick, president of the Kovalchick Corporation that owns the railroad, and Stanley G. Hall, general manager of the East Broad Top Railroad, are the key players in this historic railroad that faces significant preservation issues. With a location 19 miles north of the Pennsylvania Turnpike via United States Highway 522, the railroad makes a nice one-day trip for many potential customers. More riders could provide more revenues, which might help enhance the railroad's future. The Mount Union Connecting Railroad Company was formed in 1993 to operate from the Norfolk Southern Railroad main line in Mount Union to the Riverview Business Center Industrial Park south of the village of Allenport. The railroad includes 0.8 miles of the former Pennsylvania Railroad spur into central Mount Union and 2.9 miles of East Broad Top Railroad trackage. On July 24, 2007, filming was done on the East Broad Top Railroad for a one-hour Discovery Channel presentation *Abraham Lincoln: The Speech That Saved America*. Locomotive No. 15 was fitted with a temporary cowcatcher and balloon-style smokestack. Combination passenger-baggage car No. 15 and parlor car No. 20 were decorated with red, white, and blue bunting. With authentic original equipment in its historic location, the East Broad Top Railroad was an excellent location for a Civil War production.

Adjacent to the East Broad Top Railroad, the Rockhill Trolley Museum was established in 1960. The *Mount Union Times* newspaper of Friday, July 5, 1963, announced for Saturday (July 6, 1963) the "official opening of the Railways to Yesterday, Inc. trolley line at the site of the East Broad Top Railroad at Rockhill Furnace." Johnstown Traction Company car No. 311 made its run on the 2,000-foot-long line of the former Shade Gap branch of the East Broad Top Railroad. The article noted former Washington, D.C., snow sweeper No. 09 would be displayed along with interurban car No. 315 that "was transported to Mount Union by special rail car and then was trucked to Rockhill Furnace." Over the years the line has been extended. The 1.54-mile trolley line operates a variety of trolleys that range from a vintage 1912 open summer car from Rio de Janeiro, Brazil, to a 1947 Presidents' Conference Committee car from Philadelphia.

One

EARLY YEARS

Construction of the narrow-gauge East Broad Top Railroad began on September 16, 1872. On August 30, 1873, the line was completed from the borough of Mount Union to the borough of Rockhill Furnace. Following some lean years, the railroad made track and bridge improvements during the early 1900s. The 32.54-mile main line reached Alvan by 1916. Railroad passenger service was provided, linking an isolated area to the Pennsylvania Railroad at Mount Union where connections could be made to the rest of the country. Recognizing that a considerable amount of paving tar for road repair was being used by the Pennsylvania State Department of Highways, C. D. Jones, vice president and general manager of the East Broad Top Railroad, by an August 11, 1932, letter to J. B. Phelan, superintendent, middle division, the Pennsylvania Railroad (Altoona), noted that there was a need to deliver this material in standard-gauge tank cars to Neelyton, Shade Gap, Orbisonia, Three Springs, Saltillo, and Robertsdale. The letter stated,

> There is a very considerable quantity of this material used in our district each year and I have informed the State Highway Department that if we can make the necessary arrangements with the Pennsylvania Railroad, we will design and build special 36" gauge trucks for carrying standard gauge tank bodies and by our electric cranes or other mechanism at Mount Union Yard, transfer these standard gauge tanks to these 36" gauge trucks and deliver the material much closer to the point of consumption.

A positive reply was received by a September 6, 1932, letter from W. C. Higginbottom, general manager of the Pennsylvania Railroad, who noted, "Our company has no objection to your handling the matter in this manner, and we do not see why it could not be worked out satisfactorily." The idea of placing narrow-gauge trucks under standard-gauge cars worked and secured new business for the railroad that was formerly handled by truck. In consultation with the Motive Power Department of the Pennsylvania Railroad, the East Broad Top Railroad designed and constructed a narrow-gauge truck with sufficient capacity to handle a standard-gauge freight car.

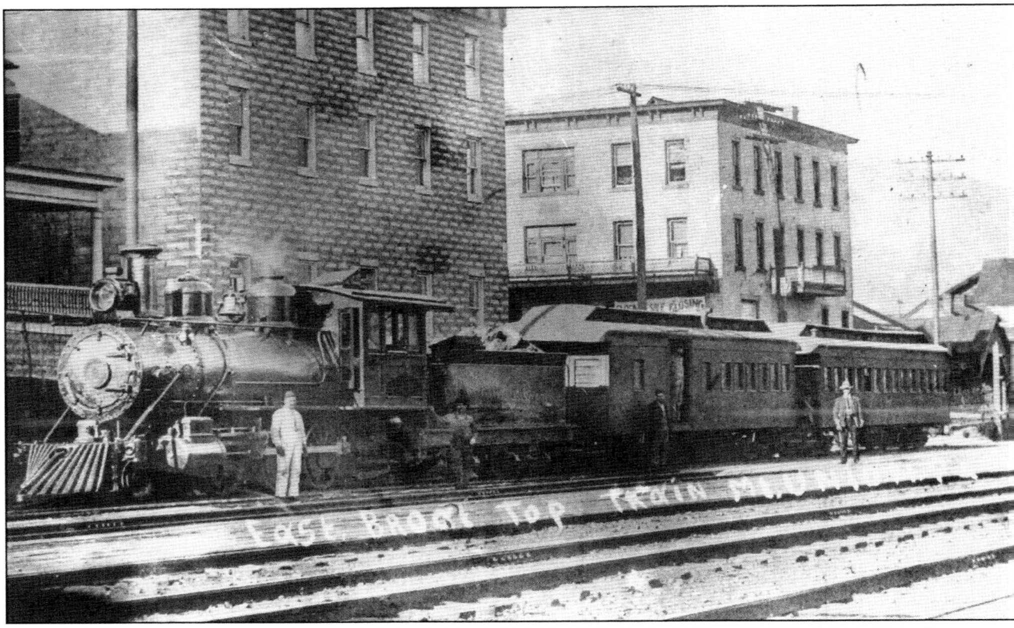

An East Broad Top Railroad passenger train pauses with its crew in this early postcard scene at the Mount Union station around the early 1900s. This was a transfer point with the Pennsylvania Railroad main line connecting west to Pittsburgh and east to Philadelphia. Steam locomotive No. 9 was a Mogul type with a 2-6-0 wheel arrangement built by Baldwin Locomotive Works in February 1889.

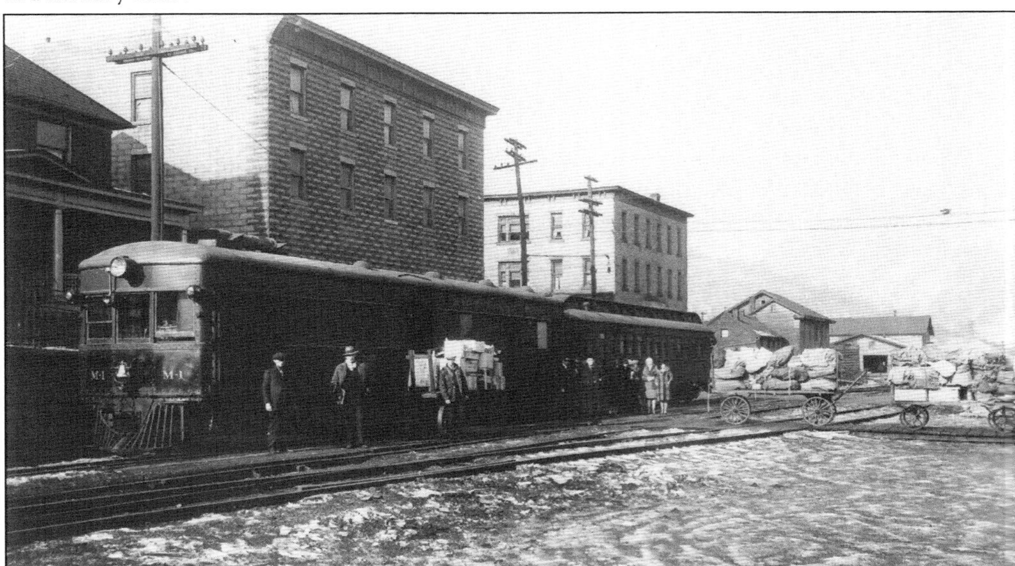

Gas-electric motor car M-1 is shown pulling passenger car No. 8 (equipped with roller bearing trucks to make it easier to pull) at the Mount Union station in this 1930s postcard scene. The M-1 entered service on January 6, 1927, and handled mail along with passenger service. Just as the East Broad Top Railroad has remained unchanged, the M-1 was still in service in 2007 with the original engine.

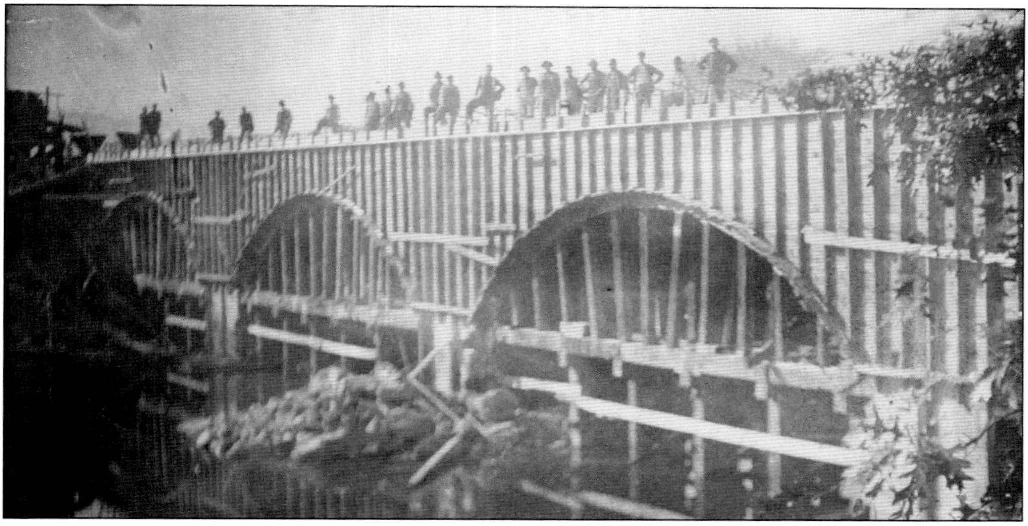

The new four-arch concrete bridge is under construction in the spring of 1914 at Aughwick. The original bridge built in 1873 was damaged by a train derailment on January 8, 1883, and was replaced. The 1889 flood washed out the bridge, and it was replaced by an iron bridge, which was later replaced by the new concrete bridge. (East Broad Top Railroad collection.)

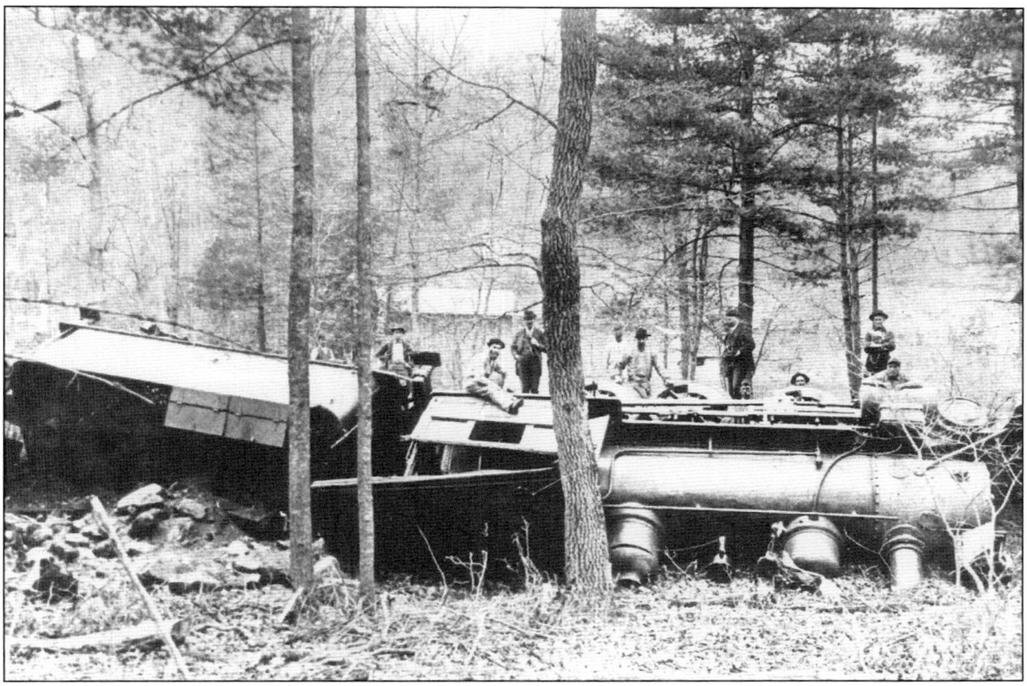

Mogul-type locomotive No. 9 with a 2-6-0 wheel arrangement has derailed at the village of Cooks in April 1896. Baldwin Locomotive Works originally built this locomotive in February 1889 for the Coeur D'Alene Railway and Navigation Company as No. 4. It was sold to the East Broad Top Railroad in December 1892. (East Broad Top Railroad collection.)

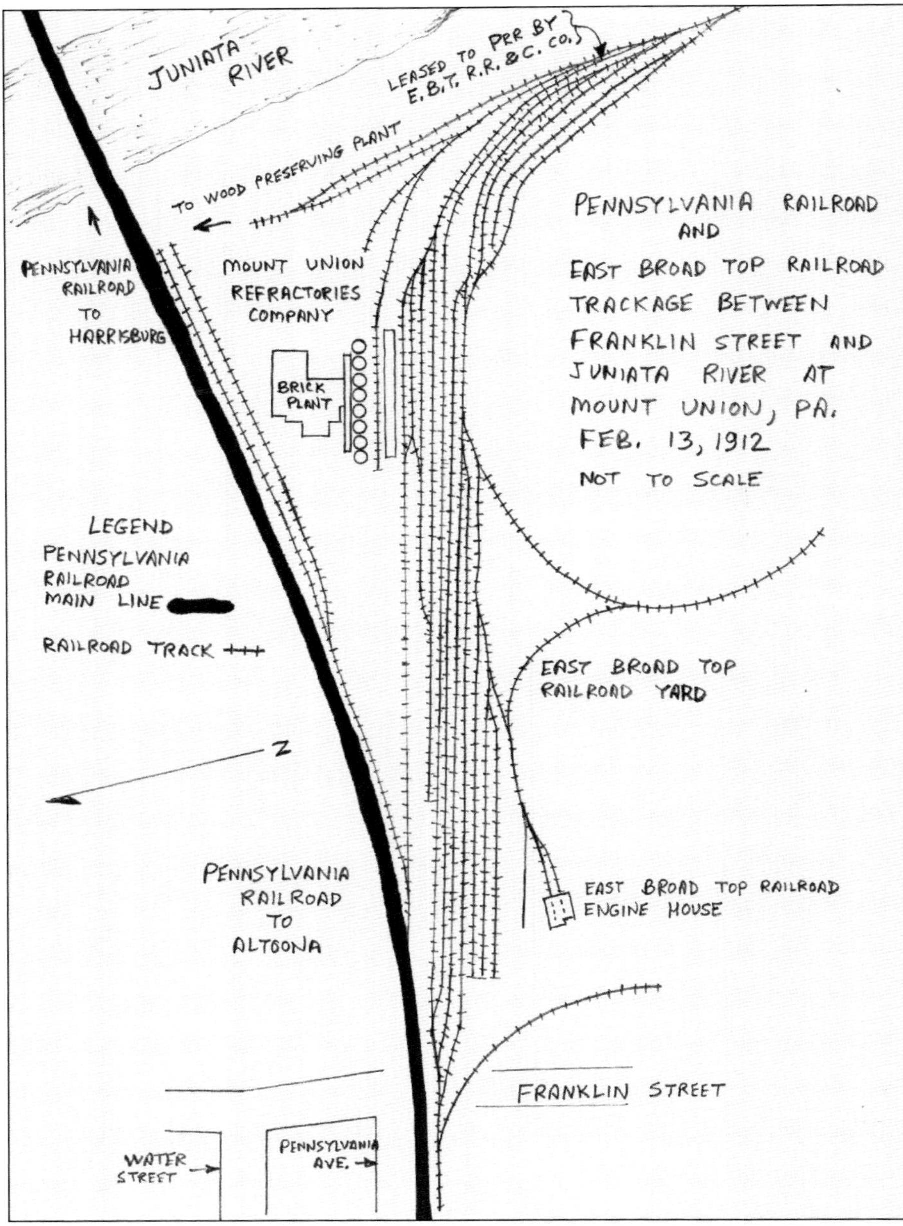

The February 13, 1912, map above shows the East Broad Top Railroad yard at Mount Union and its connection with the Pennsylvania Railroad. Mount Union received its name from the panoramic beauty of the "union of the mountains." When three brick refractories were in full operation, Mount Union was the world's largest producer of silica brick used as a lining in furnaces. The East Broad Top Railroad served the major refractories, and its yard could handle hundreds of cars. Mount Union was a consumer of coal brought in by the East Broad Top Railroad. In July 2007, the East Broad Top Railroad yard slumbers in a dense thicket of trees growing around the freight cars. The outside of the two-stall engine house has been repainted by the Mount Union Connecting Railroad, which has also removed trees from some of the trackage. (Pennsylvania Railroad, collection of Susan Yosten.)

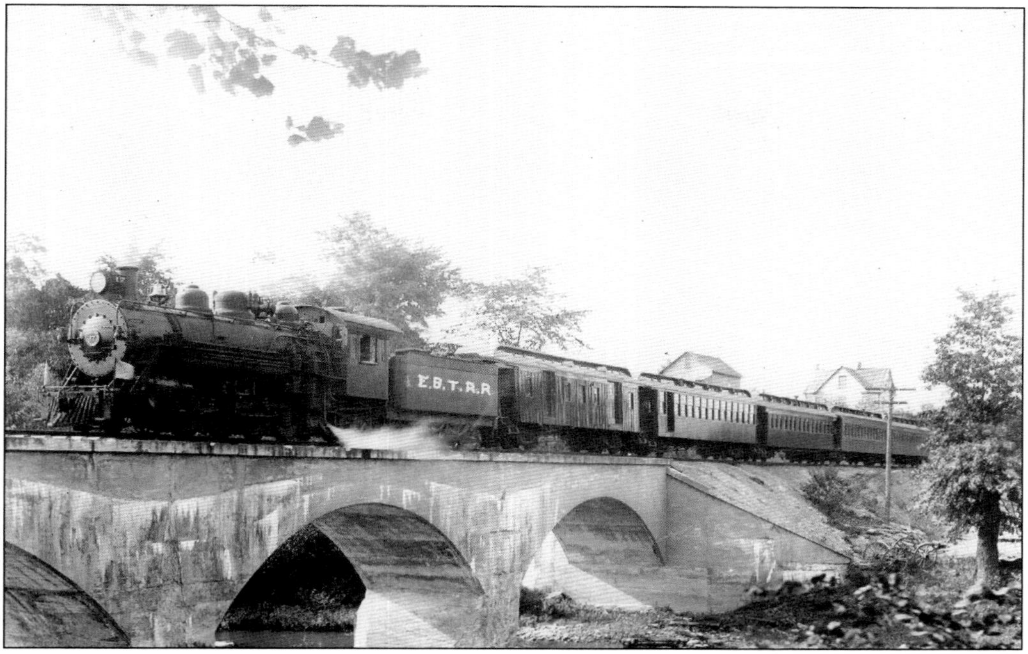

In the early 1920s, locomotive No. 17 is northbound crossing the concrete bridge reinforced with railroad rails over Aughwick Creek. This impressive bridge would normally be found on a main line railroad. Light bridge spans were normally sufficient for a narrow-gauge line, but the East Broad Top Railroad handled heavy tonnage. (East Broad Top Railroad collection.)

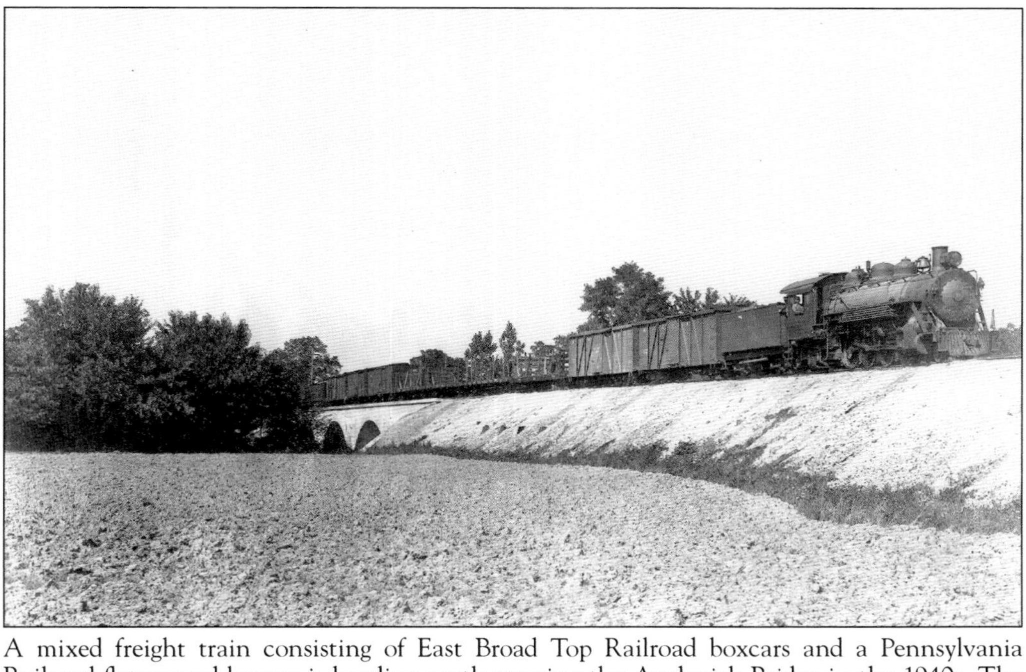

A mixed freight train consisting of East Broad Top Railroad boxcars and a Pennsylvania Railroad flatcar and boxcar is heading south crossing the Aughwick Bridge in the 1940s. The 203-foot-long, four-arch concrete bridge was completed in 1914. Hurricane Fran battered it in 1996. It can be viewed today from Aughwick Mills Road. (East Broad Top Railroad collection.)

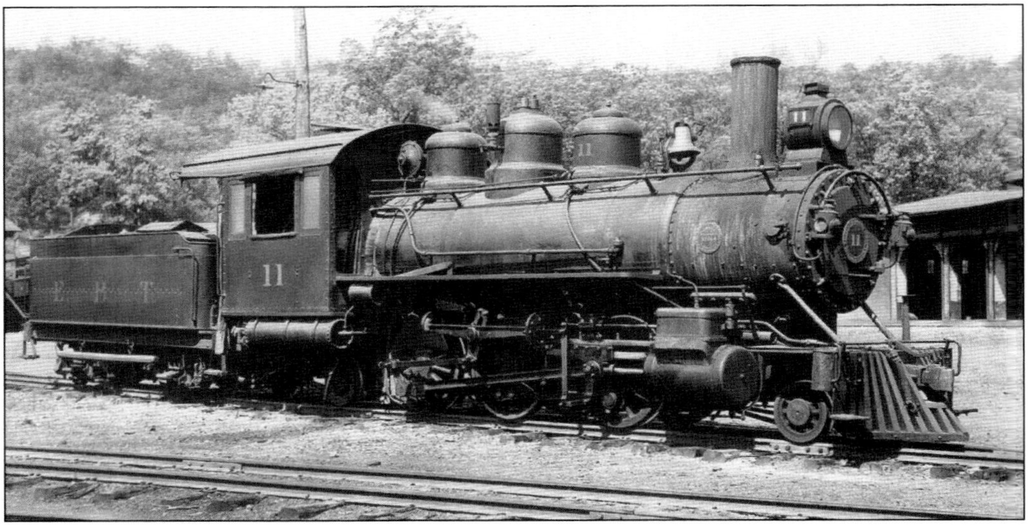

Prairie-type locomotive No. 11, with a 2-6-2 wheel arrangement and 48-inch-diameter drive wheels, is at the Rockhill Furnace yard. Baldwin Locomotive Works built this locomotive for the East Broad Top Railroad in February 1908. This was the first locomotive purchased by the East Broad Top Railroad with a trailing truck and weighed 89,780 pounds.

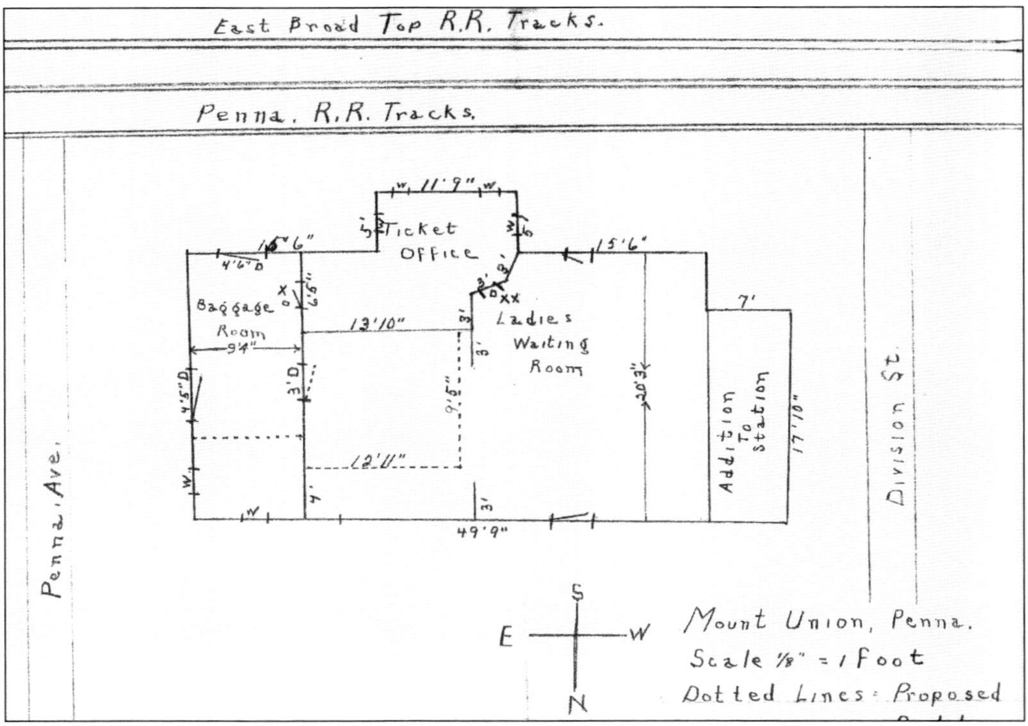

This sketch shows the interior dimensions of the East Broad Top Railroad passenger station at Mount Union. American Railway Express Company requested using a portion of the facility with a partition shown by dotted lines. Superintendent F. M. Butler of the East Broad Top Railroad responded with a December 13, 1923, letter noting, "We will not be able to spare the room to the Express Co." (Pennsylvania Railroad, collection of Susan Yosten.)

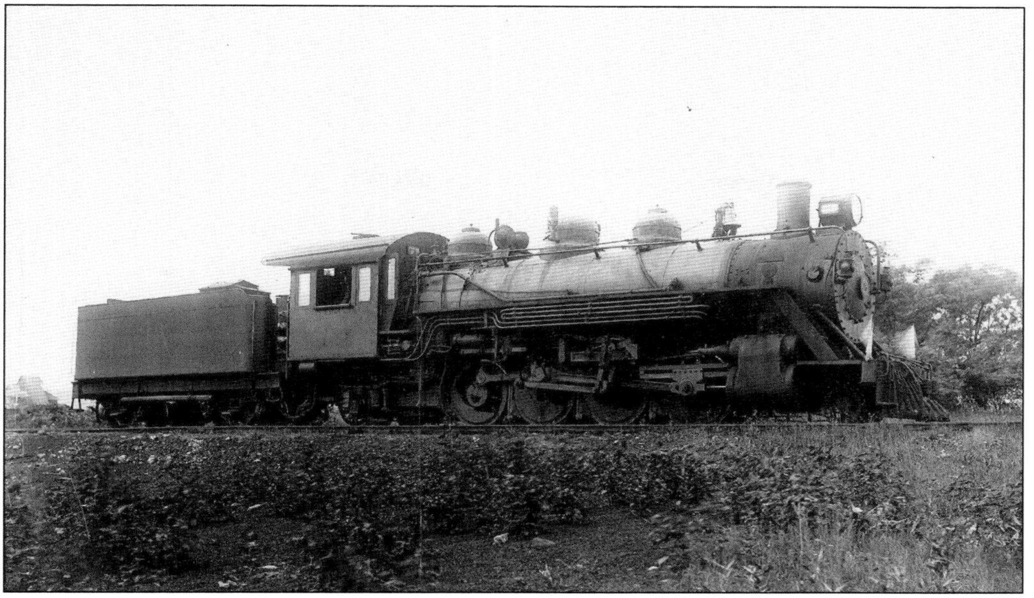

Mikado-type steam locomotive No. 18 with a 2-8-2 wheel arrangement is at Mount Union in the 1920s. This was the last and largest narrow-gauge steam locomotive purchased by the East Broad Top Railroad. Baldwin Locomotive Works built this locomotive in August 1920. It weighs 164,200 pounds and has 48-inch-diameter drive wheels. (East Broad Top Railroad collection.)

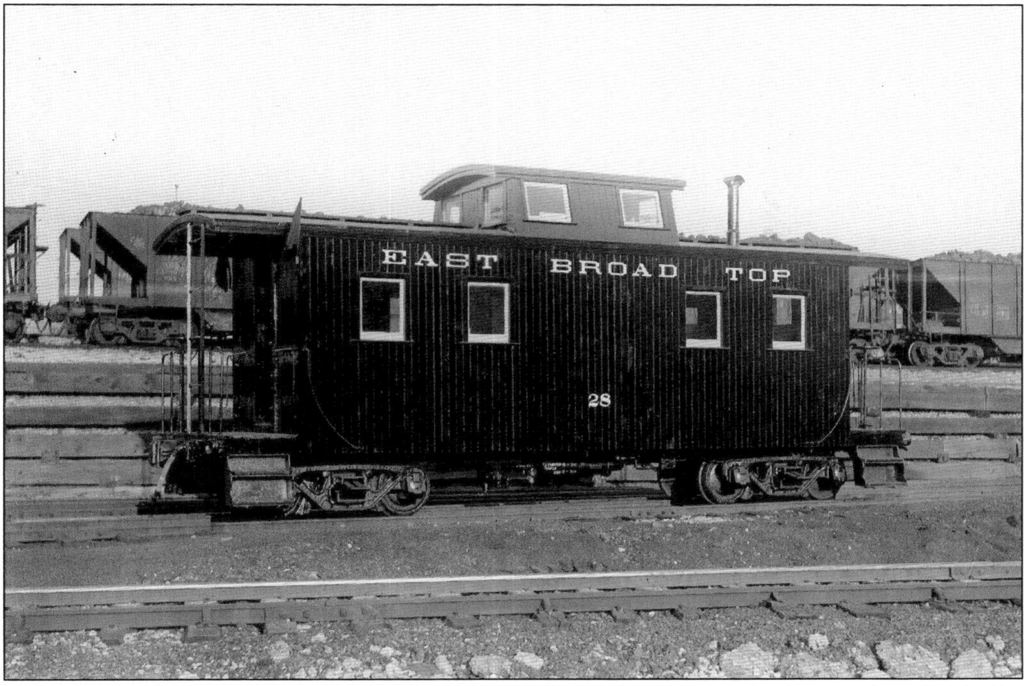

Caboose No. 28 is at the Mount Union yard with hopper cars in the background in the 1920s. This caboose was built by the East Broad Top Railroad shops in 1920 and demonstrates the outstanding capabilities of the facilities and employees. The caboose was still in excellent condition 87 years later in 2007. (East Broad Top Railroad collection.)

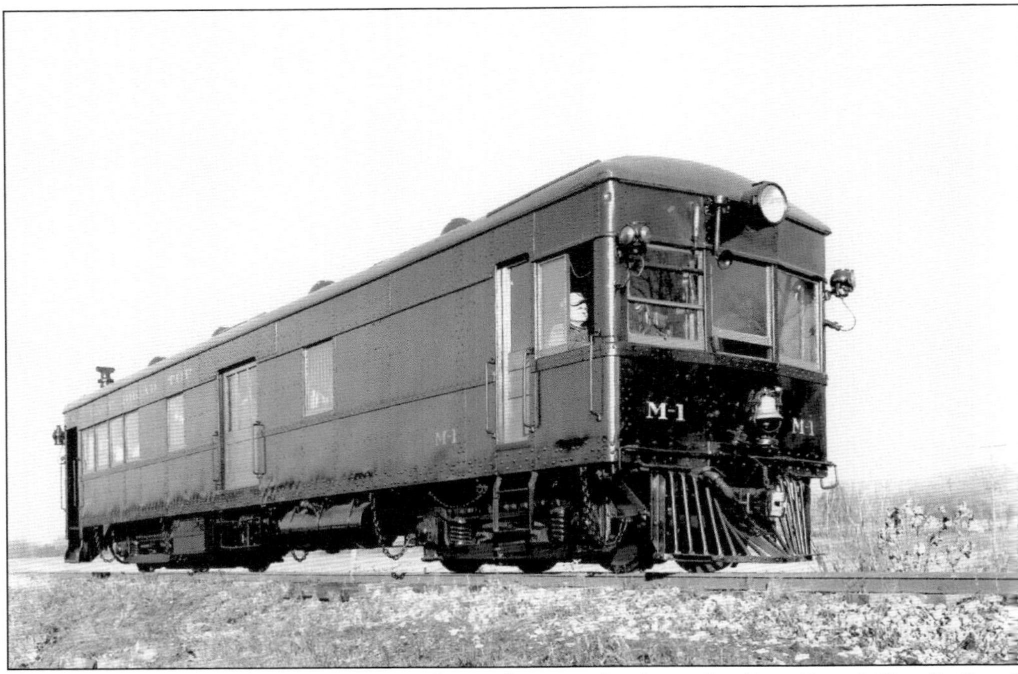

Gas-electric motor car M-1 is posing for a photograph along the East Broad Top Railroad. Recognizing a decline in passenger revenues during the 1920s, the railroad's Rockhill Furnace shops built this car, which reduced operating expenses. At times, passenger coach No. 8 was pulled behind the M-1, which also towed hopper cars and other rolling stock as needed. (Kenneth C. Springirth collection.)

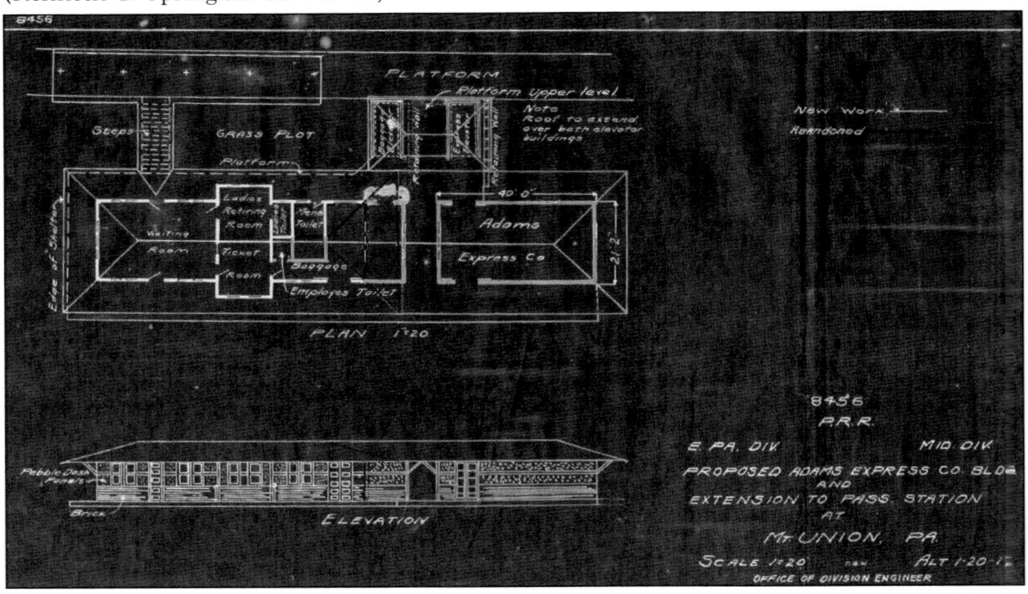

The proposed Adams Express Company addition for the Pennsylvania Railroad Mount Union station is shown in the blueprint above. In the period before World War I, railroads were expanding, and the Mount Union Pennsylvania Railroad passenger station had increased activity, as evidenced by the proposed addition. (Pennsylvania Railroad, collection of Susan Yosten.)

TIME TABLE NO. 57

EAST BROAD TOP RAILROAD COMPANY

In Effect Tuesday, January 26th, 1932

NORTHWARD							SOUTHWARD		
No. 5	No. 7	No. 3	No. 1	Car Capacity of Passing Sidings	MAIN LINE	Distance from Mt. Union	No. 8	No. 2	No. 4
P. M.	P. M.	P. M.	A. M.				A. M.	P. M.	P. M.
....	4 15	....	....		Leave....... **Alvan** .... Arrive	33.0	7 00	....	....
7 10	s4 20	12 25	6 35		Woodvale	32.0	s6 53	12 15	7 10
7 20	s4 32	s1 45	s6 45		*Robertsdale	30.0	s6 45	s12 05	s7 00
	f4 47	f1 55	f7 00	25	Cooks	27.0	f6 35	f11 52	f6 47
	f4 54	f2 01	f7 07	16	*Rocky Ridge	25.0	f6 27	f11 45	f6 40
	f4 59	f2 06	f7 12	28	*Coles	24.0	f6 22	f11 40	f6 35
	f5 04	f2 11	f7 17	30	Kimmel	23.0	f6 17	f11 32	f6 27
	f5 09	f2 16	f7 22		Fairview	22.0	f6 12	†11 25	†6 20
	s5 20	s2 30	s7 35	37	*Saltillo	19.0	s5 58	s11 05	s6 00
	s5 27	s2 38	s7 43	25	*Three Springs	17.0	s5 50	s10 55	s5 47
	f5 35	f2 46	f7 52	40	Pogue	14.0	f5 40	f10 45	f5 35
	5 45				Arrive *Orbisonia Leave	11.0	5 30	10 35	5 25
		s3 00	s8 08		Leave *Orbisonia Arrive			s10 08	s5 02
		s3 14	s8 22	40	*Shirleysburg	7.0	....	s9 54	s4 48
		f3 17	f8 26	10	Pump Station	5.0	....	f9 49	f4 43
		f3 19	f8 29		Aughwick	4.0	....	f9 46	f4 39
		†3 25	†8 35	26	Adams	2.4	....	†9 42	†4 35
		f3 28	f8 39		Allenton	1.0	....	f9 38	f4 32
		f3 32	s8 42		*Mount Union Yard	.4	....	f9 35	s4 30
		3 40	8 50		Arrive ...***Mt. Union**... Leave	.0	....	9 20	4 15

s—Regular Stop. f—Stop on signal. †Trains will not stop. *Train order stations.

No. 9		SHADE GAP BRANCH	Distance from Orbisonia	No. 10
7 00	30	Leave..... **Neelyton** ..... Arrive	10.0	6 55
s7 15	25	*Shade Gap	6.0	s6 40
f7 21	12	Locke Valley	5.0	f6 35
f7 25		Cedar Rock	4.0	f6 32
f7 33	17	Blacklog	2.0	f6 25
7 40		Arrive... ***Orbisonia** ...Leave	0.0	6 20
A. M.				A. M.

Train No. 8 will have right of track over Train No. 1 to South end of Robertsdale Wye.
All trains run daily except Sunday. The Company reserves the right to vary from the above Time Table without notice.
Trains will be run on the Shade Gap Branch either by steam or gasoline motor, or discontinued entirely, at the option of the Company.
Trains will run on the Rocky Ridge and Coles Valley branches on special orders.
Express service stands for safe and rapid transportation of shipments. Railway Express Agency operates on our lines.

Pennsylvania Railroad Trains Leave Mount Union

EAST—12.10 a. m., 1.26 a. m., 5.41 a. m., 7.56 a. m., 12.30 p. m., 12.48 p. m., 4.01 p. m., 7.29 p. m.
WEST—2.13 a. m., 6.45 a. m., 9.02 a. m., 1.22 p. m., 4.41 p. m., 6.14 p. m., 8.46 p. m., 9.28 p. m.

The "PIONEER TRAIL" Motor Coach Service

Local Service between **Saltillo and Huntingdon, Pa.**
Through Service between **Tyrone and Chambersburg, Pa.**

Through buses make direct connections for **Hagerstown, Baltimore, Washington, Winchester, Gettysburg, York, Shippensburg and Carlisle. Philipsburg, Clearfield, DuBois, State College** and points North, South and West.

Bus Time Table, Rates and Freight Rates may be obtained at any of the Company's Agents or General Office, Orbisonia, Pa.

Also operates Freight ~~Truck Service~~ Between **Huntingdon and McConnellsburg**

C. D. JONES, Vice President and General Manager

The January 26, 1932, East Broad Top Railroad timetable shows a base service of two round-trips daily, except Sunday, between Woodvale and Mount Union, plus a commuter round-trip from Orbisonia to Alvan. Compared to the schedule that was in effect on April 18, 1921, the only reduction was on the Shade Gap branch from two round-trips between Neelyton and Orbisonia to one round-trip. The 1932 timetable noted that "trains will be run on the Shade Gap Branch either by steam or gasoline motor, or discontinued entirely, at the option of the Company. Trains will run on the Rocky Ridge and Coles Valley branches on special orders." On April 18, 1921, the Pennsylvania Railroad had 10 westbound and 10 eastbound passenger train departures from Mount Union, which by 1932 were reduced to 8 westbound and 8 eastbound departures from Mount Union. (Pennsylvania Railroad, collection of Susan Yosten.)

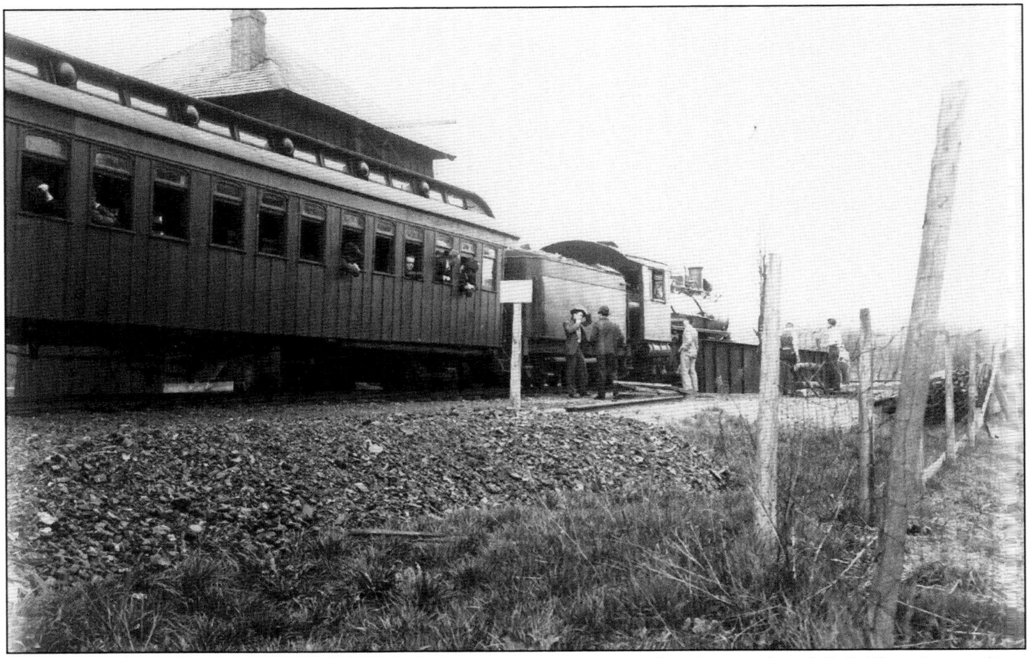

A National Railway Historical Society excursion pauses at the borough of Saltillo. According to data published by *Poor's Manual of Railroads* in 1907 and 1908 and *Poor's 1926* (manual) railroad and banking section, for the year ending June 30, 1906, the East Broad Top Railroad carried 99,013 passengers, increasing to 111,853 passengers for the year ending June 30, 1907, and 151,054 passengers for the year ending December 31, 1925. (East Broad Top Railroad collection.)

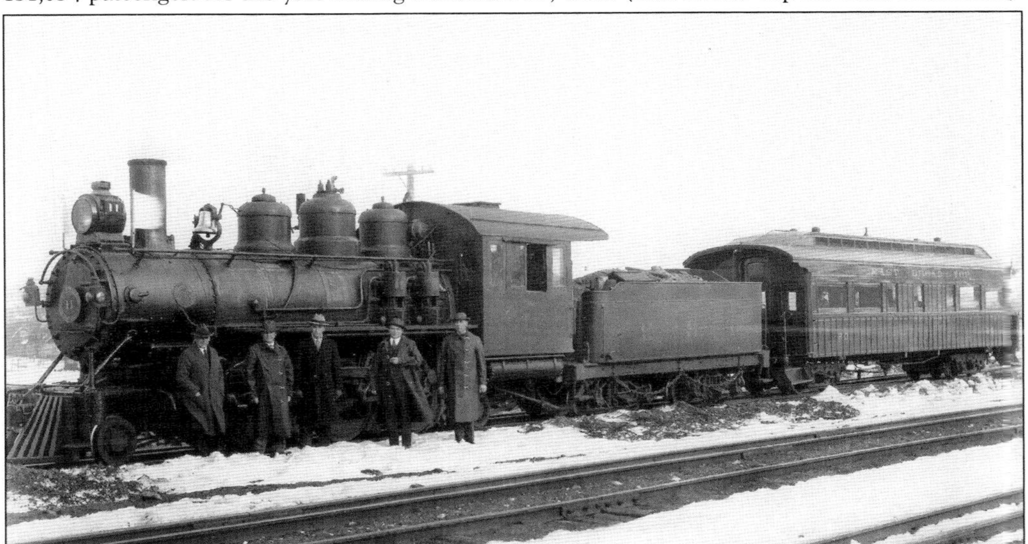

Locomotive No. 11 is pulling parlor car No. 20 on an important inspection trip in the 1930s. This may have been in connection with the December 19, 1934, bankruptcy of Madeira, Hill and Company and the July 20, 1938, reorganization under which the assets were purchased by bondholders who turned them over to a new Rockhill Coal Company. (East Broad Top Railroad collection.)

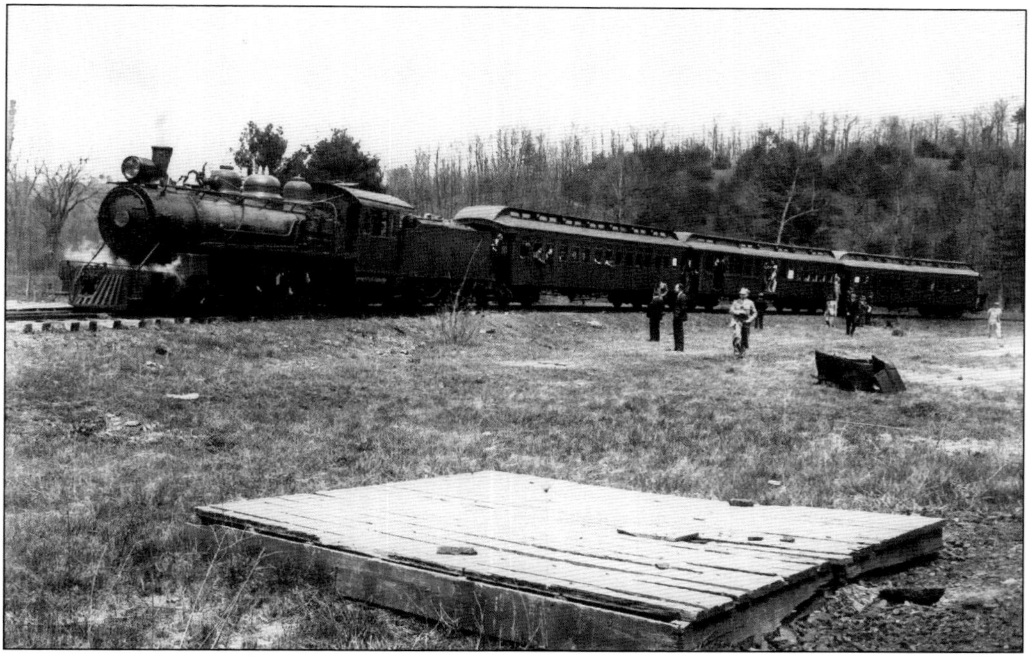

Locomotive No. 12, pulling three coaches, is on a National Railway Historical Society excursion trip in 1936. Rail enthusiasts from all parts of the country started coming on excursions to the East Broad Top Railroad as miles of narrow-gauge railroads in service in the United States declined from the peak of 11,699 miles as of December 31, 1885, to 1,729 miles by December 31, 1939. (East Broad Top Railroad collection.)

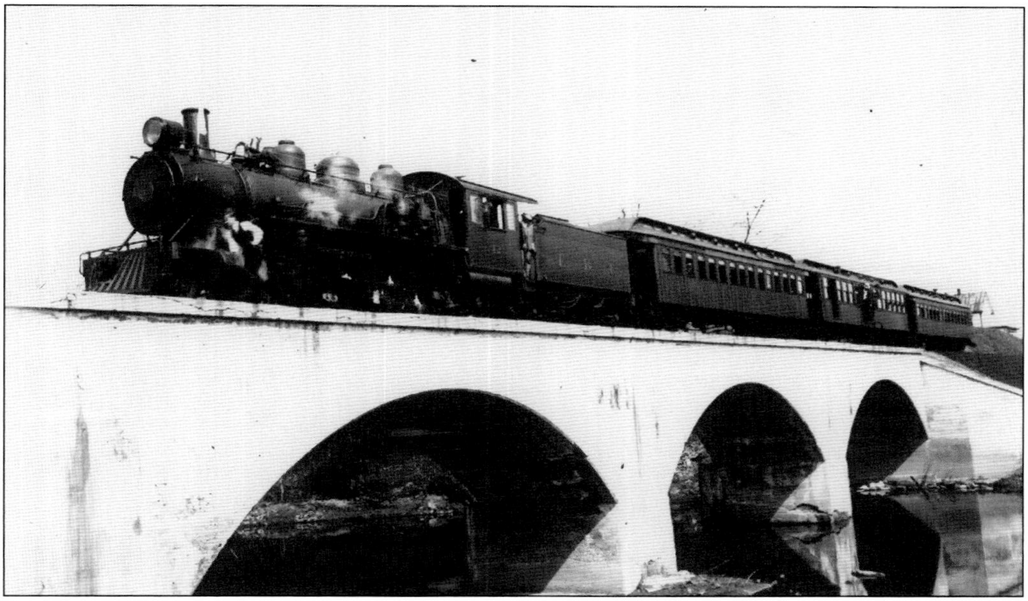

East Broad Top Railroad locomotive No. 12 is on a National Railway Historical Society excursion for a photograph stop at the four-arch concrete bridge over Aughwick Creek in 1936. This was a popular stop for students of rail transportation. Seventy-one years later in 2007, this bridge, although severely weathered, was still picturesque. (East Broad Top Railroad collection.)

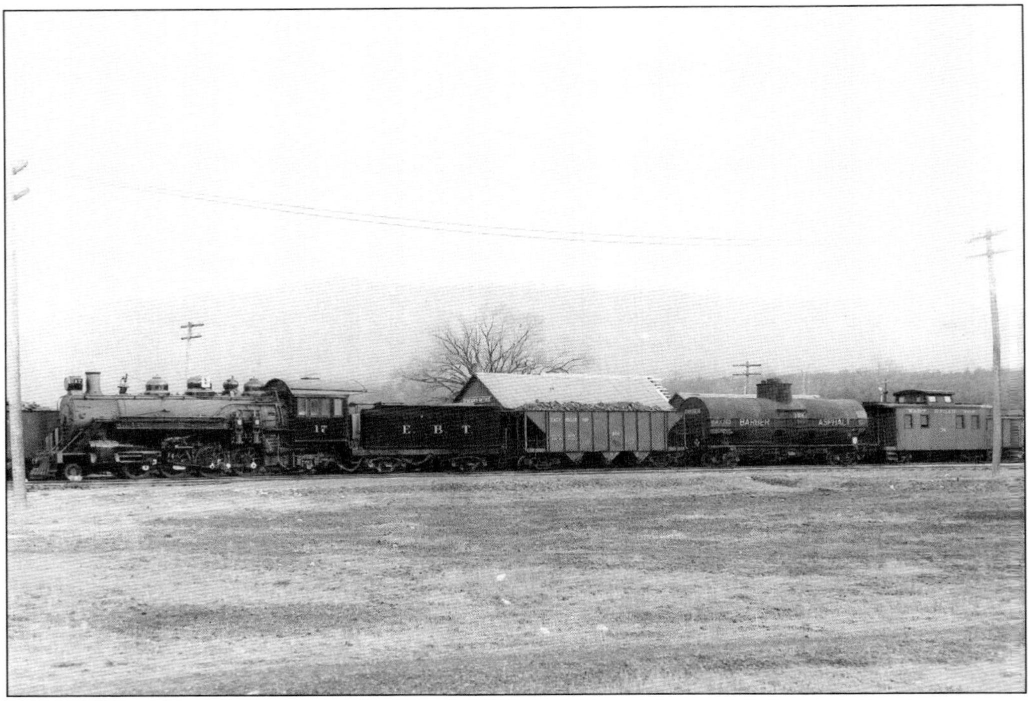

Locomotive No. 17 is pulling a train with a Barber Asphalt standard-gauge tank car with narrow-gauge trucks around 1933 at the Rockhill Furnace yard. The plan of placing narrow-gauge trucks on standard-gauge cars was developed by C. D. Jones, vice president and general manager of the East Broad Top Railroad, and the railroad shops built special trucks to use with standard-gauge cars. (East Broad Top Railroad collection.)

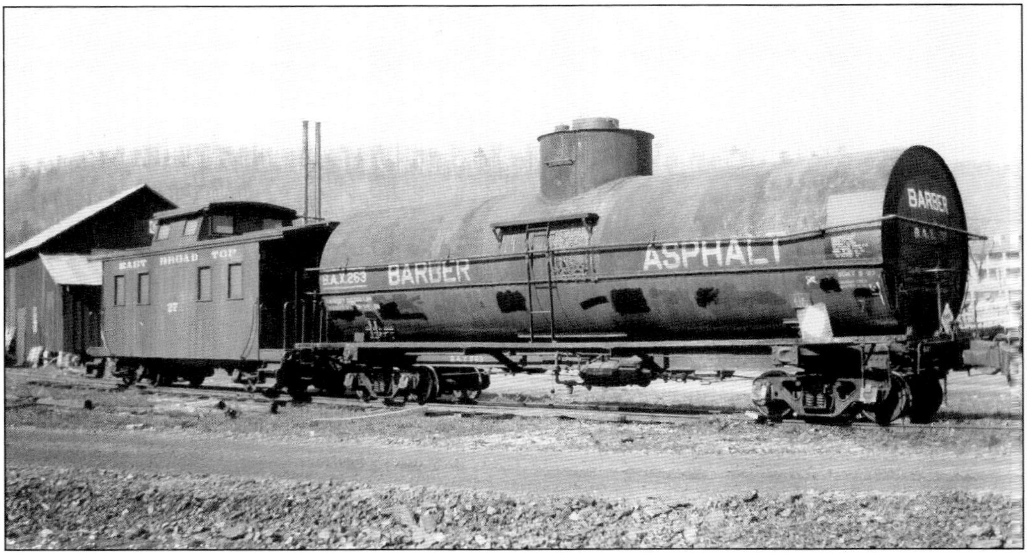

East Broad Top Railroad caboose No. 27 and a Barber Asphalt standard-gauge tank car on narrow-gauge trucks are shown in this 1933 view. A Barber Asphalt tank car was the first type of car put through the timber transfer at the Mount Union yard to change from standard gauge to special narrow-gauge trucks with oversized axles and journals. (East Broad Top Railroad collection.)

9-36 200

TIME TABLE NO. 71

EAST BROAD TOP RAILROAD COMPANY

In Effect Thursday, October 1st, 1936

NORTHWARD							SOUTHWARD		
No. 5	No. 7	No. 3	No. 1	CAR CAPACITY OF PASSING SIDINGS	MAIN LINE	DISTANCE FROM MT. UNION	No. 8	No. 2	No. 4
P. M.	P. M.	P. M.	A. M.				A. M.	A. M.	P. M.
....	3 30	....	....		Leave ....**Alvan**........ Arrive	33.0	7 00	....	....
6 55	s3 35	12 20	6 30		................Woodvale................	32.0	s6 53	12 20PM	6 55
7 05	s3 45	s1 30	s6 45		..............*Robertsdale..............	30.0	s6 45	s12 10PM	s6 50
	f3 58	f1 40	f6 55	25	..................Cooks..................	27.0	f6 35	f11 58	f6 37
	f4 05	f1 46	f7 01	16	.... *Rocky Ridge	25.0	f6 27	f11 50	f6 30
	f4 11	f1 51	f7 05	28	..................*Coles..................	24.0	f6 22	f11 44	f6 25
	f4 16	f1 56	f7 08	30	................Kimmel................	23.0	f6 17	f11 38	f6 17
	f4 21	†2 01	†7 12		.... Fairview	22.0	f6 12	†11 30	†6 10
	s4 36	s2 15	s7 22	37	...............*Saltillo................	19.0	s5 58	s11 10	s5 50
	s4 44	s2 23	s7 29	25	.... Three Springs.............	17.0	s5 50	s10 55	s5 40
	f4 52	f2 31	f7 38	40	.... Pogue................	14.0	f5 40	f10 40	f5 30
	5 05				Arrive ..... ***Orbisonia**...... Leave	11.0	5 30	10 30	5 20
		s2 50	s7 55		Leave ..... ***Orbisonia**...... Arrive		....	s10 12	s5 02
		s3 05	s8 08	40	.... *Shirleysburg	7.0	....	s9 58	s4 48
		f3 08	f8 10	10	.... Pump Station	5.0	....	f9 53	f4 43
		f3 10	f8 13		..............Aughwick..............	4.0	....	f9 50	f4 39
		†3 17	†8 17	26	.... Adams	2.4	....	†9 46	†4 35
		f3 21	f8 20		.... Allenport...............	1.0	....	f9 43	f4 32
		f3 25	s8 23		.... *Mount Union Yard	.4	....	f9 40	s4 30
		3 35	8 30		Arrive ...***Mt. Union**... Leave	.0	....	9 30	4 15

s—Regular Stop. f—Stop on signal. †Trains will not stop. *Train order stations.

Train No. 8 will have right of track over Train No. 1 to North end of Robertsdale. No. 7 will take siding at Orbisonia for No. 4
All trains run daily except Sunday. The Company reserves the right to vary from the above Time Table without notice.
Trains will run on the Shade Gap, Rocky Ridge and Coles Valley branches on special orders.

RAILWAY EXPRESS AGENCY OPERATES ON OUR LINES

Pennsylvania Railroad Trains Leave Mount Union

EAST—12.49 a. m., 4.54 a. m., 8.40 a. m., 11.04 a. m., 1.55 p. m., 4.07 p. m.
WEST—6.54 a. m., 9.26 a. m., 1.15 p. m., 5.13 p. m., 8.22 p. m.

PIONEER TRAIL

MOTOR COACH SERVICE

THROUGH and LOCAL SERVICE

ALTOONA, TYRONE, HUNTINGDON, MOUNT UNION, ORBISONIA, McCONNELLSBURG, MERCERSBURG, HAGERSTOWN, MD.

THROUGH CONNECTIONS

BUFFALO, N. Y. WARREN, PA. JAMESTOWN, N. Y. OIL CITY—ERIE	TO	WASHINGTON, D. C. BALTIMORE, MD. WINCHESTER, VA.

AND ALL POINTS SOUTH

Connections at McConnellsburg, Pa., for
Chambersburg, Gettysburg, York, Lancaster, Philadelphia and Atlentic City via Greyhound Lines
Connections at Tyrone, Pa., for
Philipsburg, Clearfield, Du Bois, Oil City, Franklin, Kane, Warren, Jamestown, N. Y., Buffalo, N. Y.
Local and through Time Tables may be obtained from any Ticket Agent or General Office, Orbisonia, Pa.

Also operates Freight Truck Service—Huntingdon to McConnellsburg

Telephones—Orbisonia 211, Mount Union 97 and 127 — **C. D. JONES,** Vice President and General Manager

Even with the hard economic times of the Depression, except for time changes, the number of daily, except Sunday, main line passenger trains remained the same from 1932 to the October 1, 1936, timetable of the East Broad Top Railroad. However, there was no longer regular railroad passenger service on the Shade Gap branch. The schedule noted, "Trains will run on the Shade Gap, Rocky Ridge and Coles Valley branches on special orders." East Broad Top Transit Company bus service (subsidiary of the East Broad Top Railroad), which began on August 3, 1929, from Huntingdon to Hagerstown, Maryland, via Mount Union and Orbisonia, was not able to make up for the decline in passenger train riders. Pennsylvania Railroad service had been reduced to six eastbound and five westbound passenger trains departing from the borough of Mount Union. (Pennsylvania Railroad, collection of Susan Yosten.)

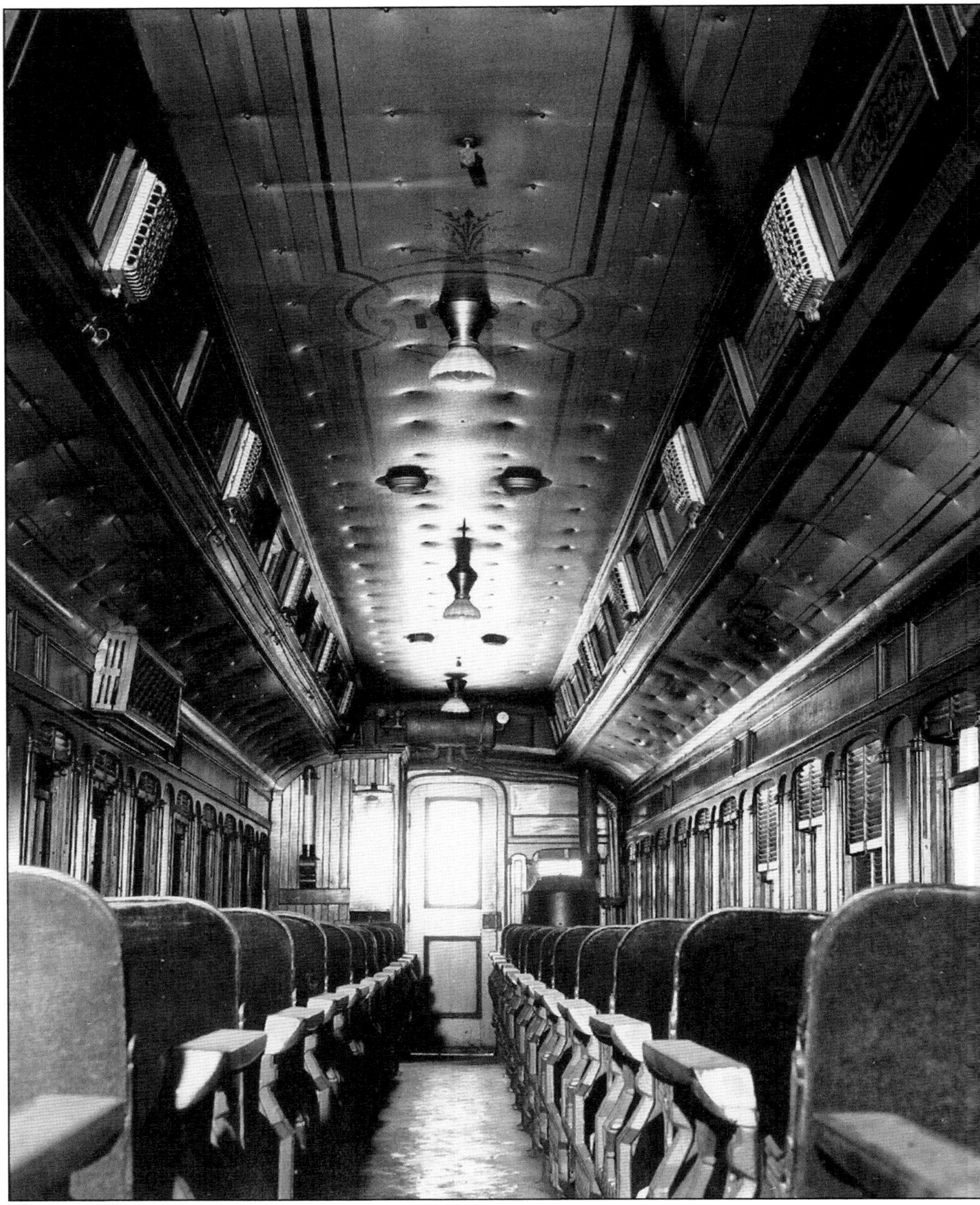

This is the interior of East Broad Top Railroad passenger car No. 8. Laconia Car Company built this car in 1882 for the Boston, Revere Beach and Lynn Railroad, which was a narrow-gauge railroad that linked suburban communities with Boston. It was sold to the East Broad Top Railroad in 1916. In 1965, Stanley G. Hall, who later became general manager of the East Broad Top Railroad, and Sam Price, from Mount Union, replaced the old ceiling with a new ceiling. They made a new template and hand painted the new ceiling. As of 2007, this car was 125 years old and still in use. (East Broad Top Railroad collection.)

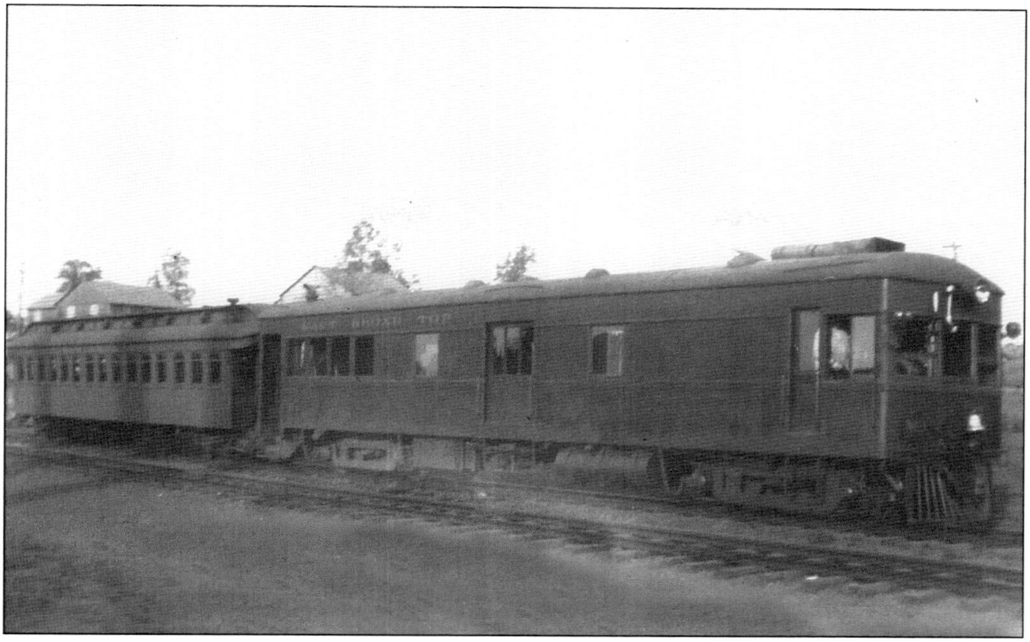

Gas-electric "doodlebug" M-1 is pictured at the town of Woodvale on September 11, 1930, hauling passenger car No. 8. The gas engine in M-1 was powerful enough to handle one or two coaches, tow freight cars, and even move disabled locomotives. Car No. 8 received new roller bearing trucks and was the passenger car generally assigned with the M-1. (Photograph by W. H. Watts, Robert G. Lewis collection.)

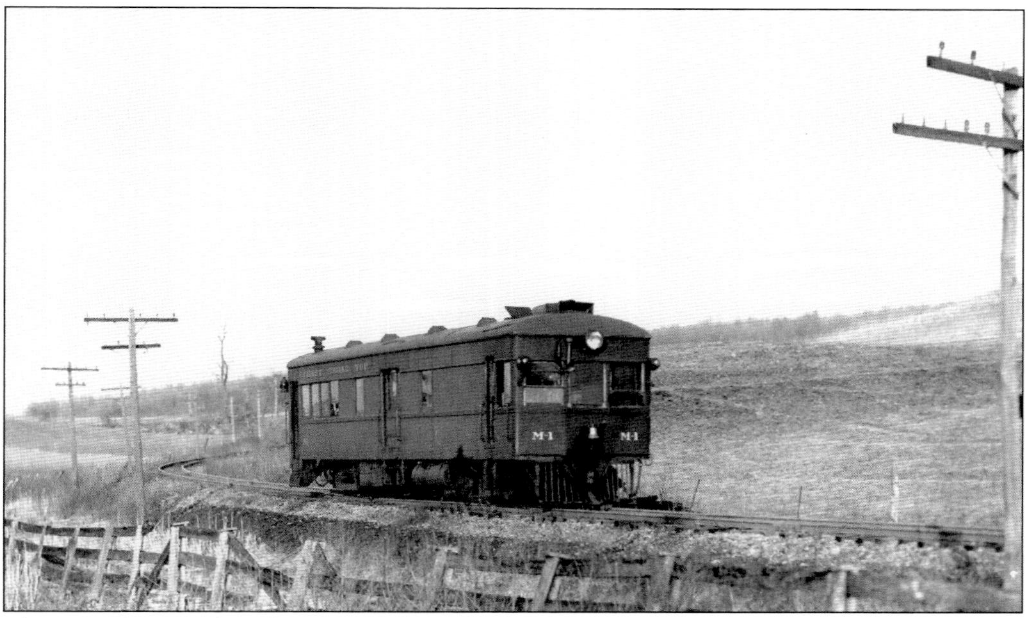

The versatile M-1 is handling an assignment on the East Broad Top Railroad on February 7, 1953. The M-1 handled passenger service on Saturdays and the annual two-week miners' vacation period. Still in service in 2007, the M-1 celebrated its 80th birthday, which was a tribute to the railroad and its employees. (Photograph by Robert G. Lewis.)

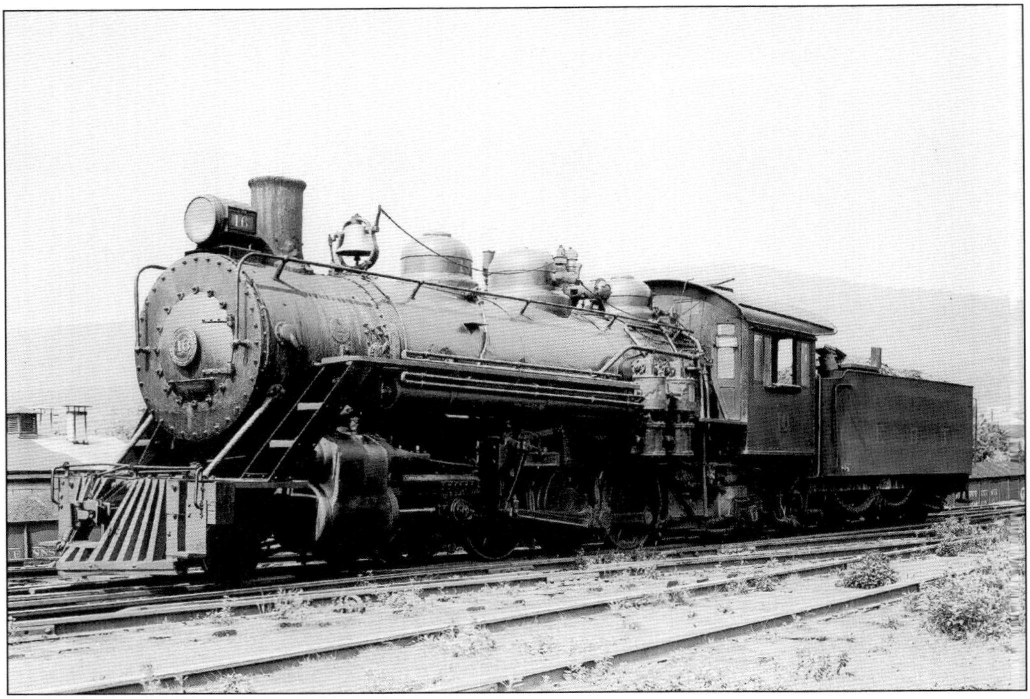

Locomotive No. 16 is at the brickyard in the borough of Mount Union in the early 1930s. Baldwin Locomotive Works delivered this locomotive to the East Broad Top Railroad in June 1916. This Mikado-type locomotive, with a 2-8-2 wheel arrangement, weighed 163,000 pounds and had 48-inch-diameter drive wheels. (East Broad Top Railroad collection.)

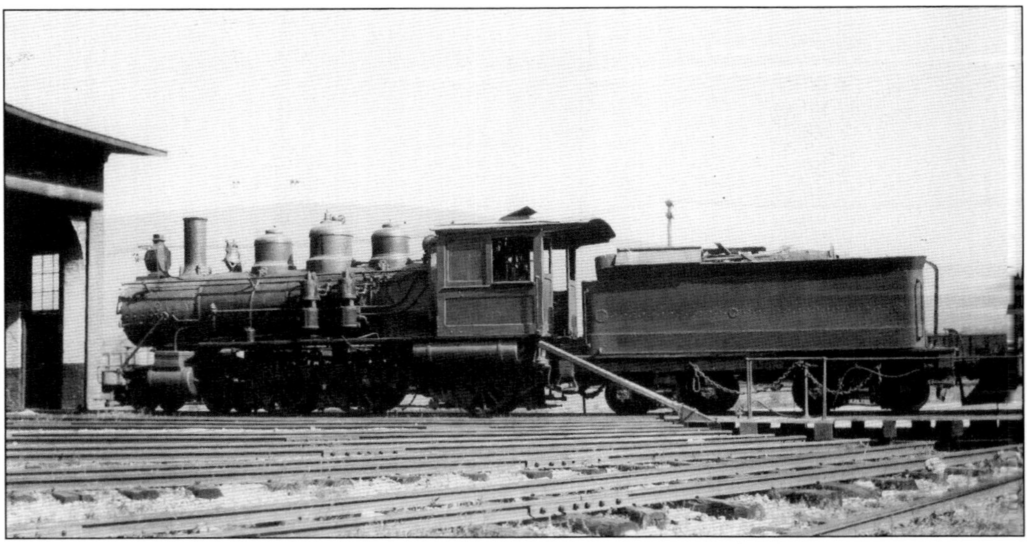

A Ten Wheeler–type locomotive, the second No. 4 with a 4-6-0 wheel arrangement, is going into stall No. 1 at the Rockhill Furnace roundhouse. Baldwin Locomotive Works built this locomotive in December 1901, and it was retired during 1927. The first No. 4 locomotive was built by Baldwin Locomotive Works with a 2-8-0 wheel arrangement in May 1874 and was off the roster by 1895. (East Broad Top Railroad collection.)

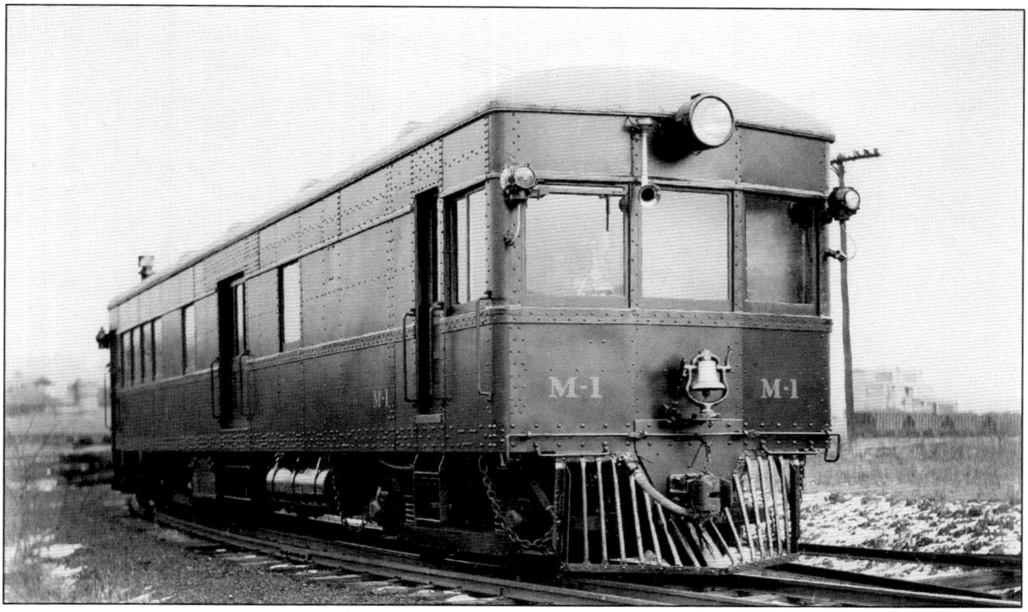

Gas-electric motor car M-1 is at the Mount Union yard heading south in the 1930s. Built at the Rockhill Furnace shops from parts obtained from J. G. Brill Car Company and complete electrical equipment from Westinghouse Electric Company, it began service on January 5, 1927, and its operating cost was about 50 percent of the operating cost of a steam locomotive. (East Broad Top Railroad collection.)

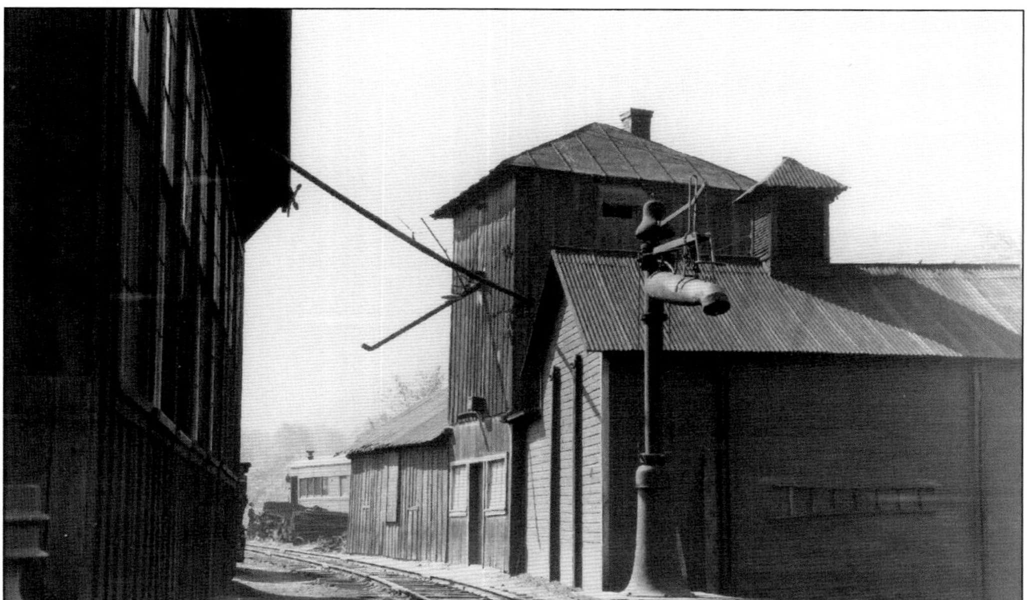

Waiting for the next assignment, gas-electric motor car M-1 is behind the ice/sand house adjacent to the shop complex at the Rockhill Furnace yard in the early 1940s. Passenger traffic on the East Broad Top Railroad declined as rural roads were paved. The railroad operated passenger service for the miners. On days the mines were closed, the M-1 operated to handle mail and express. (East Broad Top Railroad collection.)

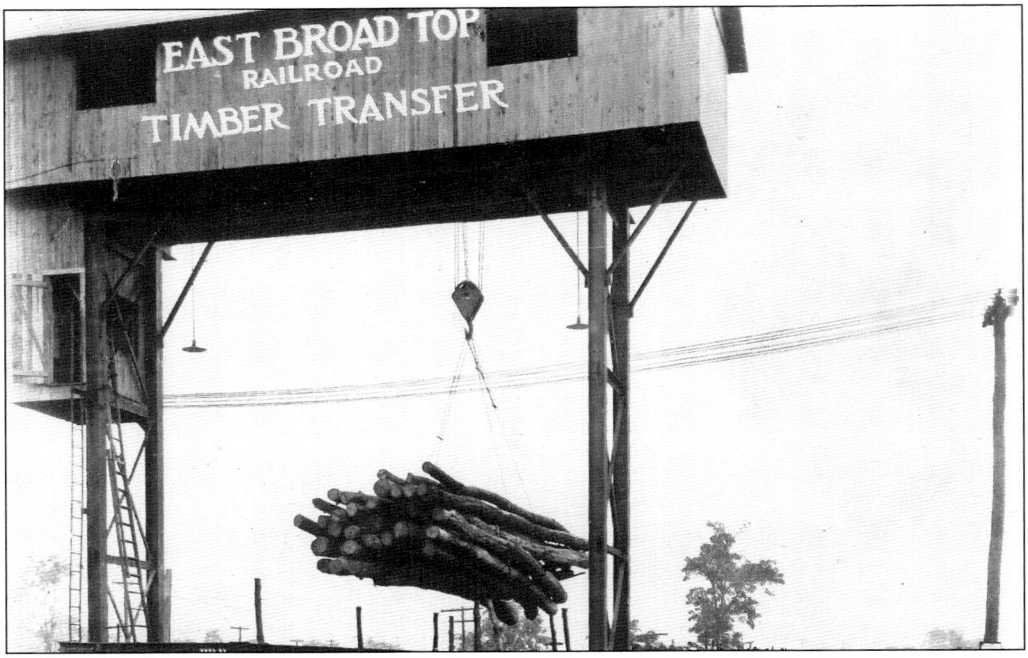

The East Broad Top Railroad timber transfer at the Mount Union yard is loading pulpwood from an East Broad Top Railroad flatcar to a Pennsylvania Railroad gondola. This timber transfer was later used to lift standard-gauge car bodies off their trucks and place them on narrow-gauge trucks. (East Broad Top Railroad collection.)

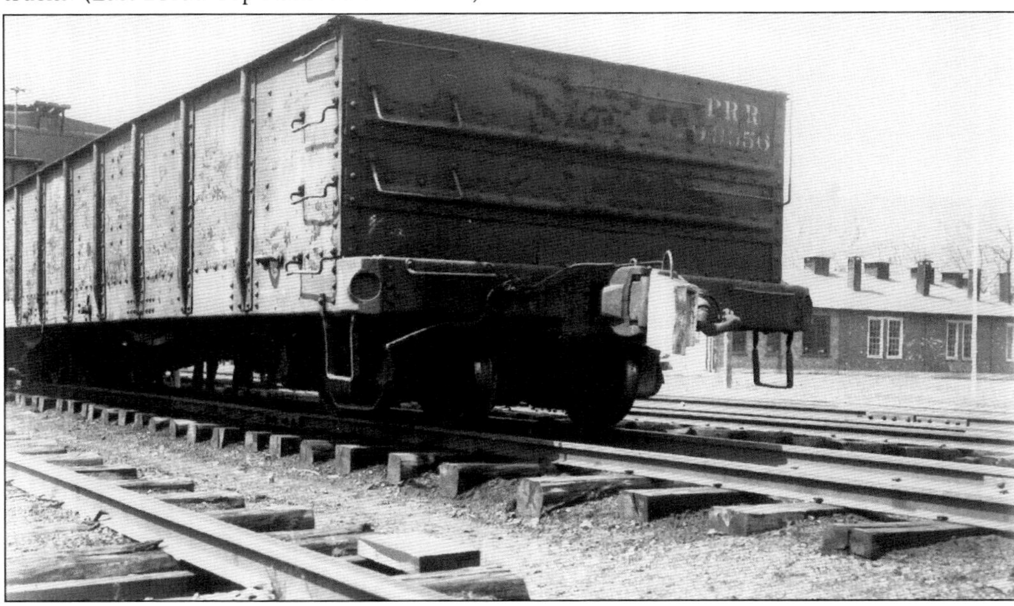

A Pennsylvania Railroad standard-gauge gondola car on narrow-gauge trucks with the aluminum alloy–designed adapter is at the Rockhill Furnace yard. Replacing the standard-gauge trucks of incoming car bodies to narrow-gauge trucks was successful because the East Broad Top Railroad's well-maintained track minimized the sway of standard-gauge cars on narrow-gauge track. (East Broad Top Railroad collection.)

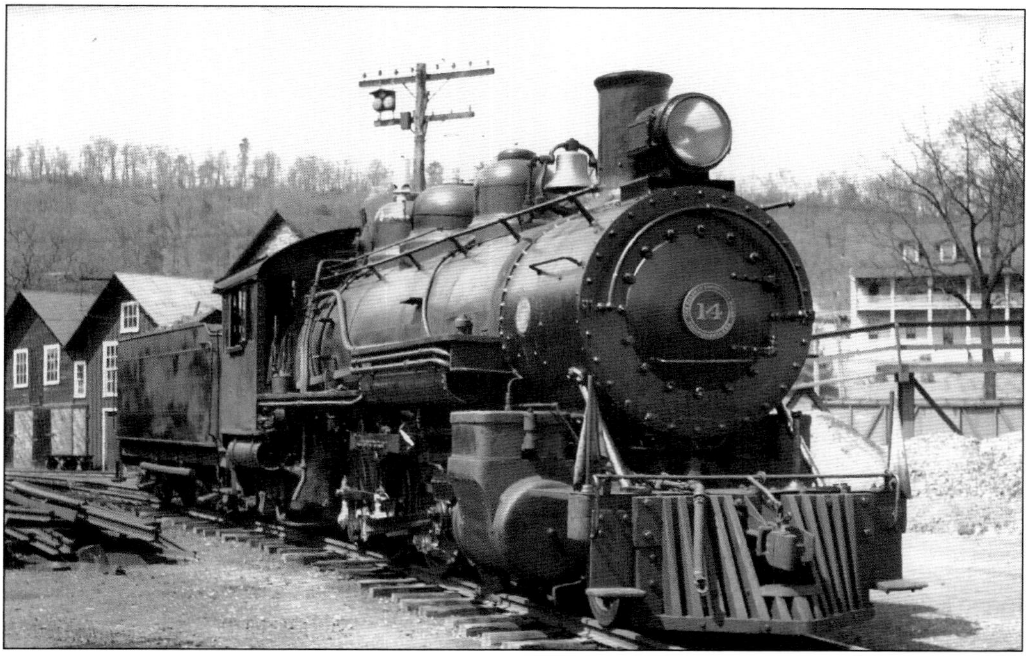

East Broad Top Railroad locomotive No. 14 is shown at the Rockhill Furnace yard on May 3, 1936. During the construction of the Pennsylvania Turnpike, freight trains carried highway construction material over the Shade Gap branch to the town of Neelyton. Once the highway was completed, business on the Shade Gap branch declined, and the branch was cut back to the Blacklog station in 1948. (Photograph by Robert G. Lewis.)

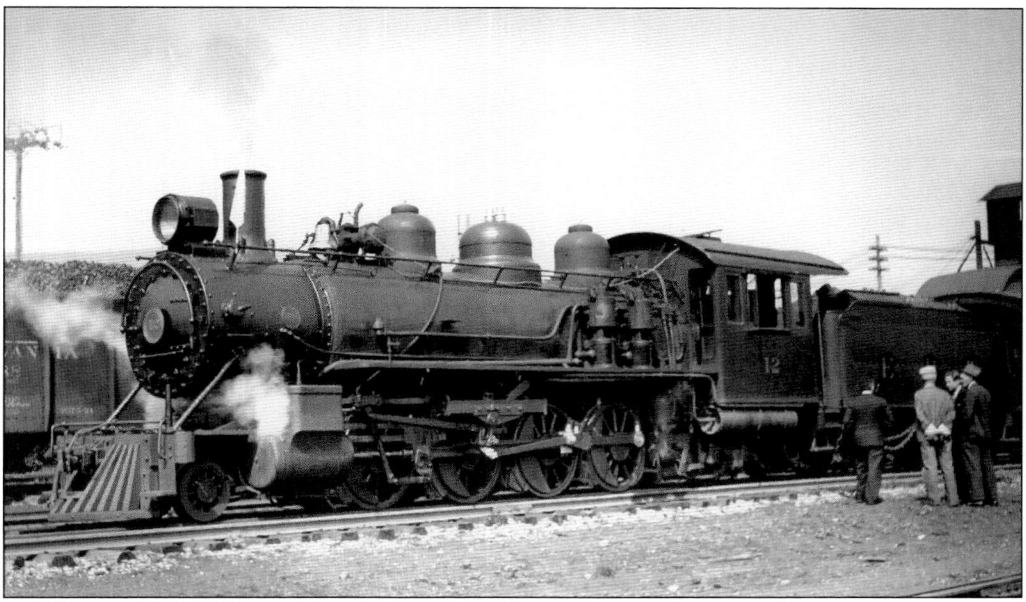

Mount Union yard finds several well-dressed passengers on the Lancaster Chapter of the National Railway Historical Society excursion gathered near the cab of East Broad Top Railroad locomotive No. 12 on May 3, 1936. This railroad featured a variety of vintage equipment that was attracting attention throughout the United States. (Photograph by Robert G. Lewis.)

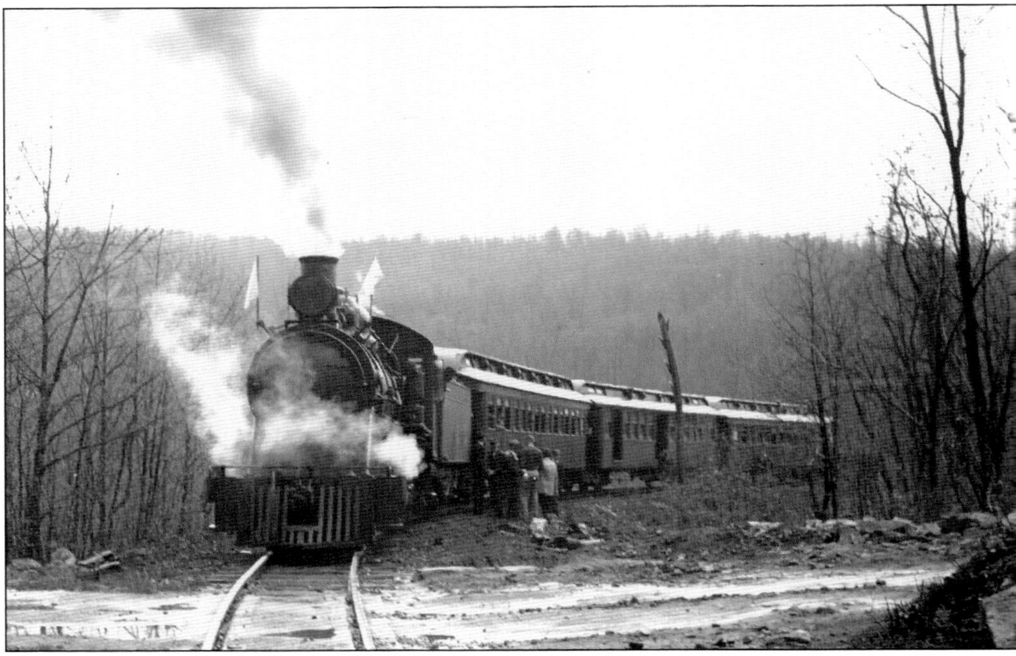

A three-car special train is on the Shade Gap branch on May 3, 1936. The Lancaster Chapter of the National Railway Historical Society chartered the train pulled by East Broad Top Railroad locomotive No. 12. Many of the students of transportation on the train wore suits as noted by the group congregated at the first passenger car. (Photograph by Robert G. Lewis.)

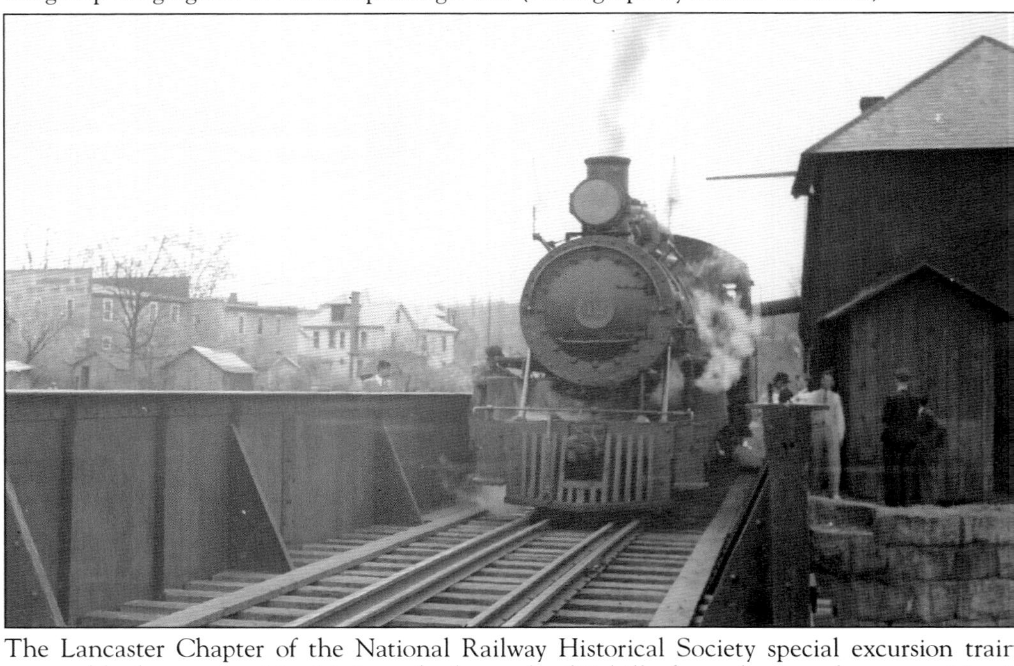

The Lancaster Chapter of the National Railway Historical Society special excursion train, powered by locomotive No. 12, is at the borough of Saltillo for a photograph stop on May 3, 1936. Additional excursions were held on the railroad, which over a period of time generated interest throughout the United States and around the world. (Photograph by Robert G. Lewis.)

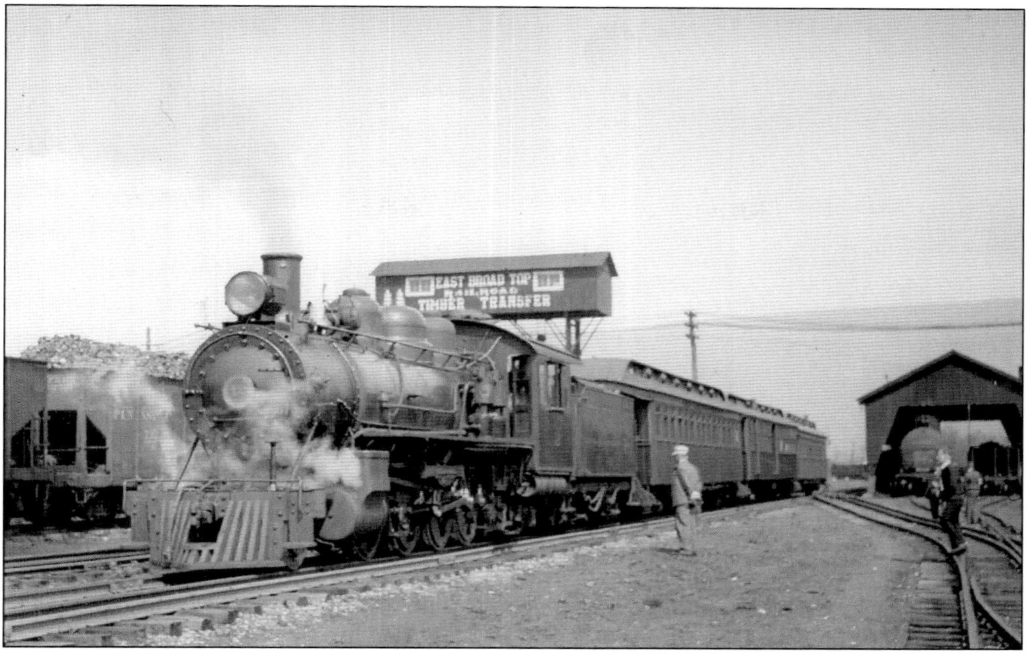

Locomotive No. 12 is powering the Lancaster Chapter of the National Railway Historical Society's excursion on May 3, 1936, at the Mount Union yard. The East Broad Top Railroad timber transfer, in view, had an electric-powered overhead gantry crane that was used to lift a standard-gauge freight car off its trucks one end at a time and roll in a narrow-gauge truck. (Photograph by Robert G. Lewis.)

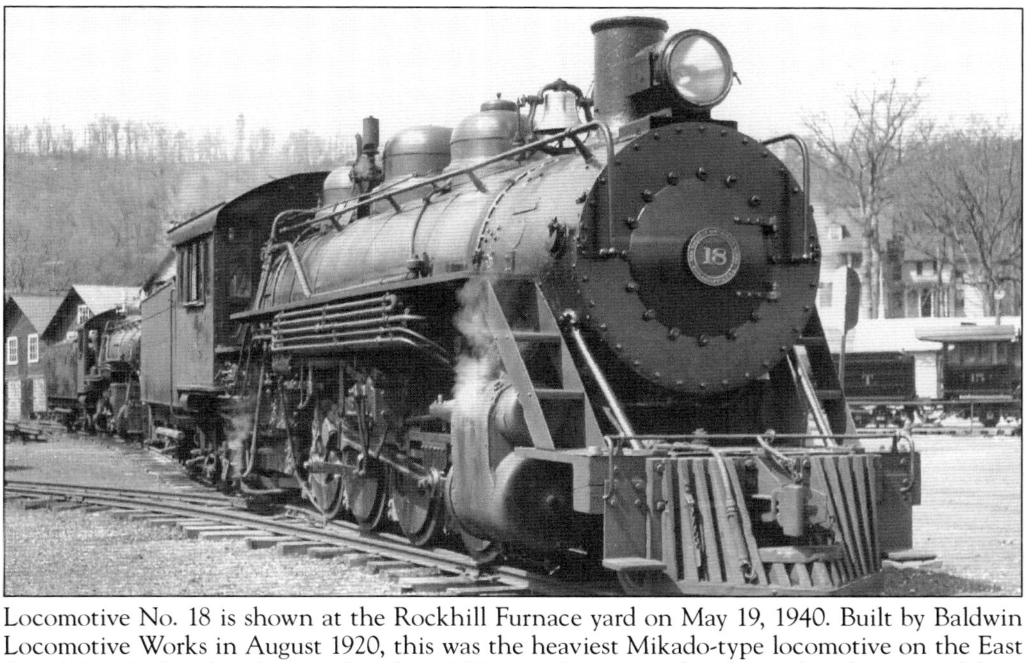

Locomotive No. 18 is shown at the Rockhill Furnace yard on May 19, 1940. Built by Baldwin Locomotive Works in August 1920, this was the heaviest Mikado-type locomotive on the East Broad Top Railroad with a weight of 164,200 pounds compared with weights that ranged from 112,000 pounds for No. 12 to 163,500 pounds for No. 17. (Photograph by Robert G. Lewis.)

A. M. Light Type — **EFFECTIVE MAY 1st, 1932** — **P. M. Dark Type**

RUNS NO.		11	1	3	5	13	7	9	15	17
Northbound		Week day	Week day	Daily	Week Day	Week Day	Week Day	Daily	Saturday	Saturday
Saltillo—E. B. T. Station	...	...	7 45	Through	...	...	5 35	Through	...	...
3 Springs—Wilson's Ser. Sta.	...	...	7 53	Coach	...	...	5 42	Coach	...	...
Pogue	...	...	8 00	...	...	...	6 50	...	...	...
Rockhill Furnace—E. B. T.	...	...	8 07	...	1 55	...	6 00		...	...
Orbisonia—Allender's	...	...	8 10	12 35	2 00	...	...	10 15	...	...
Shirleysburg—P. O.	...	...	8 18	12 42	2 08	...	...	10 22	...	...
Allenton—Buckley & Fegan	...	...	8 30	12 52	2 20		...	10 32		
Mt. Union—Peduzzi's	...	5 55	8 35	12 55	2 25	3 55	...	10 35	11 05	6 15
Mt. Union—E B. T. Station	...	6 00	8 40	12 57	2 30	4 00	...	10 37	11 07	6 17
Mapleton	...	6 10	8 50	1 04	2 42	4 10	...	10 44	11 17	6 27
Mill Creek	...	6 20	9 00	1 12	2 52	4 20	...	10 52	11 27	6 37
Ardenheim	...	6 25	9 07	1 20	3 00	4 30	...	11 00	11 35	6 45
Huntingdon—Leister House	...	...	9 15	1 25	3 05	4 35	...	11 05	11 40	6 50
5th & Penn Sts.	...	6 30	9 17	1 27	3 08	4 37	...	11 07	11 42	6 52
7th & Wash.Sts.	...	6 32	...	...	3 10	4 40	...	...	11 45	6 55
Silk Mill	...	6 36		...	...		...	...		...
Post Office	...	6 45	9 12	...	3 15	4 45	...		11 50	7 00
Alexandria—Imperial Hotel	...	...	9 32	1 40	...	...	...	11 20	...	
Water Street—Inn	...	...	9 40	1 45	...	...	...	11 25	...	...
Birmingham	...		10 00	2 00	...		...	11 43	...	...
Tyrone—Arlington Hotel	...	...	10 10	2 10	...			11 50		

Run 1: Subject to cancellation without notice Huntingdon-Tyrone

RUNS NO.	8	10	12		2	4	6	14	16	18
Southbound	Week day	Daily	Week day		Week day	Daily	Week day	Week day	Saturday	Saturday
Tyrone—Arlington Hotel	...	6 10	...	...	10 30	3 25	...	...	...	...
Birmingham	...	6 17	...	...	10 40	3 32	...	...	...	...
Water Street—Inn	...	6 40	...	...	11 00	3 50	...	...	...	...
Alexandria—Imperial Hotel	...	6 45	...	...	11 10	3 55	...	...	...	...
Huntingdon—Post Office	...	...	7 35	...	11 35	...	3 40	5 20	11 50	10 10
Silk Mill	...	...	...	...	...	...	...	5 35	12 00	...
7th & Wash.Sts.	...	...	7 38	...	...	...	3 45	5 40	12 03	10 15
5th & Penn Sts.	...	6 53	7 40	...	11 28	4 08	3 48	5 42	12 07	10 18
Leister House	...	6 55	7 45	...	11 30	4 10	3 50	...	...	10 20
Ardenheim	...	7 00	7 50	...	11 40	4 15	3 58	5 47	12 15	10 25
Mill Creek	...	7 08	8 00	...	11 50	4 22	4 07	5 53	12 25	10 35
Mapleton	...	7 14	8 10	...	12 00	4 31	4 20	6 00	12 35	10 45
Mt. Union—E. B. T. Station	...	7 20	8 20	...	12 07	4 38	4 33	6 08	12 43	10 55
Mt. Union—Peduzzi's	...	7 22	8 23	...	12 10	4 40	4 35	6 10	12 45	10 58
Allenton—Buckley & Fegan	...	7 25	8 35	...	...	4 43	4 40	...	...	...
Shirleysburg—P. O.	...	7 33	8 45	...	...	4 53	4 52	...	...	...
Orbisonia—Allender's	7 20	7 40	8 55	...	...	5 00	5 00	...	...	...
Rockhill Furnace—E. B. T.	7 23	...	9 00	...	...	...	5 05	...	...	...
Pogue	7 30	...	...	...	...	...	5 12	...	...	...
3 Springs—Wilson's Ser. Sta.	7 37	Through	Note	...	Note	Through	5 22	...	...	...
Saltillo—E. B. T. Station	7 45	Coach	2	...	3	Coach	5 30	...	...	...

Run 2: Subject to cancellation without notice Huntingdon-Tyrone

The East Broad Top Transit Company local motor coach schedule from Saltillo to Tyrone effective May 1, 1932, shows most of the bus service was between Mount Union and Huntingdon with six trips weekdays in each direction and four trips on Saturday in each direction. There were two daily through northbound trips leaving Orbisonia at 12:35 p.m. and 10:15 p.m. and arriving at Tyrone at 2:10 p.m. and 11:50 p.m., respectively, and two daily through southbound trips leaving Tyrone at 6:10 a.m. and 3:25 p.m. and arriving at Orbisonia at 7:40 a.m. and 5:00 p.m., respectively. Through motor coach service operated from Tyrone via Huntingdon and McConnellsburg to Hagerstown, Maryland. There were two weekday northbound trips leaving Saltillo at 7:45 a.m. and 5:35 p.m. and arriving at Rockhill Furnace at 8:07 a.m. and 6:00 p.m., respectively, and two weekday southbound trips leaving Rockhill Furnace at 7:23 a.m. and 5:05 p.m. and arriving at Saltillo at 7:45 a.m. and 5:30 p.m., respectfully. (John C. Corson collection.)

PENNSYLVANIA RAILROAD

The Standard Railroad of the World

Pittsburgh Night Express. Sleeping Cars.
The American. Sleeping Cars. Lounge Car. No Baggage Service.
The Buckeye Limited. No Coaches.
Manhattan Limited.
The St. Louisan. Dining Car.
"Spirit of St. Louis." Dining Car. Lounge Car.
The Red Arrow. Dining Car.
Broadway Limited. *Special Service Charge.* No Coaches.
The Liberty Limited. Dining Car.
The Cincinnati Limited. Dining Car. Lounge Car.
The Golden Arrow. Dining Car. Lounge Car.
The Pennsylvania Limited. Parlor Car. Dining Car.
The Fort Dearborn. The Duquesne. Dining Car. Parlor Car. Sleeping Car.
Buffet Parlor Car Lock Haven to Pittsburgh.
Sleeping Car. Parlor Car. Dining Car. Observation Car.
Parlor Coach. Cafe Coach.
Sleeping Car. Buffet Parlor Car.
No Baggage Service.
The Pittsburgher. No Coaches. Sleeping Cars.
The Statesman. Sleeping Cars. Drawing-room Sleeping Car Scranton to Pittsburgh (via D. L. & W. R.R., Sunbury and Harrisburg.) Drawing-room Sleeping Car Harrisburg to Pittsburgh (open 9 00 p.m.).
Iron City Express. Sleeping Car. Lounge Car.

Table 105. HOLLIDAYSBURG, MORRISON'S COVE AND MARTINSBURG BRANCHES. MIDDLE DIVISION.

EAST BROAD TOP RAILROAD & COAL CO.

P. C. MADEIRA, President, Philadelphia, Pa.
C. D. JONES, Vice-President and Gen. Manager, Philadelphia and Orbisonia, Pa.
L. W. HICKS, Vice-President, Pittsburgh, Pa.
JOHN GILBERT, Secretary and Asst. Treas., Philadelphia, Pa.
J. W. POWELL, Treasurer, "
G. H. SHRYOCK, Asst. Sec'y and Asst. Treas., Philadelphia, Pa.
J. D. DORRIS, General Counsel, Huntingdon, Pa.
C. C. HAHN, Auditor, Philadelphia, Pa.
P. F. YEAGER, Traffic Manager, Orbisonia, Pa.
N. P. BERNHARDT, Chief Engineer, Orbisonia, Pa.
J. O. BOWMASTER, Master Mechanic, Orbisonia, Pa.
A. M. CHILCOAT, Trainmaster, "
E. C. SHILEY, Supt.—Coal Transfer Plant, Mt. Union, Pa.

General Office—Orbisonia, Pa.
Philadelphia Office—1421 Chestnut Street.

■4	■2	8	Mls	April 27, 1936.	■1	■3	7	■5
	A M			LEAVE] [ARRIVE	P M	P M		
A M	4 06			North Philadelphia	4 04	9 14		
8 30				Phila. (Broad St.)		8 40		
8 34				Phila. Pa. Sta. (30th St.)		8 31		
11 10	4 25			lve.. Pittsburgh ..arr.	1 30	9 35		
P M	A M			LEAVE] [ARRIVE	A M	P M		
†4 15	†9 20		0	Mount Union	8 42	3 35		
f4 32	f9 38		1	Allenton	f8 31	f3 21		
f4 39	f9 46		4	Aughwick	f8 21	f3 10		
f4 43	f9 49		5	Pump Station	f8 18	f3 08		
4 48	9 54		7	Shirleysburg	8 14	3 05		
5 02	10 08	A M	11	arr.. Orbisonia ..lve.	8 00	2 50	P M	
5 20	10 30	†5 30	11	lve.. Orbisonia ..arr.	8 00	2 50	5 05	
f5 30	f10 40	f5 40	14	Pogue	f7 44	f2 31	f4 52	
5 40	10 55	5 50	17	Three Springs	7 36	2 23	4 44	
5 50	11 10	5 58	19	Saltillo	7 29	2 15	4 36	
– –	– –	f6 12	22	Fairview	– –	– –	f4 21	
f6 17	f11 38	f6 17	23	Kimmel	f7 12	f1 56	f4 16	
f6 25	f11 44	f6 22	24	Coles	f7 07	f1 51	f4 11	
f6 30	f11 50	f6 27	26	Rocky Ridge	f7 02	f1 46	f4 05	
f6 37	f11 58	f6 35	27	Cooks	f6 55	f1 40	f3 58	P M
6 50	12 10	6 45	30	Robertsdale	6 45	1 30	3 45	7 05
6 55	12 20	6 53	32	Woodvale	†6 30	†12 20	3 35	†6 55
P M	P M	7 00	33	arr..... Alvan ....lve.	A M	P M	†3 30	P M

Standard gauge cars are handled over the entire line by transferring bodies to specially designed 3-ft. gauge trucks with no extra cost for this service.

THE EAST BROAD TOP TRANSIT CO.

Motor Coach Schedule. *Pioneer Trail Route*

Read Down.				Mls.	July 4, 1936.	Read Up.			
A M			P M		LEAVE] [ARRIVE		P M		A M
*7 00			*9 10		Buffalo		9 00		7 2?
9 35			11 50		lve... Bradford ...arr.		6 35		4 4?
10 25			12 40		arr...... Kane .....lve.		5 50		4 0?
1 15		A M	3 15		lve.. Punxsutawney .lve.		3 15	P M	1 1?
5 20		*11 30	8 00	0	lv. { ..Altoona.. P. R.R. Station } ar.		10 40	4 50	8 2?
5 25		11 35	8 05	0.6	lve.. { Altoona Bus Depot } .arr.		10 35	4 45	8 1?
5 55		12 05	8 35	16.4	arr..... Tyrone ....lve.		10 05	4 15	7 4?
	P M			37.8	lve.. Huntingdon .arr.	A M			
6 40	†4 15	1 05	9 40		*Leister House*	6 46	9 00	3 20	6 4?
7 05	4 40	1 35	10 10	50.9	lve. Mount Union arr.	6 15	8 30	2 55	6 2?
7 18	4 53	1 48	10 23	58.0	Shirleysburg	6 02	8 17	2 46	6 0?
7 25	5 00	1 55	10 30	62.5	arr. .. Orbisonia .. lve.	5 55	8 10	2 35	6 0?
7 30	5 05			63.0	ar.. Rockhill Furnace .lv.	†5 50	*8 05		
P M	P M	2 00	10 35	62.5	lve. .. Orbisonia ..arr.	A M	A M	2 35	5 5?
		2 50	11 25	91.7	.. McConnellsburg ..			1 45	5 0?
		3 10	11 45	102.5	Mercersburg			1 25	4 4?
		3 30	12 05	113.6	Greencastle			1 05	4 2?
		3 50	12 25	125.0	arr.. Hagerstown .lve.			12 45	4 0?
		4 00	1 30		lve.. Hagerstown .arr.			12 40	3 5?
		6 30	4 00		arr... Baltimore ..lve.			*10 15	1 1?
		6 25	4 00		Washington			*10 15	*11 ?
		P M	P M		ARRIVE] [LEAVE			A M	P M

* Daily; † daily, except Sunday; *f* stops on signal. ■ Gas-electric train.
STANDARD—*Eastern time.*

The April 27, 1936, East Broad Top Railroad schedule and East Broad Top Transit Company bus schedule is shown along with a portion of the Pennsylvania Railroad passenger train schedule of July 12, 1936, from Harrisburg to Altoona. Orbisonia was a stop on the Buffalo to Washington, D.C., bus route. A one-day trip from Philadelphia involved the westbound Pennsylvania Railroad train leaving the North Philadelphia station at 4:06 a.m. and arriving in Mount Union at 8:55 a.m. The East Broad Top Railroad train left Mount Union at 9:20 a.m. and arrived in Orbisonia at 10:08 a.m. An afternoon East Broad Top Railroad train left Orbisonia at 2:50 p.m., arriving at Mount Union at 3:35 p.m. The eastbound Pennsylvania Railroad train left Mount Union at 3:57 p.m., arriving at the North Philadelphia station at 9:14 p.m. A day trip from Pittsburgh involved using the eastbound Pennsylvania Railroad train that left Pittsburgh at 4:25 a.m., arriving at Mount Union at 8:40 a.m. The westbound Pennsylvania Railroad train left Mount Union at 5:17 p.m., arriving in Pittsburgh at 9:35 p.m.

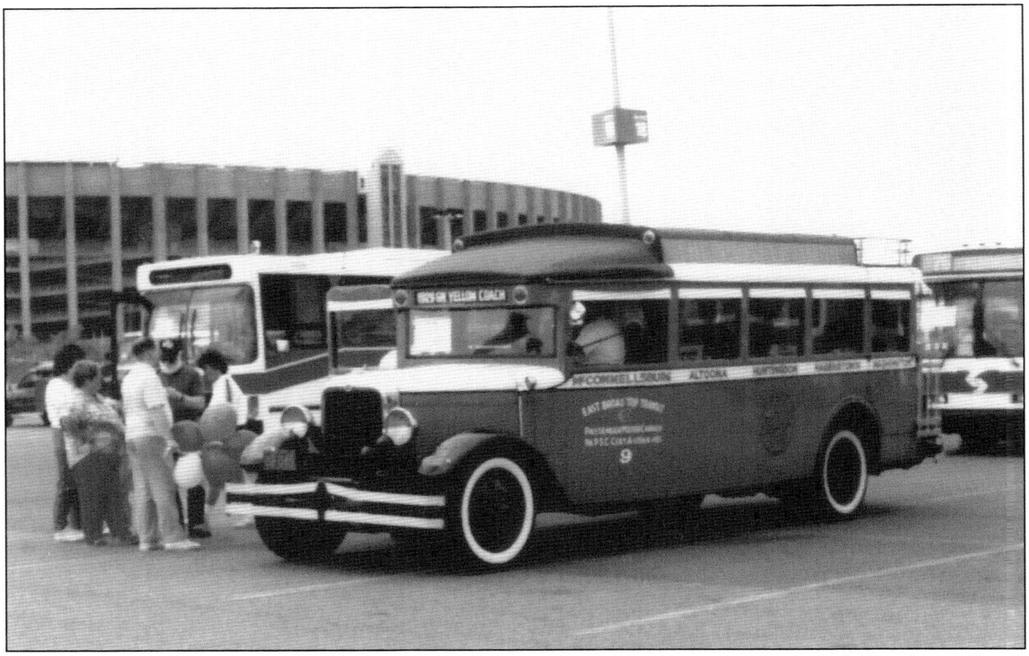

A restored East Broad Top Transit Company bus No. 9 (chassis No. 130564 with Buick overhead valve six-cylinder engine) is at Veterans Stadium in Philadelphia for a bus rodeo on July 23, 1990. On August 3, 1929, bus service began from Huntingdon via Mount Union and Orbison a to Hagerstown, Maryland. Two buses were destroyed in the July 8, 1933, Orbisonia bus garage fire. Two replacement buses manufactured by General Motors Truck, Division of Yellow Truck and Coach Manufacturing Company of Pontiac, Michigan, were purchased from White Star Lines of Washington, Pennsylvania (a Greyhound Lines subsidiary). They did not match the East Broad Top Transit Company red and white paint scheme but were relettered and retained their Greyhound blue and white paint scheme. The bus system was sold in the early 1940s. (Oliver J. Ogden, Museum of Bus Transportation photographs.)

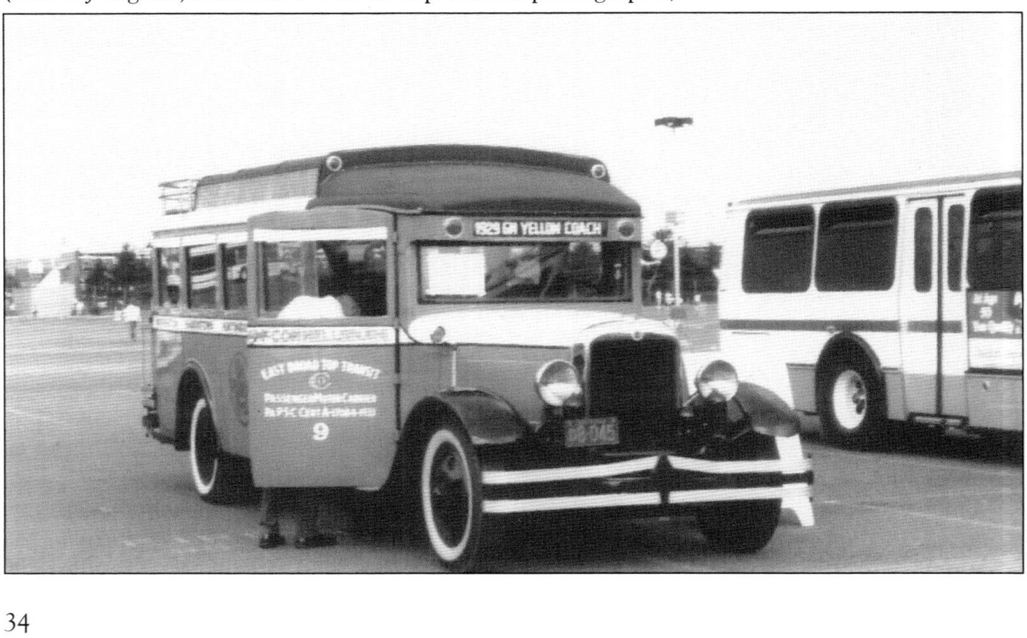

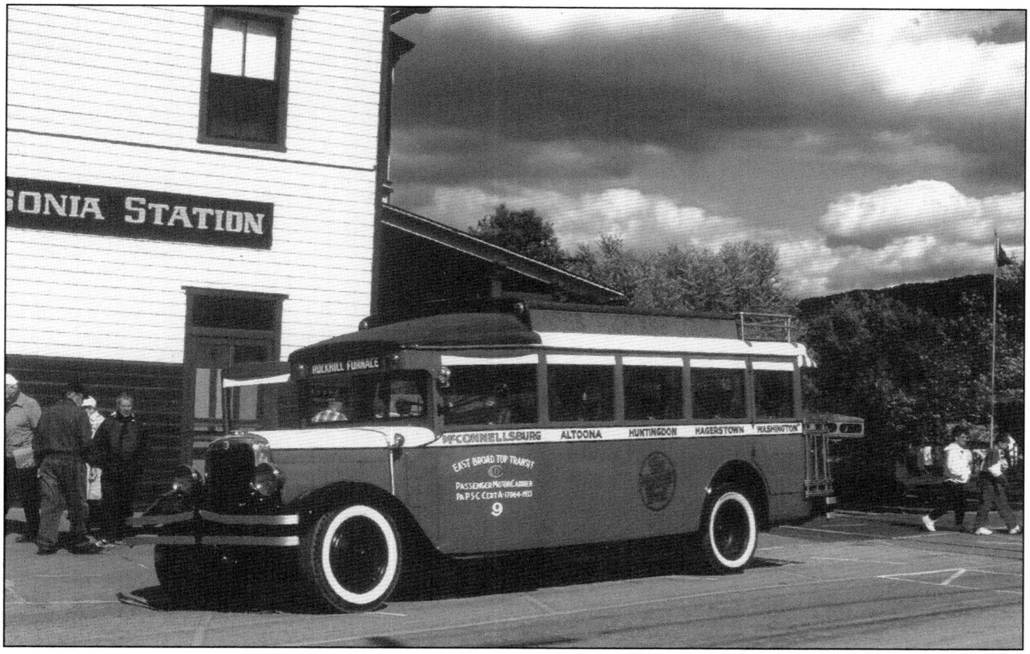

Yellow Coach model W bus is at the Orbisonia station on October 6, 2001. Built by General Motors Truck, Division of Yellow Truck and Coach Manufacturing Company of Pontiac, Michigan, in August 1929 as a sales demonstrator, Iowa Railway and Light Company of Cedar Rapids, Iowa, purchased it December 1929. John C. Corson acquired it and restored it as East Broad Top Transit Company bus No. 9. (Photograph by Kenneth C. Springirth.)

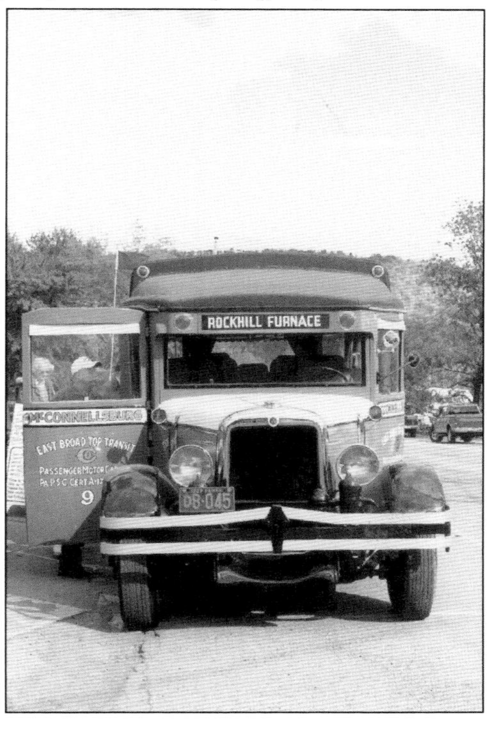

In this October 6, 2001, view at Rockhill Furnace this bus has been restored to match East Broad Top Transit Company bus No. 9. Weighing 10,000 pounds, the 21-passenger bus is 24 feet long and is 90 inches wide. With the bus owned by John C. Corson, restoration began in 1986 by Kelso Restoration in McConnellsburg and was finished in 1987. (Photograph by Kenneth C. Springirth.)

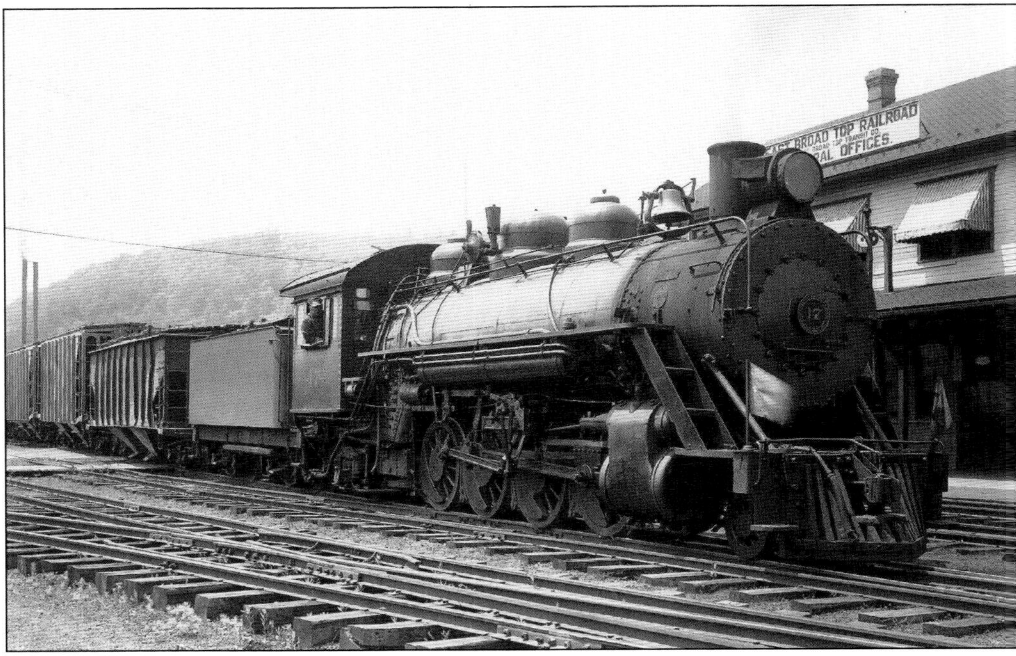

A train of standard hopper cars and covered hopper cars is passing the Orbisonia station in the 1940s. The high standard of track maintenance made it possible to handle standard-gauge cars and provided the East Broad Railroad the ability to retain tonnage that would have been lost to trucks. (East Broad Top Railroad collection.)

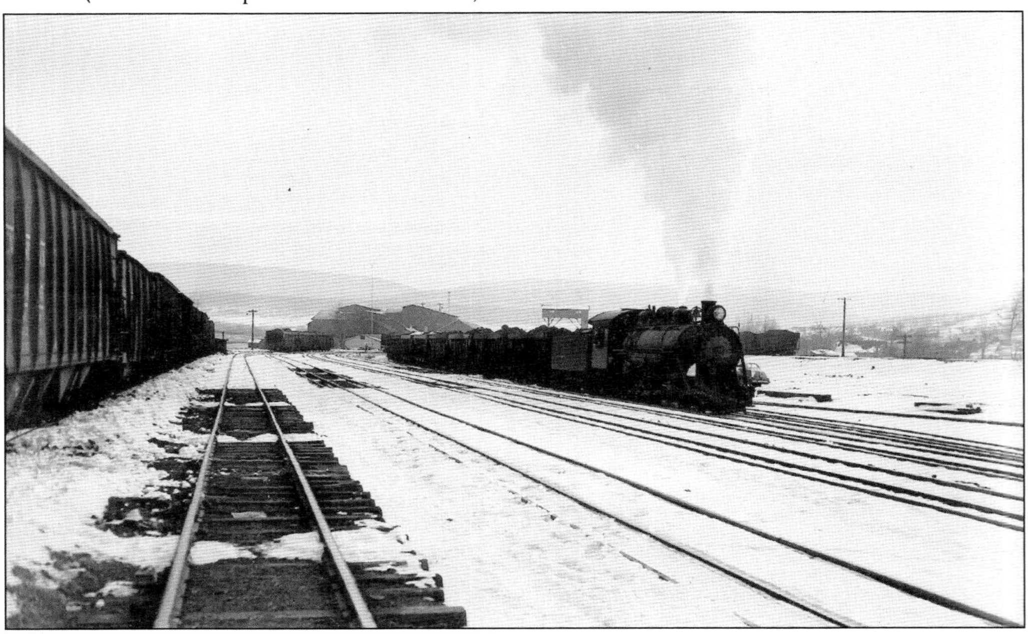

Locomotive No. 17 is making its way through the Mount Union yard in the early 1940s. The timber transfer is in the picture just behind the locomotive. Winter in south-central Pennsylvania can be snowy, but the East Broad Top Railroad operated in all types of weather conditions. (East Broad Top Railroad collection.)

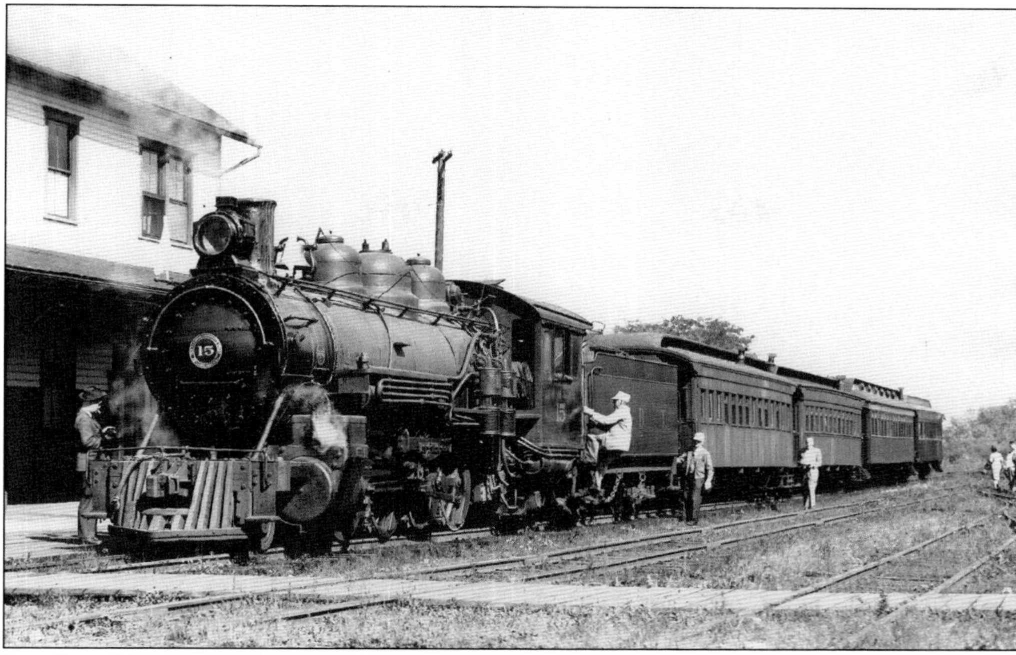

East Broad Top Railroad locomotive No. 15, with four passenger cars, is at the Orbisonia station on an October 6, 1946, rail excursion. Sixty-one years later, this scene could be retaken at the same station with locomotive No. 15, passenger car No. 8 (third car from the tender), and parlor car No. 20, which is the last car on the train. (East Broad Top Railroad collection.)

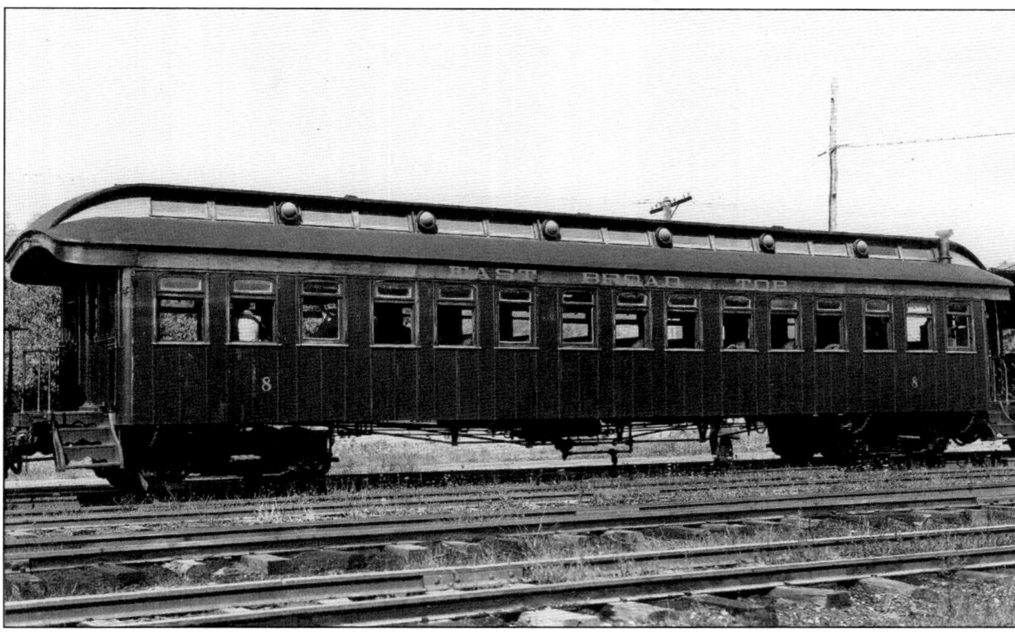

On October 6, 1946, East Broad Top Railroad passenger car No. 8 is at the Rockhill Furnace yard. Originally built by the Laconia Car Company in 1882, this 44-foot-long car, seating 52, was acquired in 1916 from the Boston, Revere Beach and Lynn Railroad. It was rebuilt in January 1927. (East Broad Top Railroad collection.)

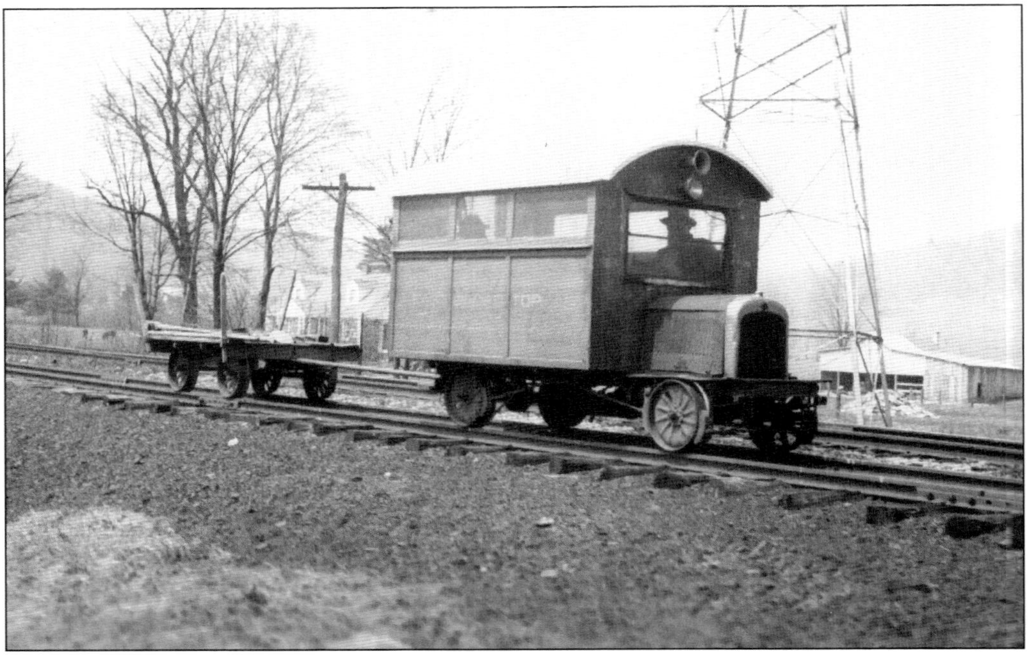

Motor car M-3 is at the village of Cooks on May 4, 1950. On the motor car is Horace Corbin, who was head policeman and track inspector for the East Broad Top Railroad and Rockhill Iron and Coal Company. Built at the East Broad Top Railroad shops in 1928, this motor car was used for inspection trips and to ferry maintenance crews over the line. (East Broad Top Railroad collection.)

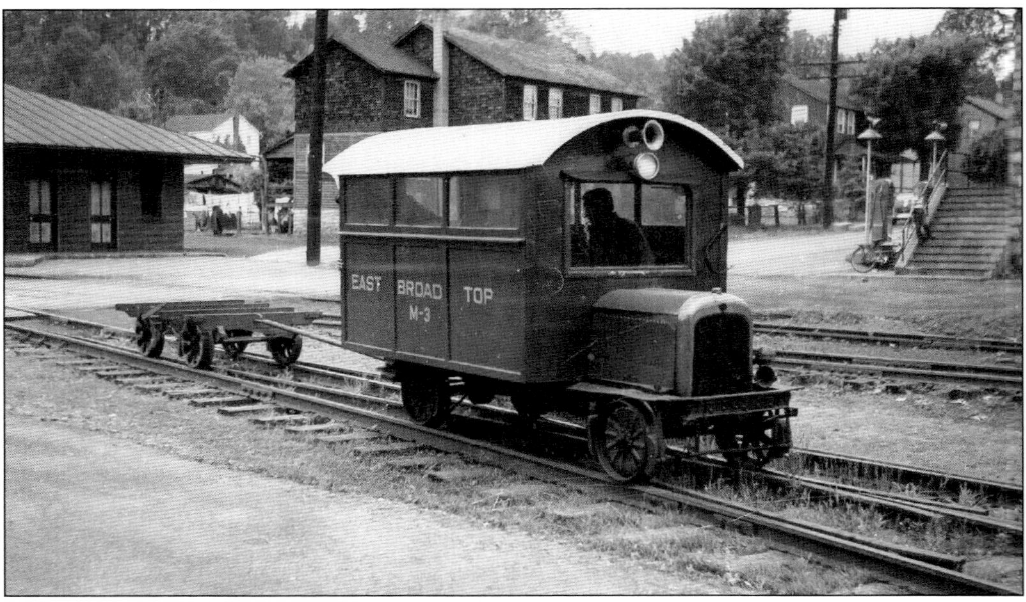

With the Robertsdale station in the background, motor car M-3 has just crossed Main Street and is on the Robertsdale wye on June 24, 1952. The East Broad Top Railroad shops built this motor car from scratch with a Maxwell engine and transmission. It was rebuilt with a Nash drive train. (East Broad Top Railroad collection.)

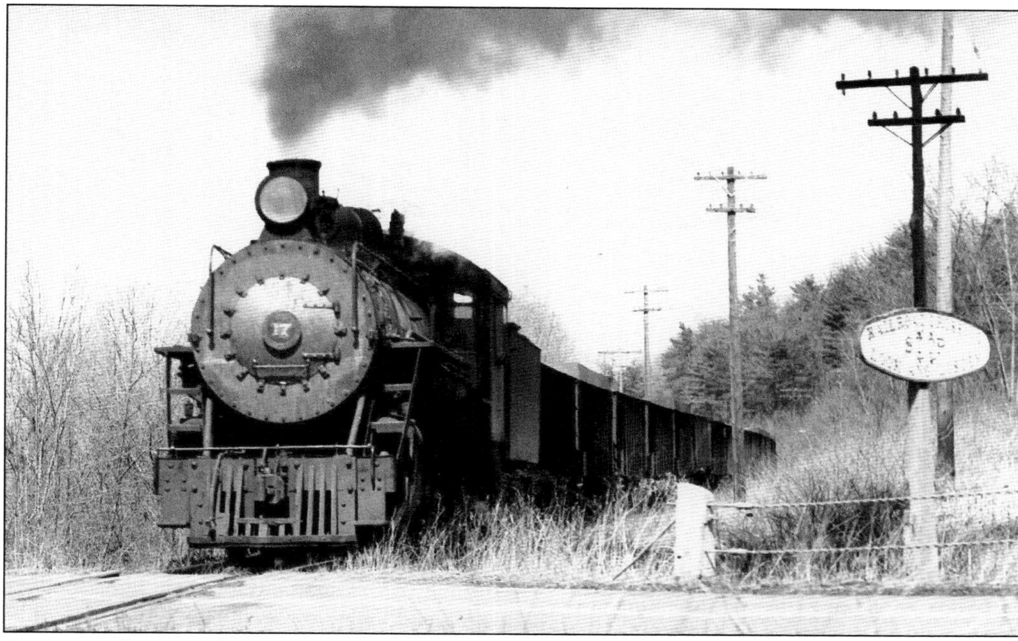

A train of empty hopper cars is being pulled by locomotive No. 17 northbound at the Pennsylvania State Highway 994 crossing north of Southern Huntingdon County High School in the 1950s. The East Broad Top Railroad was a specialized coal hauler, and its steel hopper cars were essentially scaled-down versions of standard-gauge hopper cars. (East Broad Top Railroad collection.)

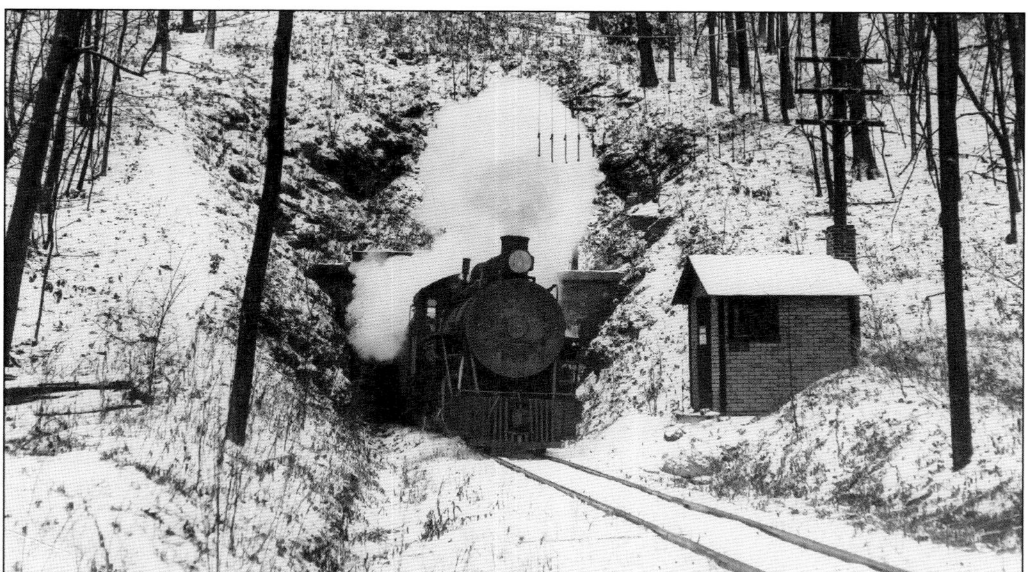

Amid the winter snow, East Broad Top Railroad locomotive No. 16, with a trainload of coal, is emerging from the north portal of Wray's Hill Tunnel northbound in the early 1950s. The grade from the Robertsdale station northward to the village of Pogue was downhill. Southbound trains encountered a continuous uphill grade from the village of Pogue to the mining town of Robertsdale. (East Broad Top Railroad collection.)

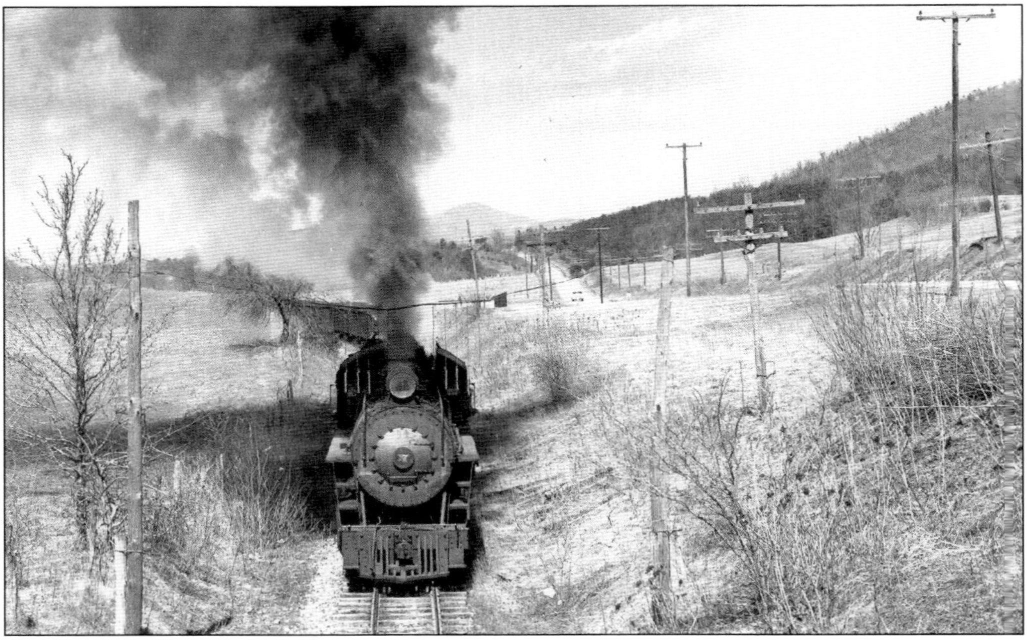

Locomotive No. 17 is heading south on March 26, 1956, with a train of hopper cars, with United States Highway 522 on the right. The East Broad Top Railroad had received Interstate Commerce Commission permission to abandon the railroad. In less than a month, service would end. As strip mines closed and independent coal producers switched to trucks, the railroad was no longer financially viable. (East Broad Top Railroad collection.)

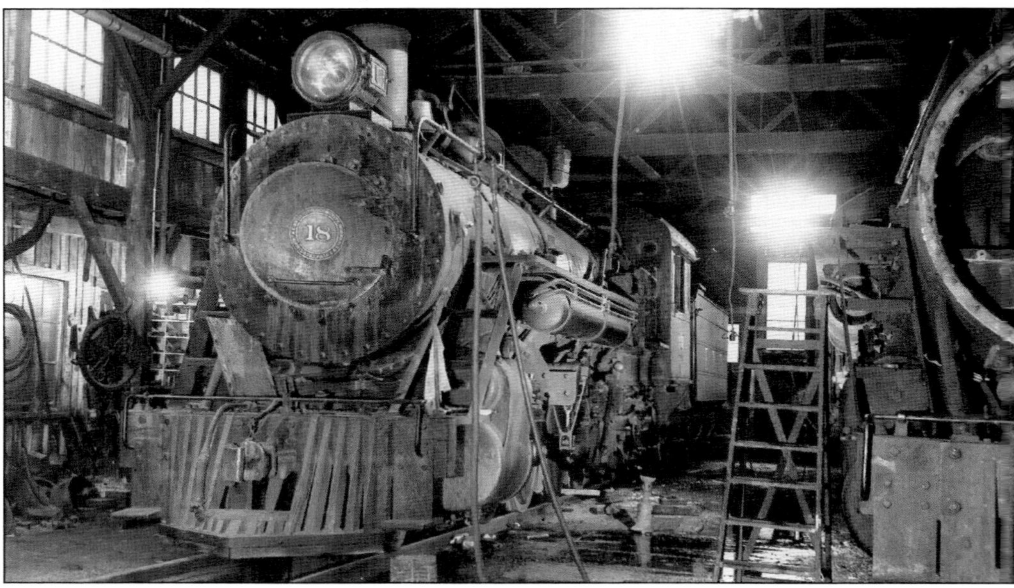

Locomotives No. 18 and No. 16 are at Rockhill Furnace shops in 1960. Well-equipped shops and a skilled workforce yielded a long life for the locomotives and rolling stock. The East Broad Top Railroad had the foresight to maximize ton miles by constructing 70,000-pound capacity hopper cars and boosting their capacity by adding a 14-inch steel band around the top edge of the car. (East Broad Top Railroad collection.)

Two

Time Stands Still

After World War II, the East Broad Top Railroad was faced with rising labor costs, labor strikes, declining coal deposits, and a decreasing market. The last run was made at the Mount Union yard on April 13, 1956. Kovalchick Salvage Company purchased the railroad on May 1, 1956. With the exception of the removal of trackage on the Narco and Shade Gap branch lines in 1957, the 32.54 miles of remaining trackage has been kept in place and can be viewed along public roads and highways along with the shop facilities and most of the rolling stock. Among the surviving bridges on the out-of-service portion of the line that can be viewed are the four-arch concrete bridge at Aughwick Mills, the truss bridge at Pogue, and the Robertsdale wye bridge. Heavy underbrush and trees have grown around and over many of the hopper cars at the Mount Union yard. The Mount Union Connecting Railroad, formed to service some businesses in the Mount Union area, has repainted the Mount Union engine house of the East Broad Top Railroad that still houses standard-gauge switcher No. 3. In addition, trackage has been cleared of brush. Where United States Highway 522 parallels the railroad, new ballast can be seen from the village of Allenport south to the Pennsylvania State Highway 103 grade crossing. At the Rockhill Furnace yard, many freight cars can be viewed, including hopper cars, boxcars, and a tank car. The Kovalchick family and railroad employees have done their best to save this historic railroad. The Friends of the East Broad Top have refurbished rolling stock, restored key structures on the railroad, set up a visitors center at the Robertsdale depot, and promoted the importance of the East Broad Top Railroad. At the August 18, 2007, Community Appreciation Day, Friends of the East Broad Top volunteers were involved in restoration of buildings in the shop area, the rebuilding of side-dump hopper car No. 802, and the rebuilding of boxcar No. 168 for passenger service. There is not another railroad in North America that is so complete and original.

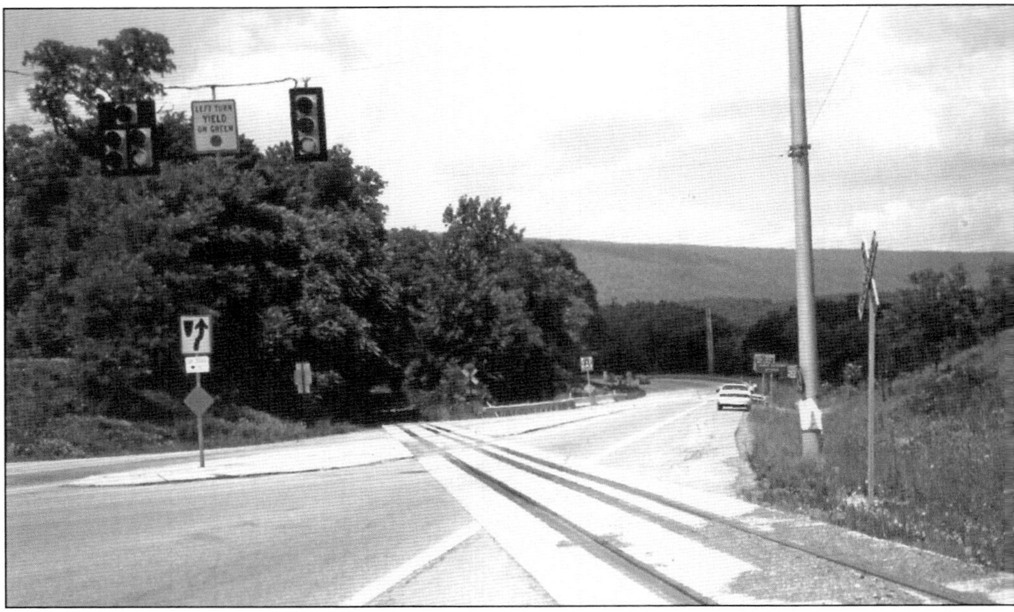

Looking north on July 7, 2007, the dual-gauge East Broad Top Railroad track crosses United States Highway 522 just north of Shirley Street in the borough of Mount Union. When this bypass was constructed in the late 1990s, the Pennsylvania Department of Transportation installed the crossing to maintain the railroad right-of-way in recognition of its historical significance. (Photograph by Kenneth C. Springirth.)

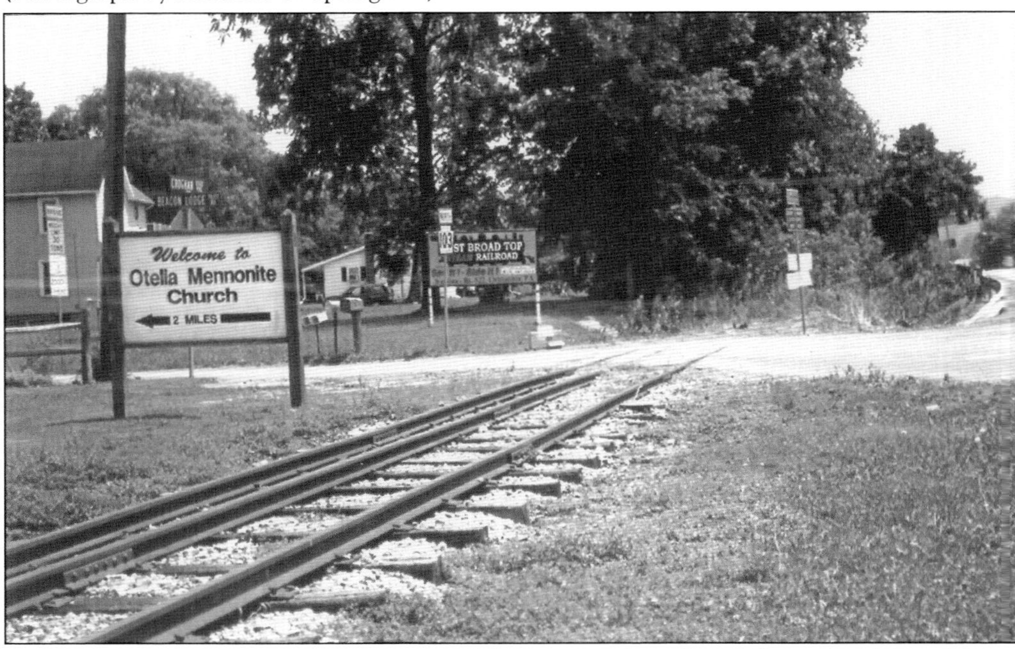

South of the borough of Mount Union and looking south with Croghan Pike (United States Highway 522) on the right at Beacon Lodge Road (Pennsylvania State Highway 103), the East Broad Top Railroad trackage has received new ballast to this crossing. South of this road the tracks disappear into the woods in this July 7, 2007, view. (Photograph by Kenneth C. Springirth.)

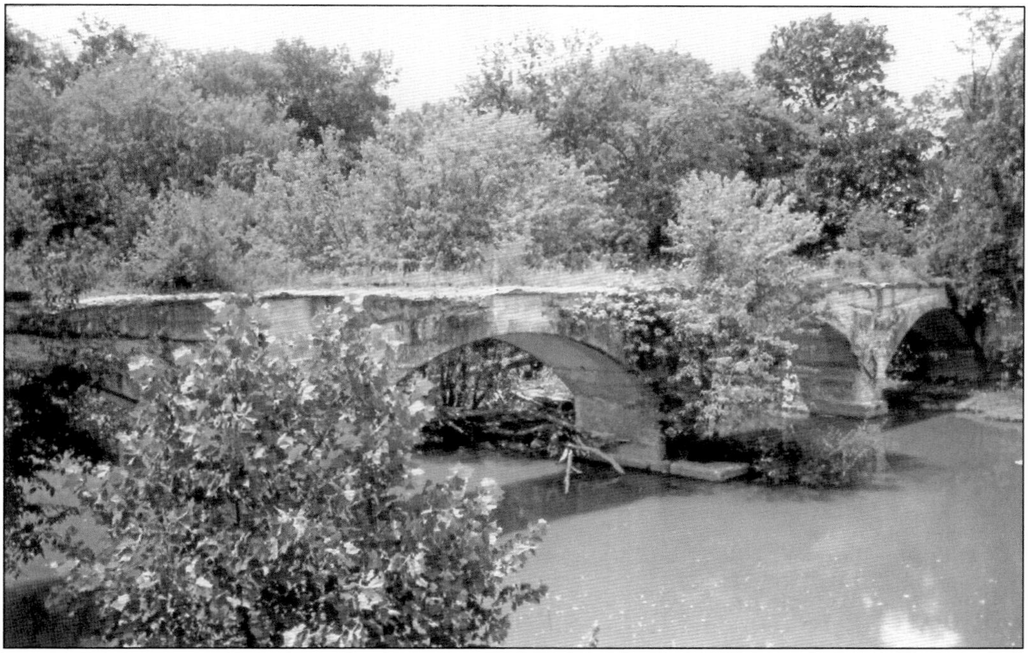

The East Broad Top Railroad bridge over Aughwick Creek north of the borough of Shirleysburg is visible in this July 7, 2007, view. This 203-foot-long, four-arch reinforced-concrete bridge, built during 1914, is adjacent to and on the west side of the Aughwick Mills Road bridge over Aughwick Creek. The bridge can be accessed from United States Highway 522 via Aughwick Mills Road. (Photograph by Kenneth C. Springirth.)

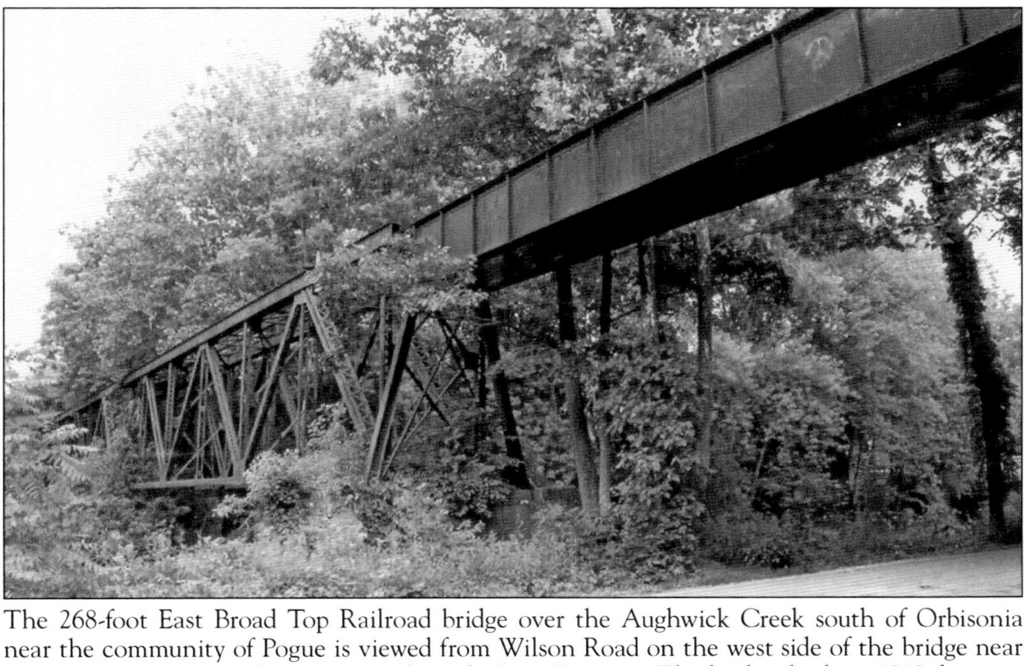

The 268-foot East Broad Top Railroad bridge over the Aughwick Creek south of Orbisonia near the community of Pogue is viewed from Wilson Road on the west side of the bridge near Pennsylvania State Highway 994 in this July 7, 2007, scene. The bridge, built in 1910, has two steel truss spans and one steel plate girder span. (Photograph by Kenneth C. Springirth.)

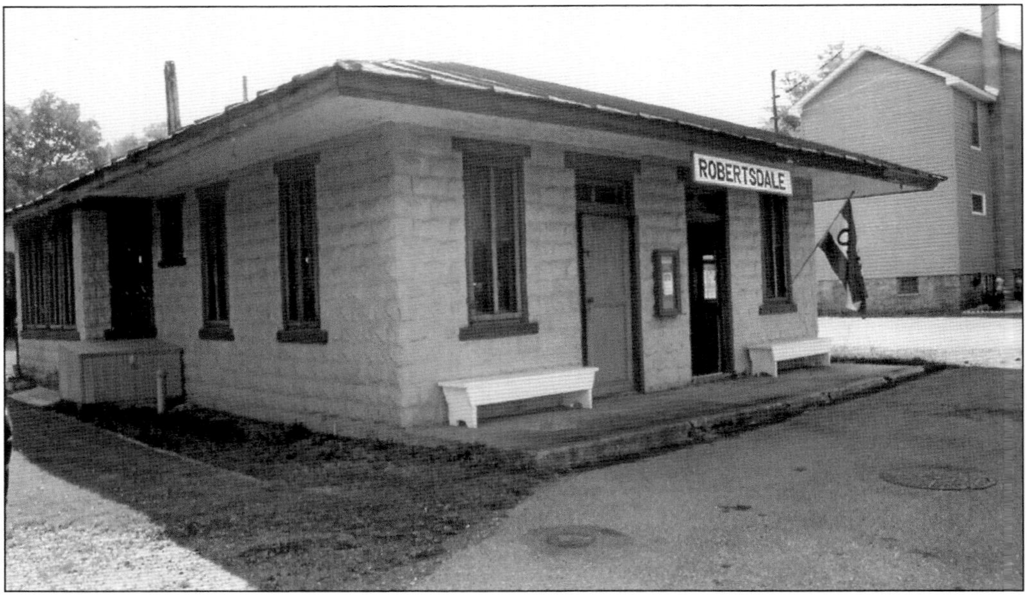

The former East Broad Top Railroad station at Robertsdale is shown in this July 21, 2007, view. This is part of the museum complex of the Friends of the East Broad Top. The mining town of Robertsdale was the original southern terminus of the East Broad Top Railroad. The railroad was later extended south to Alvan, which was a stop for No. 9 Mine, No. 10 Mine, and No. 11 Mine. (Photograph by Kenneth C. Springirth.)

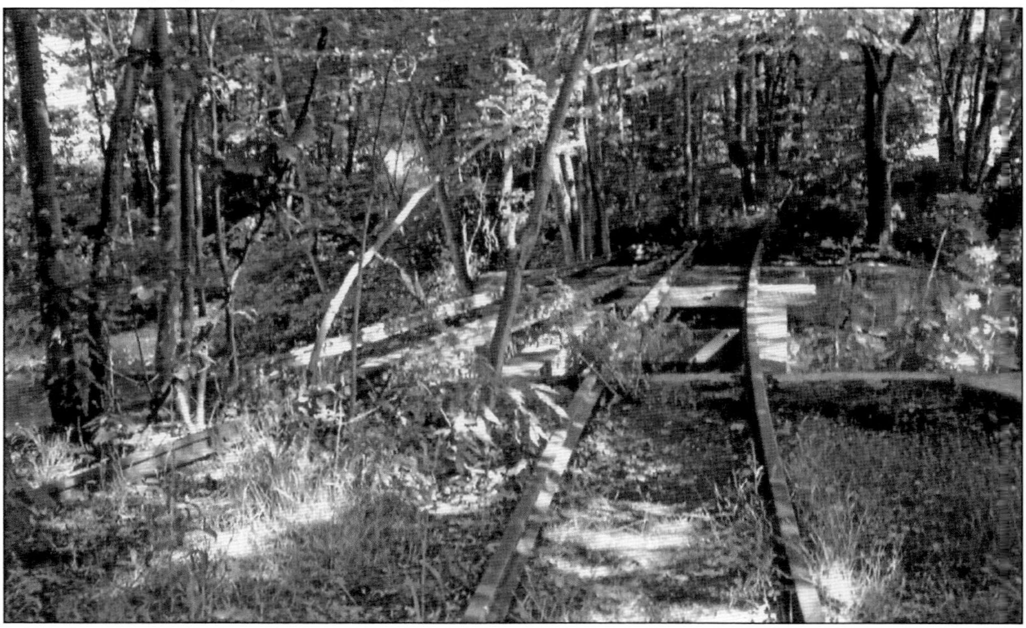

The Robertsdale wye of the East Broad Top Railroad ended at a bridge over Trough Creek, and the rail is still in place as noted in this July 21, 2007, scene. Erected in 1900, this steel plate girder bridge was 23 feet long. The landscape has remained virtually intact. Tied together with the coal-mining area, the railroad provides a unique story of coal production and railroad transportation. (Photograph by Kenneth C. Springirth.)

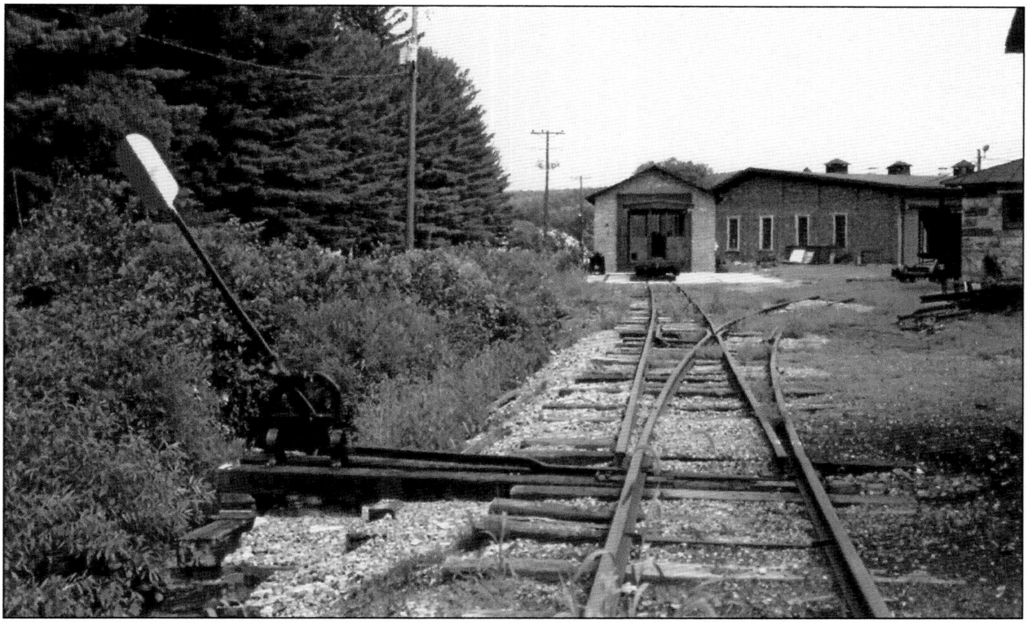

This two-way stub switch is at the Rockhill Furnace yard. A stub switch enables the train to be guided from one track to another, but it does not have the tapered points of a typical switch. Both the movable rails and the ends of the rails of the diverging route have their ends cut off square. (Photograph by Kenneth C. Springirth.)

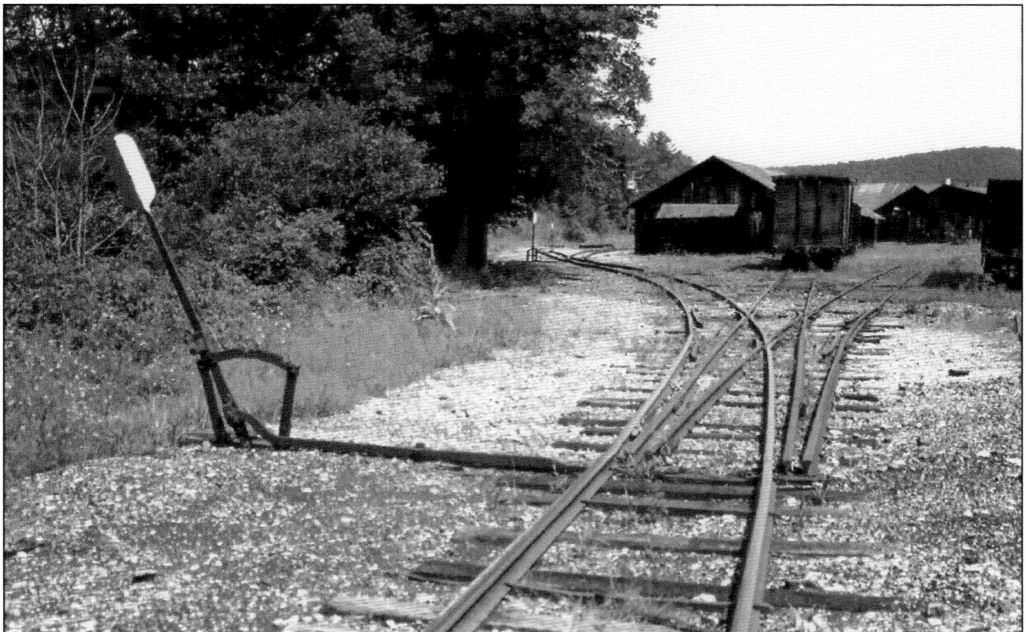

The Rockhill Furnace yard is the location for the last three-way narrow-gauge stub switch in the United States east of the Rocky Mountains. Stub switches were once very common in the early days of railroads. Off to the left is a vintage harp-type switch stand, which is a simple lever, used to move the rails to the desired diverging route. (Photograph by Kenneth C. Springirth.)

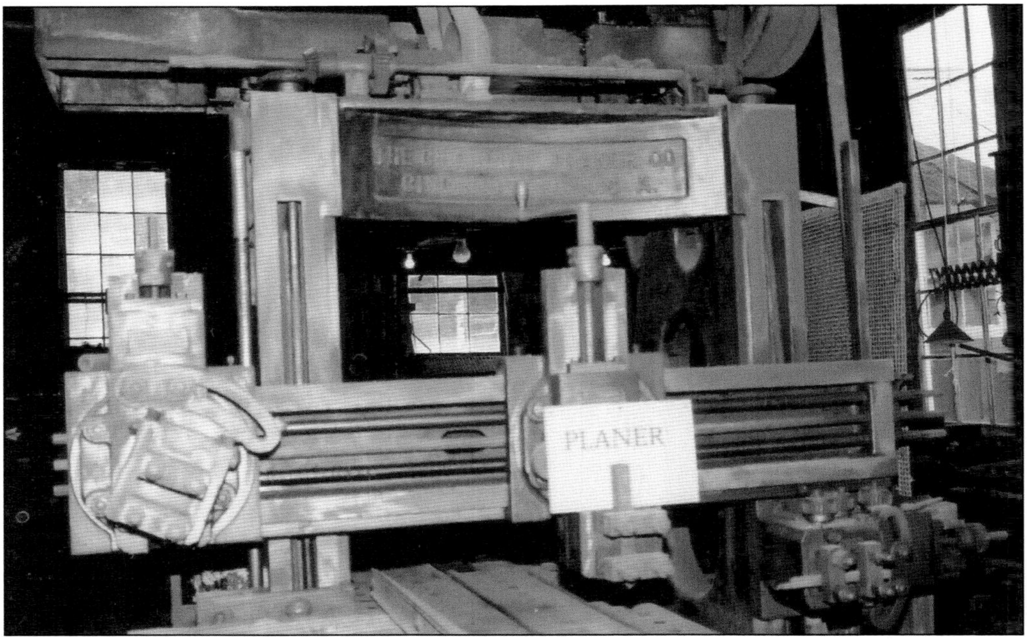

Inside the machine shops of the East Broad Top Railroad is this Cincinnati-built planer where the cutting tool is in a rigid position and the piece moves against it. The rail shown in the lower portion of the picture was being machined down to a fine point for a switch when the railroad closed in 1956. (Photograph by Kenneth C. Springirth.)

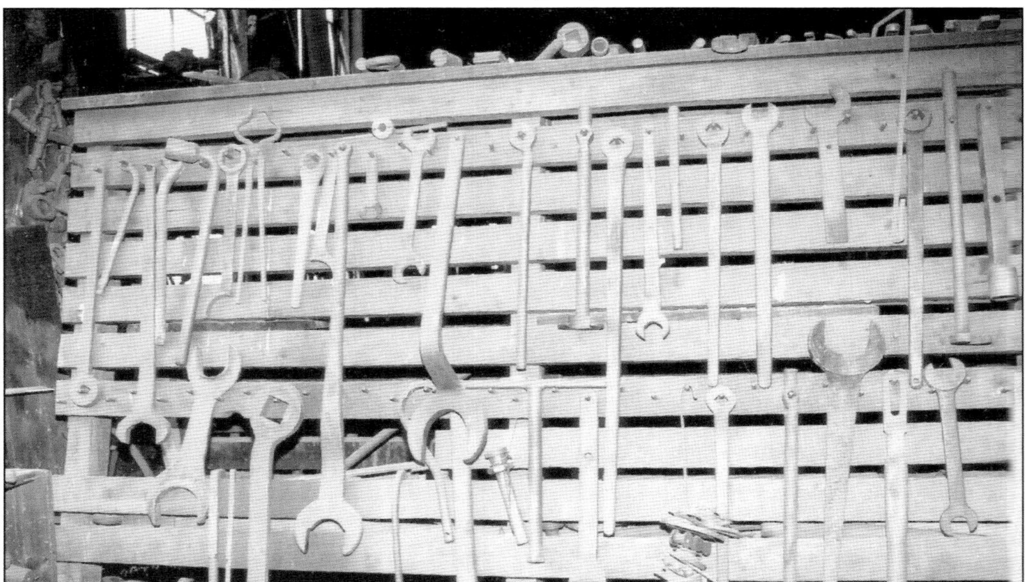

Specialized railroad shop tools are shown in the rack at the East Broad Top Railroad machine shops. When these shops closed in June 1956, the workers cleaned, oiled machinery, and hung up their tools. Most of the shop employees thought this would be a short-term shut down. On August 18, 2007, the tools are still in the rack waiting for the call that never came. (Photograph by Kenneth C. Springirth.)

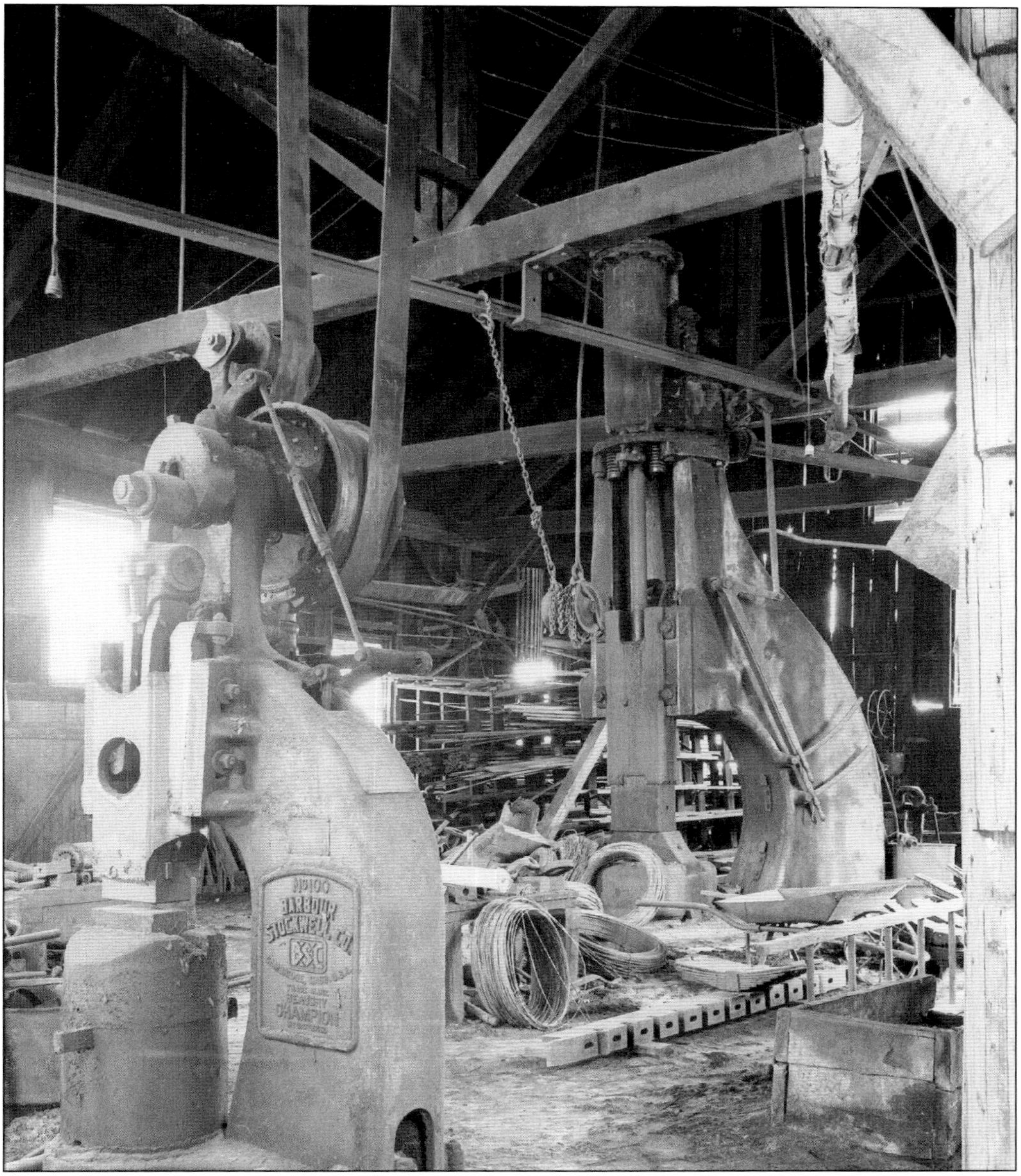

This 1977 scene is inside the blacksmith shop at the Rockhill Furnace yard of the East Broad Top Railroad. The Rockhill shops developed hopper cars that would maximize ton miles handled per train. During 1913 and 1914, 40 hopper cars, Nos. 800 to 839, with each car having 60,000-pound capacity, were purchased from Pressed Steel Car Company of Pittsburgh. Between 1927 and 1936, the shops rebuilt these hopper cars, raising their capacity to 70,000 pounds. The East Broad Top Railroad shops built about 290 freight cars during the years 1913 to 1930. Some of the hopper cars received a 14-inch-high steel band on top of the car, increasing the car capacity to 80,000 pounds, which enabled the East Broad Top Railroad to move a greater volume of coal and increased revenue by improving the hauling capacity of the railroad. (East Broad Top Railroad collection.)

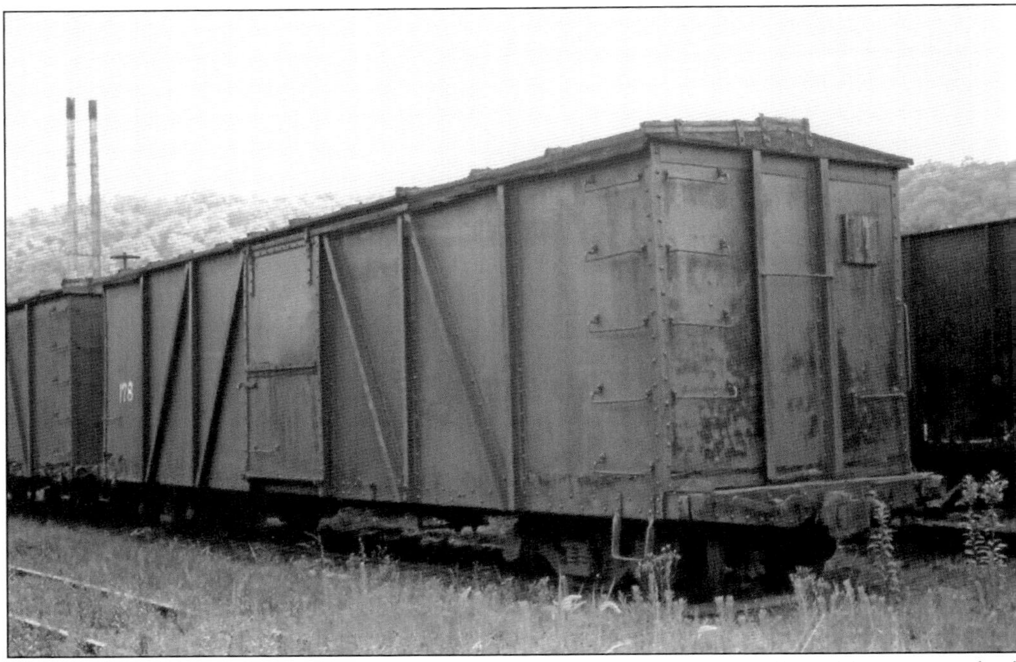

Boxcar No. 178 is at the Rockhill Furnace yard on July 7, 2007. This all-steel boxcar was built in 1916 at the Rockhill Furnace shops of the East Broad Top Railroad. When the railroad shut down in 1956, much of the rolling stock remained in place and, 51 years later, can be viewed. (Photograph by Kenneth C. Springirth.)

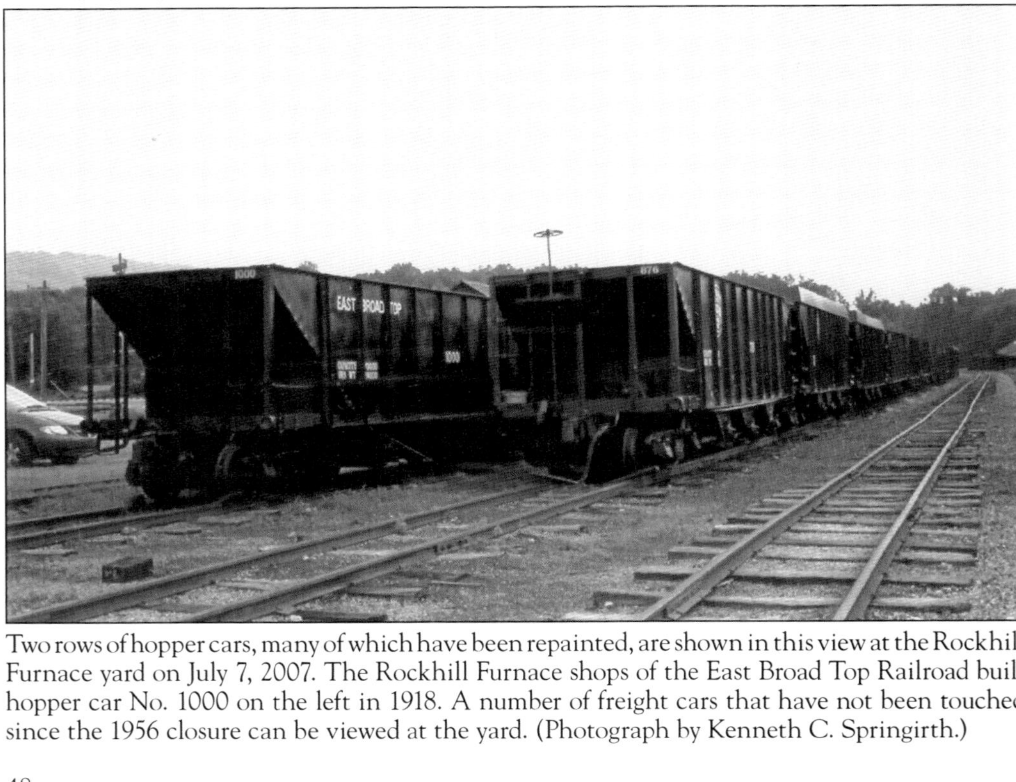

Two rows of hopper cars, many of which have been repainted, are shown in this view at the Rockhill Furnace yard on July 7, 2007. The Rockhill Furnace shops of the East Broad Top Railroad built hopper car No. 1000 on the left in 1918. A number of freight cars that have not been touched since the 1956 closure can be viewed at the yard. (Photograph by Kenneth C. Springirth.)

Three

Excursion Service Begins

To celebrate the bicentennials of the boroughs of Orbisonia and Rockhill Furnace, special trains were operated during 1960 over a portion of the line. As a result of the success of those excursions, service has continued on a year-by-year basis. For a number of years on Saturdays and Sundays from June through October, trains have left the well-kept cream, green, and brown Orbisonia station at 11:00 a.m., 1:00 p.m., and 3:00 p.m. for a ride along the picturesque Aughwick Valley. Extra trains were run on Community Appreciation Day held yearly in August. The Fall Spectacular, held Columbus Day weekend, has been the biggest event of the year with extra trains. Five miles of the line are in use from the Orbisonia station north to the Colgate Grove picnic area. Portions of the historic shop complex have been refurbished by volunteers of the Friends of the East Broad Top. A number of hopper cars, along with other freight cars, have been rehabilitated at the Rockhill Furnace yard. The East Broad Top Railroad, a privately owned operating tourist railroad, is the most original preserved railroad in the United States that has retained much of its original rolling stock and station buildings and has a complete railroad yard with machine and car shops, a blacksmith shop, a foundry, a turntable, and an eight-stall roundhouse. In its shops, the original machinery and tools are in place. There are no re-creations or replacements. During its working history, the East Broad Top Railroad can be noted for a well-maintained main line that could handle standard-gauge cars, maximizing capacity of its hopper cars to increase tonnage hauled per train, the ability to transfer standard-gauge freight cars onto special-designed narrow-gauge trucks so that freight did not have to be reloaded from standard-gauge freight cars to narrow-gauge freight cars preserving business that might have gone to highway transportation, shop facilities that built hundreds of freight cars, and working with locomotive suppliers to incorporate improvements in the next locomotive ordered. This is a railroad that is well worth visiting and supporting by riding.

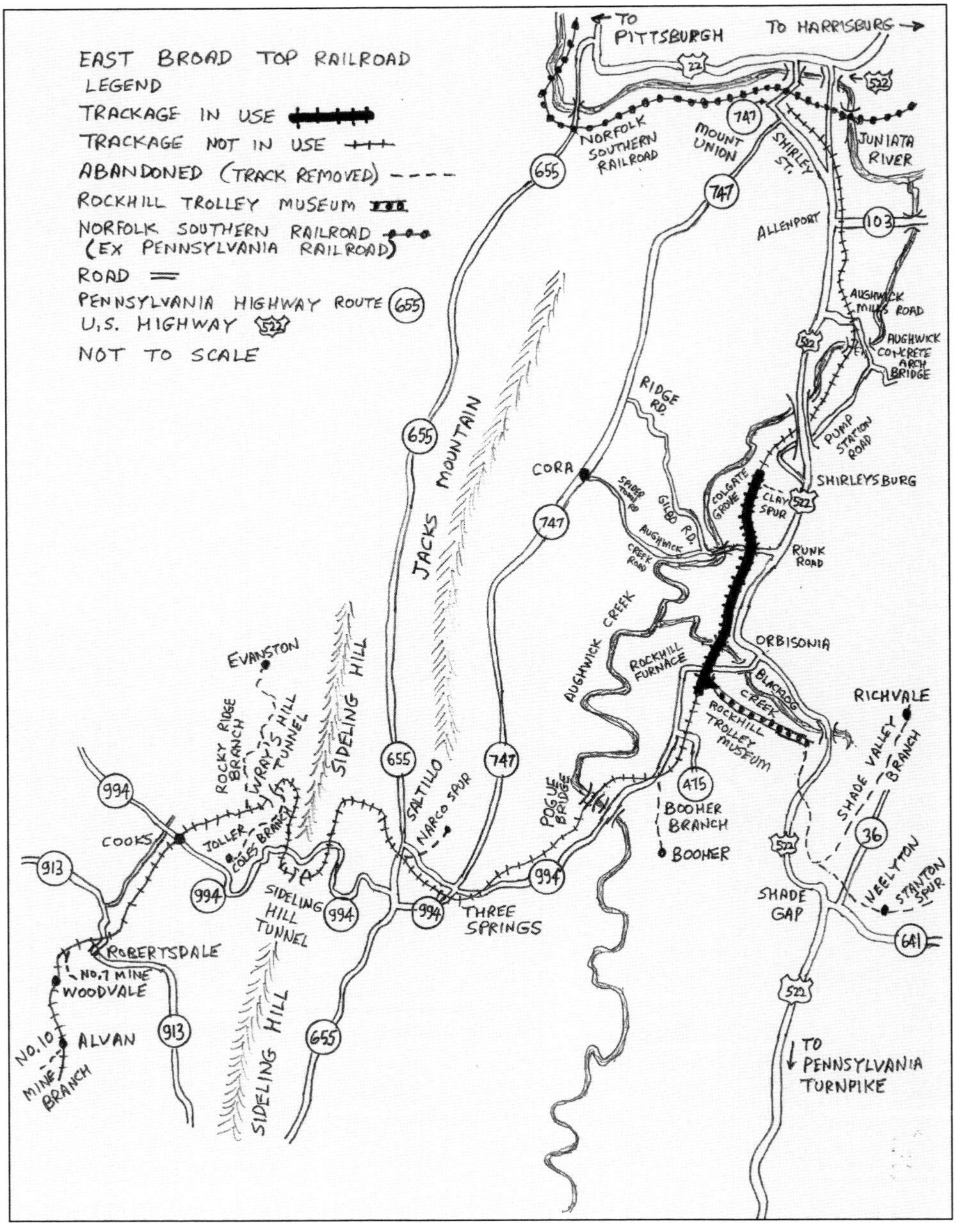

This map shows the East Broad Top Railroad. The Evanston (Rocky Ridge) branch was dismantled in 1940. In 1942, the Narco branch was constructed. On January 24, 1943, the Shade Gap branch was cut back from Neelyton to Shade Gap and in 1948 was cut back to Blacklog. The Coles Valley branch was dismantled during 1955 followed in 1957 by the Narco and Blacklog branches. With abandonment of all the branch lines, the 32.54-mile main line from Mount Union to Alvan remained. At the borough of Mount Union, the former East Broad Top Railroad yard can be viewed on North Franklin Street just south of East Pennsylvania Avenue. United States Highway 522, just north of Shirley Street in Mount Union, features a restored railroad grade crossing with the East Broad Top Railroad. South on United States Highway 522 to Orbisonia, there are a number of places to view the narrow-gauge trackage still in place.

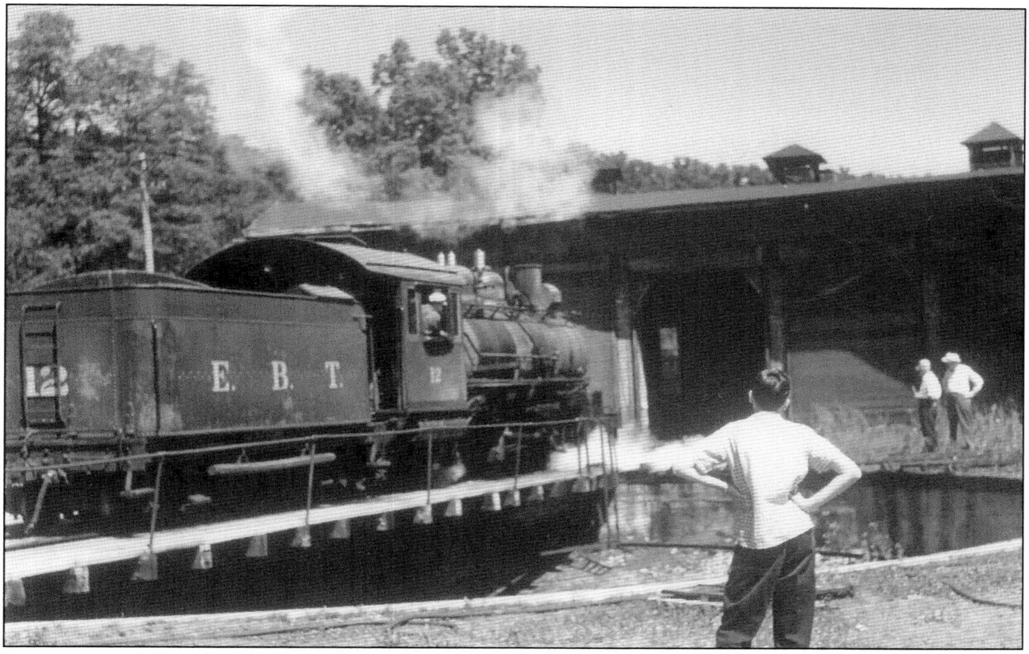

Locomotive No. 12 is moving from the roundhouse and is on the turntable for a trial run on June 25, 1960, in preparation for the August 13, 1960, reopening. When it was announced that the East Broad Top Railroad would reopen, a lot of rehabilitative work had to be done to make it possible for this special run. (Photograph by Louis J. G. Buehler, Rockhill Trolley Museum collection.)

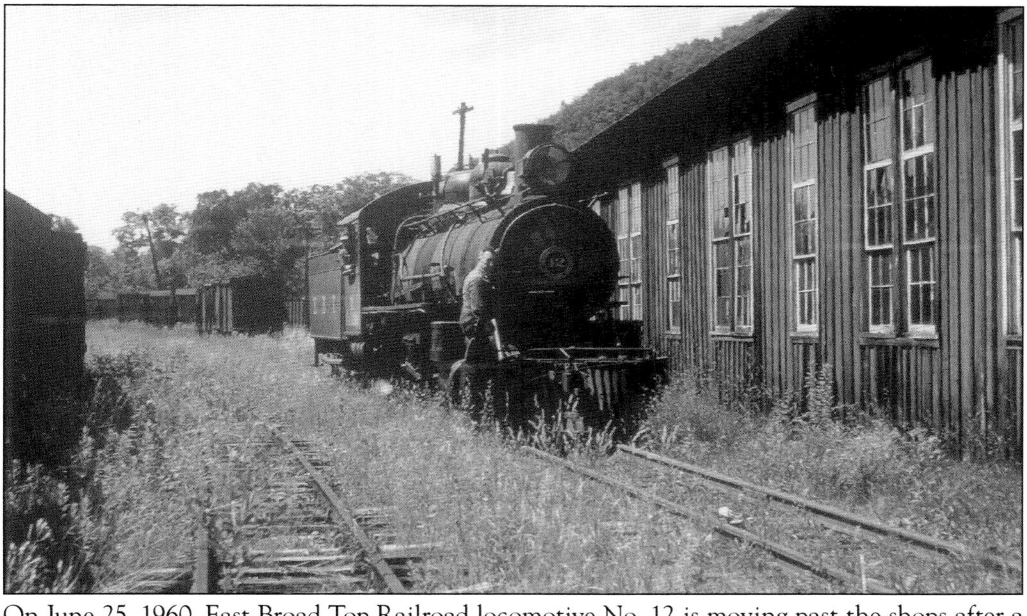

On June 25, 1960, East Broad Top Railroad locomotive No. 12 is moving past the shops after a four-year hibernation. Everything remained intact in the Rockhill Furnace yard, but vegetation was rapidly taking over the trackage areas, and buildings along with rolling stock had that weathered look. (Photograph by Louis J. G. Buehler, Rockhill Trolley Museum collection.)

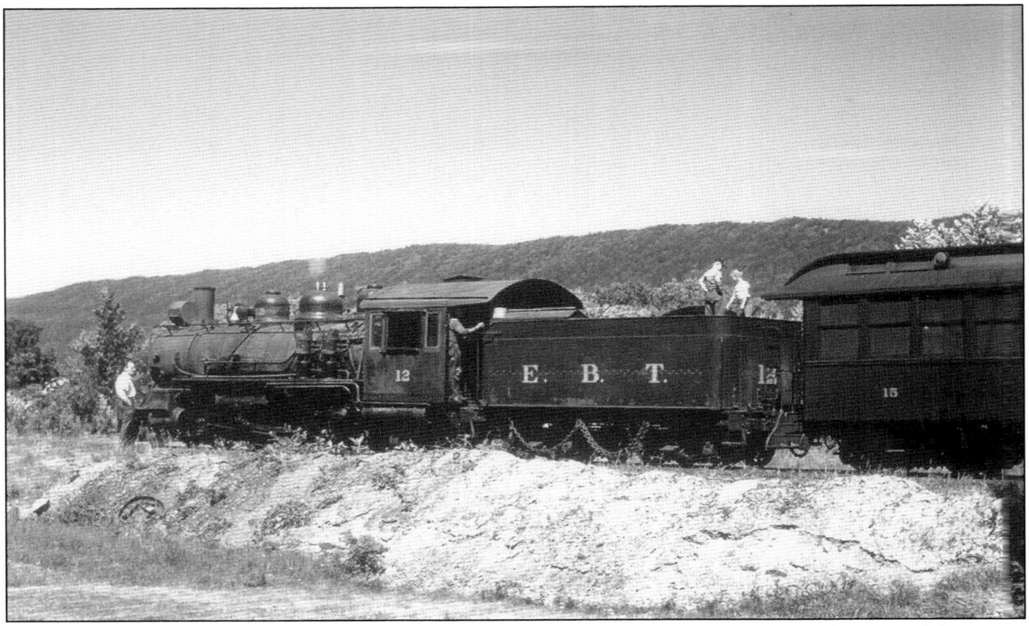

The Orbisonia station is the location for locomotive No. 12, pulling a special train of four cars for a trial run on June 25, 1960, over a restored section of the East Broad Top Railroad. There was a lot of excitement in the boroughs of Orbisonia and Rockhill Furnace over the reactivated railroad. (Photograph by Louis J. G. Buehler, Rockhill Trolley Museum collection.)

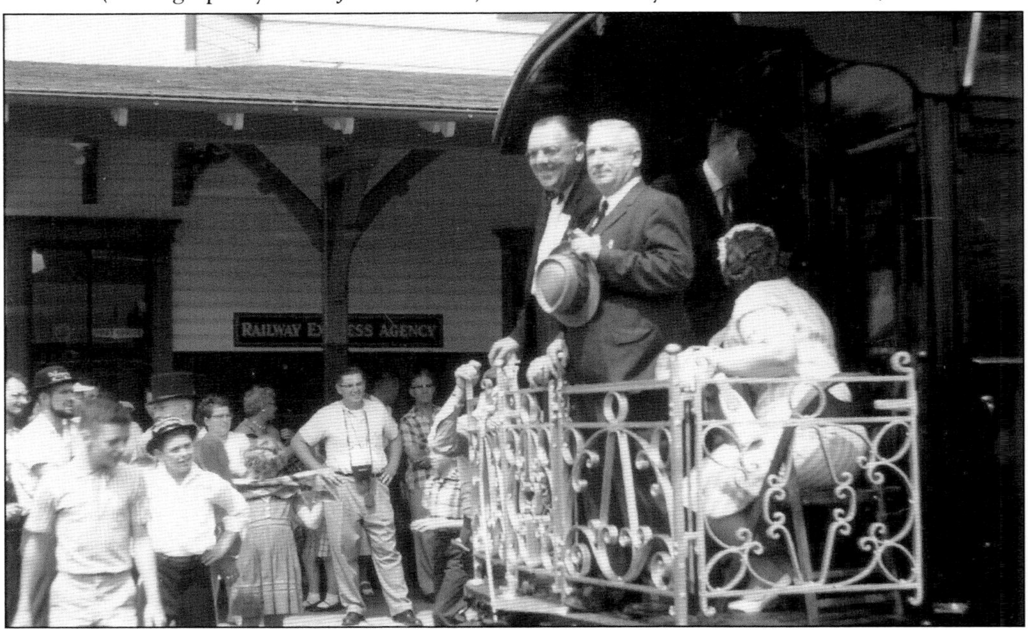

C. Roy Wilburn (left), East Broad Top Railroad operating vice president, and Nick Kovalchick, president of the Kovalchick Salvage Company, are standing on the platform of parlor car No. 20 on the inaugural run of the reopened East Broad Top Railroad on August 13, 1960. Thousands of people rode the restored section of the railroad in its first week of tourist service. (Joel Salomon collection.)

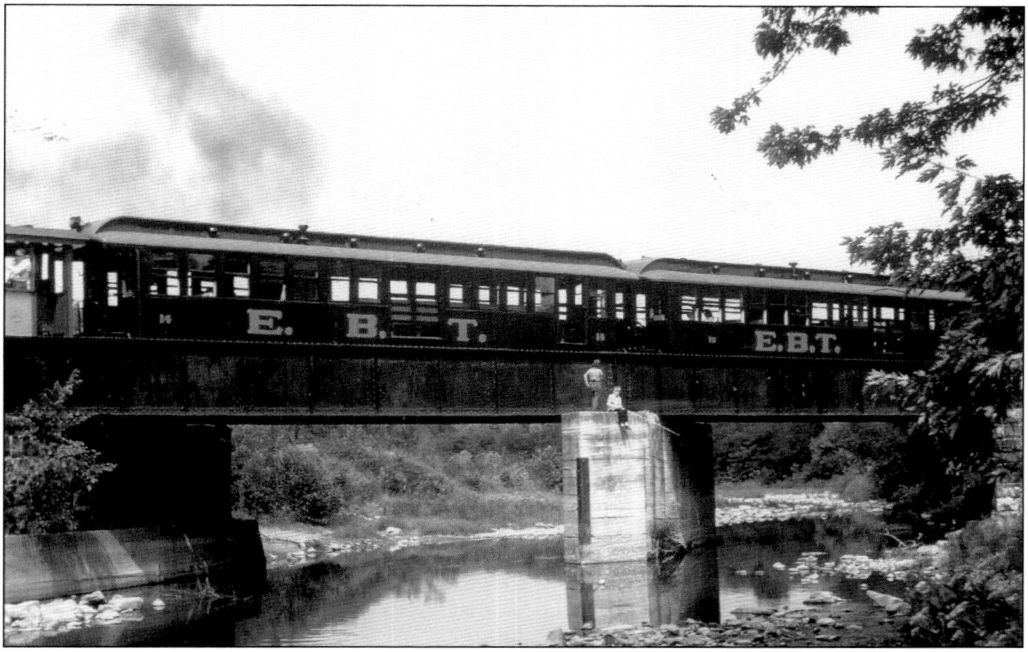

Two youngsters are fishing on the pier of the Blacklog Creek Bridge north of the Orbisonia station as an East Broad Top Railroad passenger train crosses over with combination passenger-baggage cars No. 14 and No. 15 on August 27, 1960. The large letters painted on the side of the cars were soon removed to retain the historic appearance of the railroad. (Photograph by Louis J. G. Buehler, Rockhill Trolley Museum collection.)

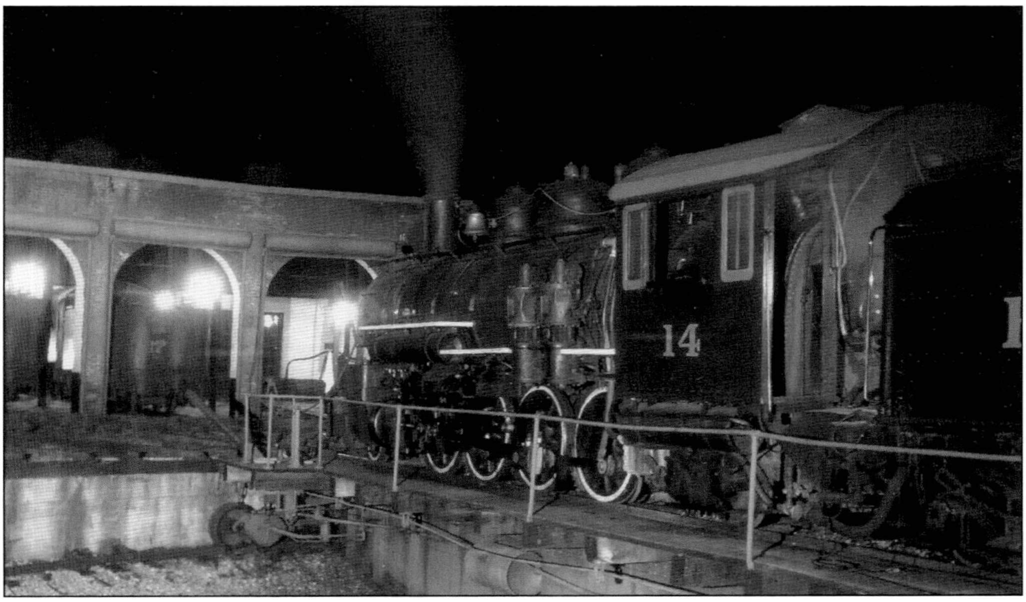

On midnight, October 20, 1962, locomotive No. 14 is on the turntable at the Rockhill Furnace yard preparing to go into the roundhouse. The turntable is a pivoted circular apparatus that rotates in a pit and is used to position the locomotive for movement to a different track. (Photograph by Louis J. G. Buehler, Rockhill Trolley Museum collection.)

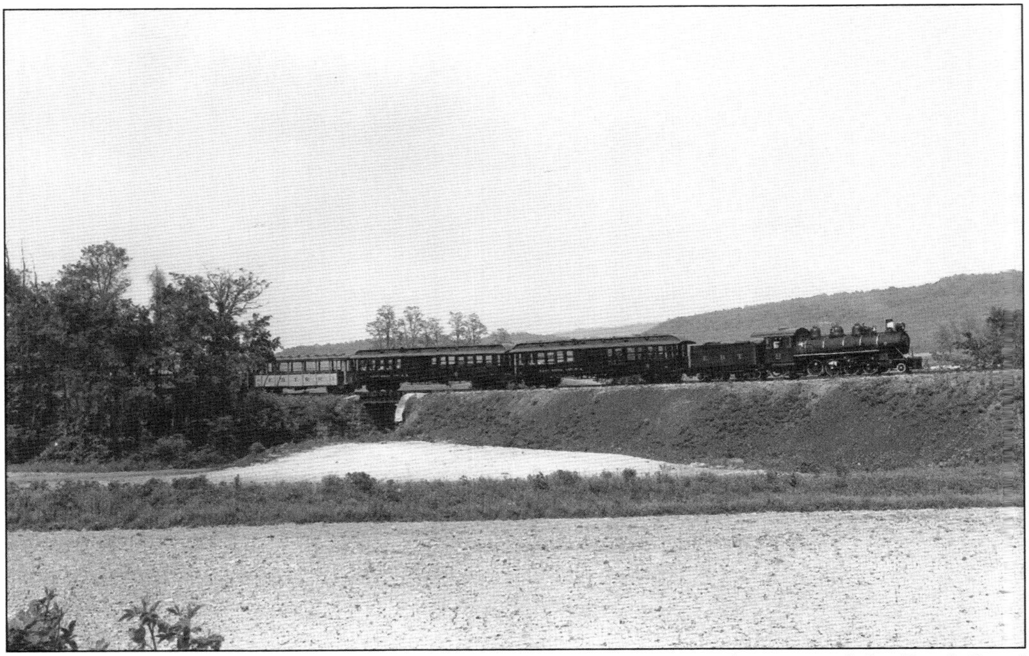

Heading southbound for the Orbisonia station, locomotive No. 12 has crossed the Runk Road Bridge in the picturesque Aughwick Valley in the early 1960s. When this locomotive was received from the Baldwin Locomotive Works in December 1911, it represented the first Mikado-type locomotive for the East Broad Top Railroad. (Photograph by James Kelly.)

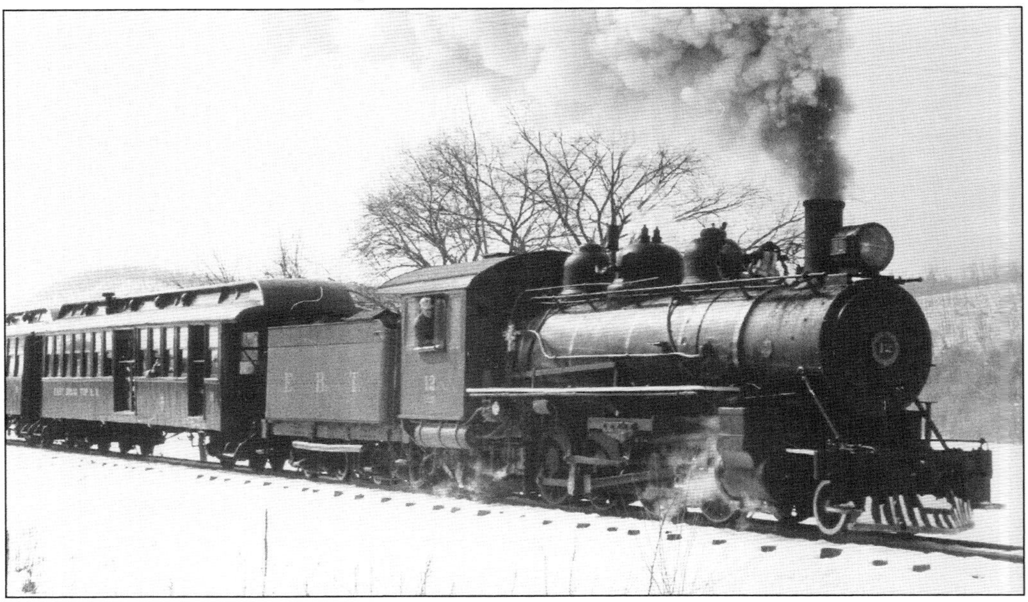

On a winter excursion in the 1960s, locomotive No. 12 is a photographer's delight over the snow-covered landscape. Combination passenger-baggage car No. 14, immediately behind the tender, was acquired from the Boston, Revere Beach and Lynn Railroad in 1916. Laconia Car Company built this car in 1882. (East Broad Top Railroad photograph, Kenneth C. Springirth collection.)

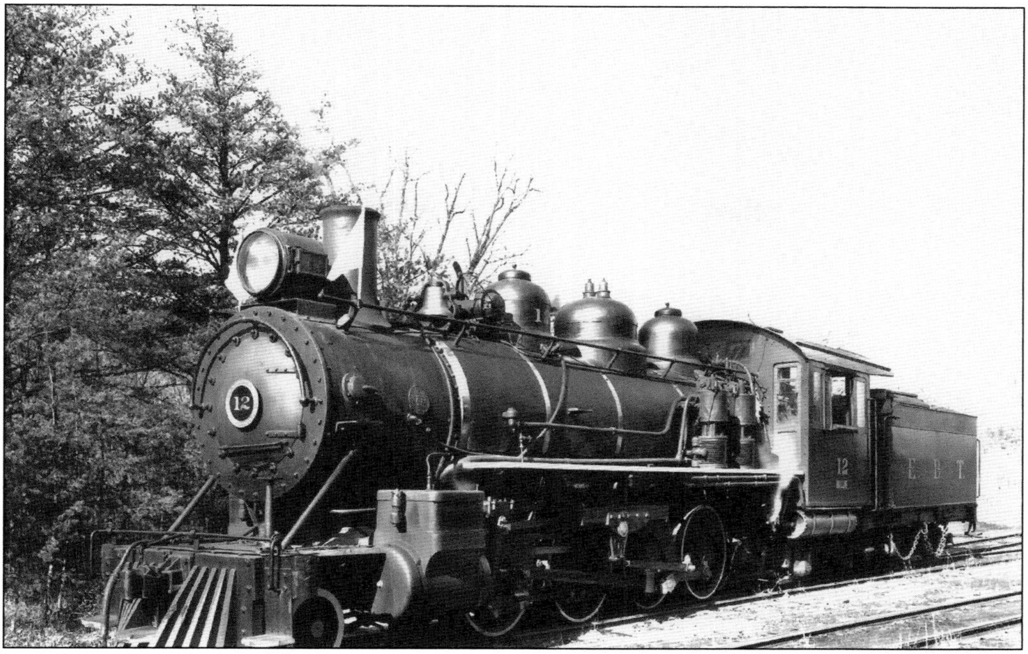

East Broad Top Railroad locomotive No. 12 is shown at the Rockhill Furnace yard with the name *Millie* painted on the cab under the locomotive number. Millie Kovalchick, daughter of Nick Kovalchick, dedicated the reopening of the railroad with a bottle of ginger ale over the front coupler on August 13, 1960. (East Broad Top Railroad photograph, Kenneth C. Springirth collection.)

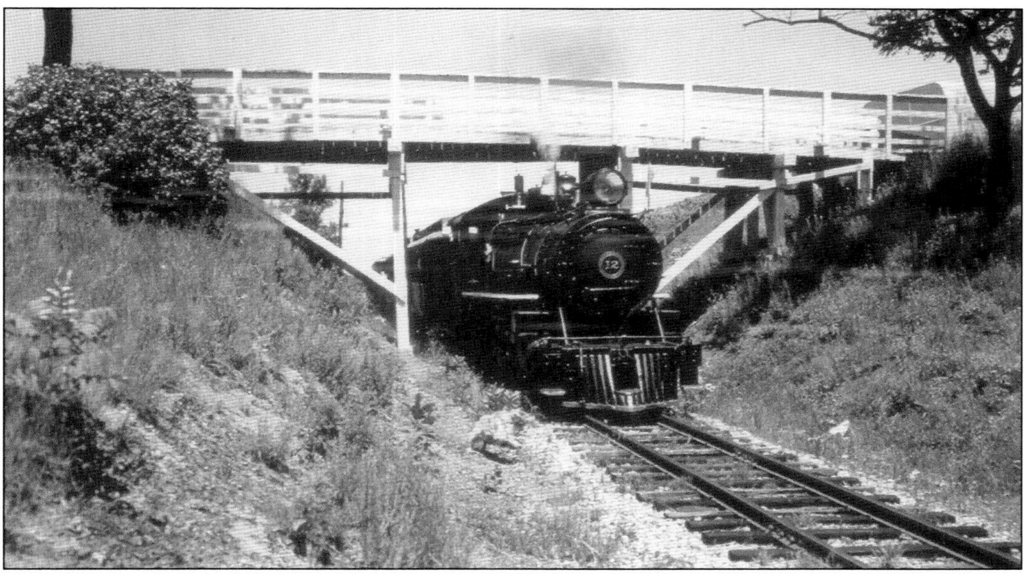

The wooden bridge for a farm road is the setting for East Broad Top Railroad locomotive No. 12 in the 1960s. This point, known as McMullins Summit, represents the highest elevation north of the borough of Rockhill Furnace. The watershed of Aughwick Creek is north of this point, and the watershed of Blacklog Creek, which feeds into Aughwick Creek, is south of this point. (East Broad Top Railroad photograph, Kenneth C. Springirth collection.)

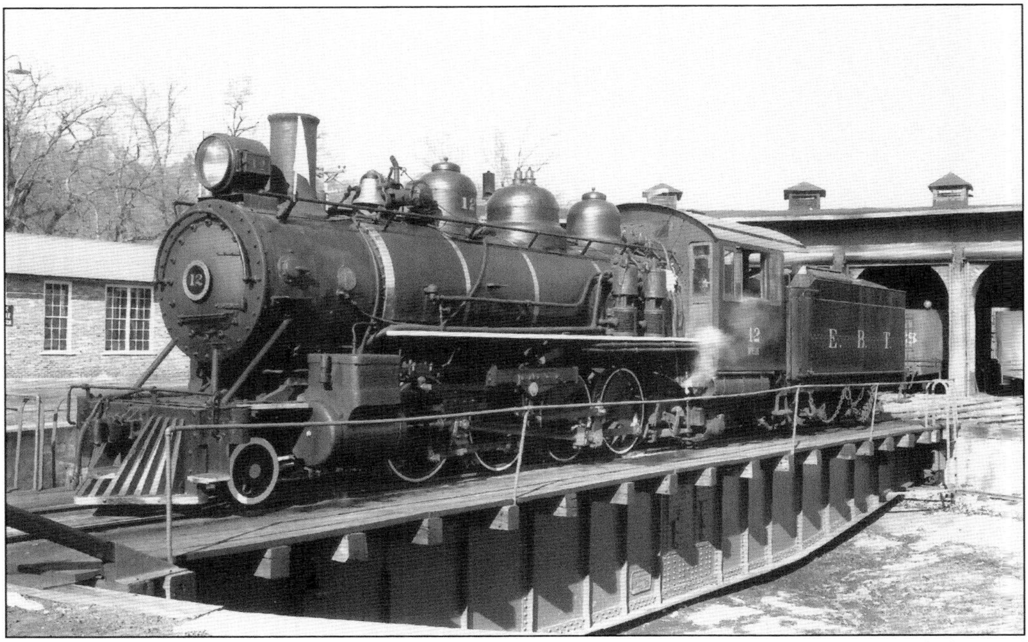

Locomotive No. 12 is on the Rockhill Furnace turntable in the 1960s. Stroebel Steel Construction Company of Chicago, Illinois, built the turntable. When the East Broad Top Railroad reopened in 1960, the turntable was redecked. The paint shop is on the left, and the roundhouse is immediately behind the locomotive. (East Broad Top Railroad photograph, Kenneth C. Springirth collection.)

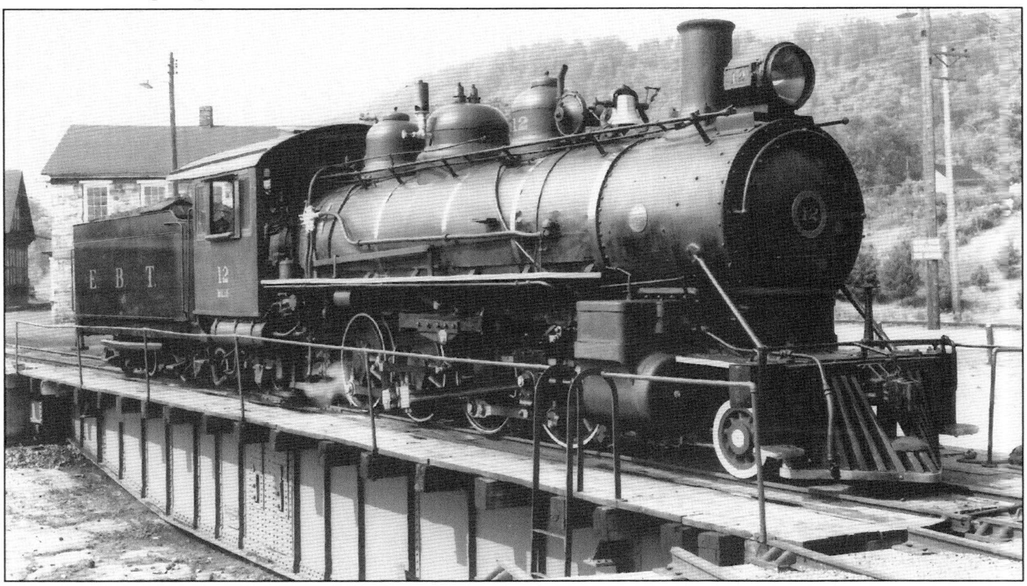

Mikado-type locomotive No. 12 is shown on the Rockhill Furnace turntable in the 1960s. The original stone farmhouse, built in the 1800s, is directly behind the locomotive. In 1873, the farm became the Rockhill Furnace yard, and the farmhouse housed the general offices of the East Broad Top Railroad. When the Orbisonia station was built, the house became the yard office. (East Broad Top Railroad photograph, Kenneth C. Springirth collection.)

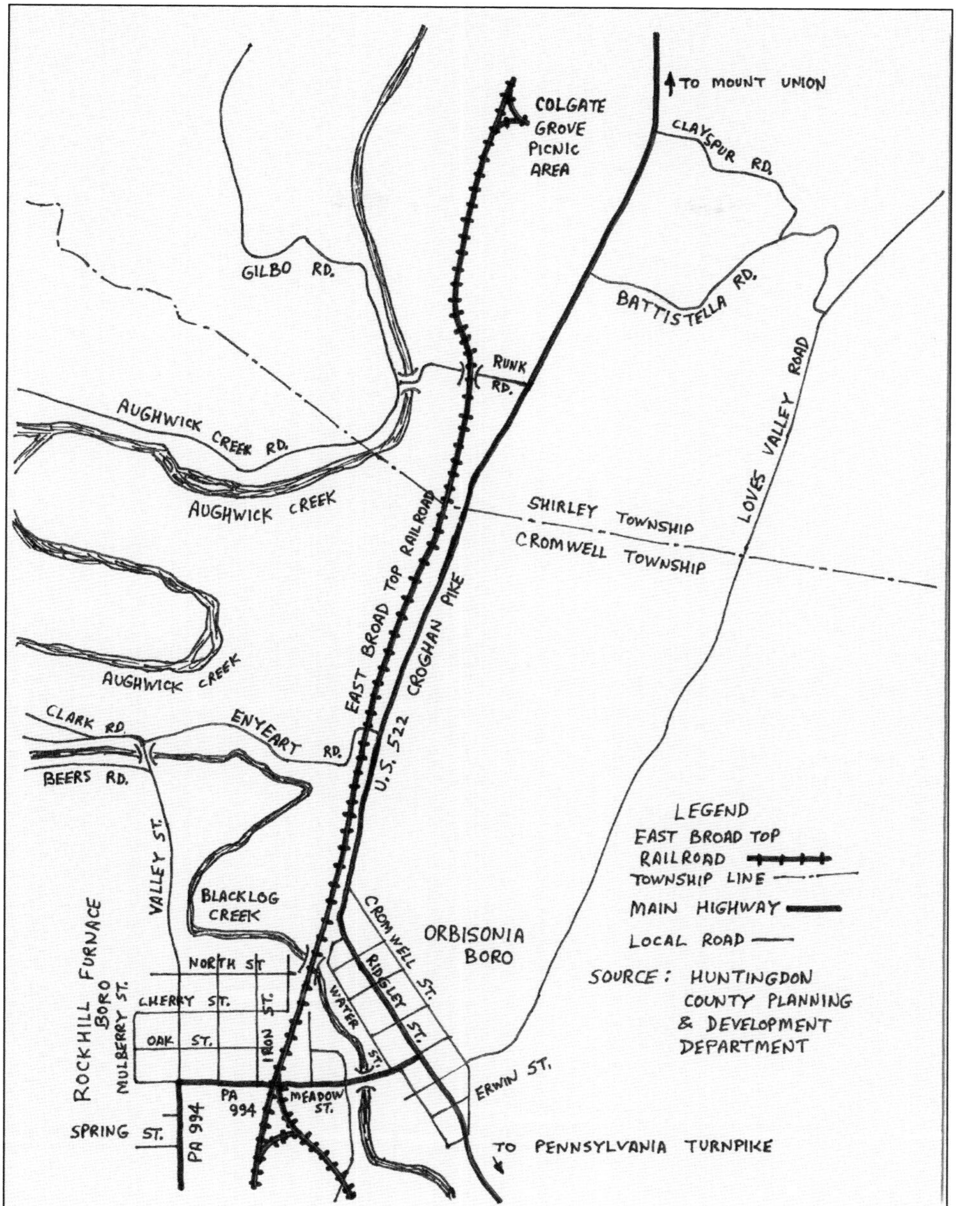

The map above shows the five-mile portion of the East Broad Top Railroad that has been restored for tourist train service from the borough of Rockhill Furnace, where the Orbisonia station and the Rockhill Furnace yard are located, to the Colgate Grove picnic area. It is the best remaining example in the United States of a narrow-gauge steam railroad system. While all the branch lines were dismantled, the main line from Mount Union to Alvan was left virtually intact; however, time, weather, and development have taken their toll on the right-of-way that was left in place when the line closed. United States Highway 522 closely follows the railroad from Orbisonia to Runk Road and parallels some of the railroad right-of-way northward to the borough of Mount Union and links with the Pennsylvania Turnpike on the south and United States Highway 22 at Mount Union.

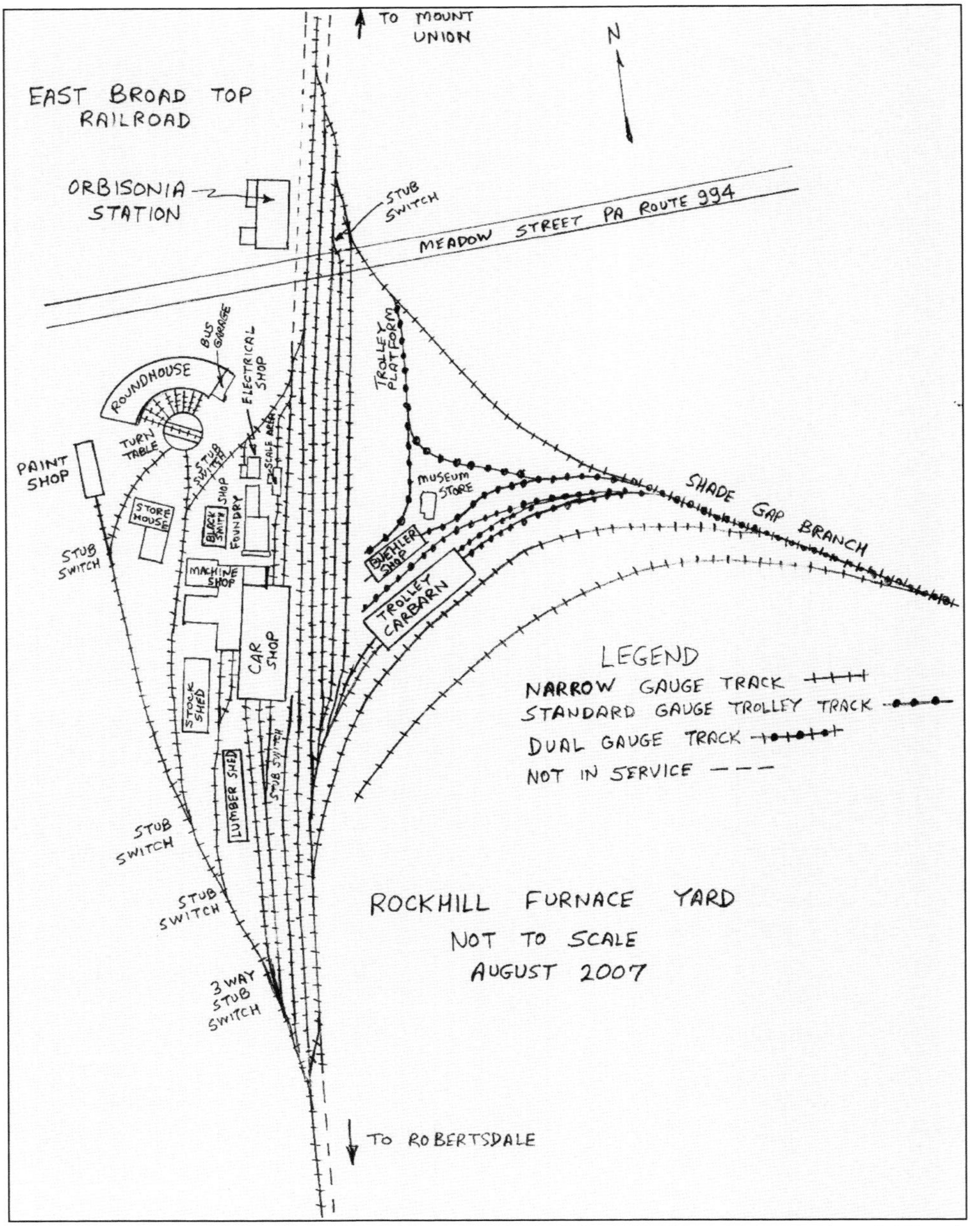

This is a map of the current Rockhill Furnace yard of the East Broad Top Railroad. The shop complex was built in 1873 on farmland, and the original 1800s farmhouse is still in place and is used as a storehouse. The steam-powered, belt-driven machinery produced castings, forgings, and machined parts for the railroad and the mines. A skilled workforce constructed a variety of freight cars in this well-equipped facility. Gas-electric motor car M-1 was constructed in these shops using parts from J. G. Brill Car Company and Westinghouse Electric Company. The shops made the railroad almost self-sufficient. When the railroad closed in 1956, virtually everything was kept in place at the shops. These shops are a transportation treasure with their historic facilities that represent an example of a complete maintenance facility based on 19th-century technology.

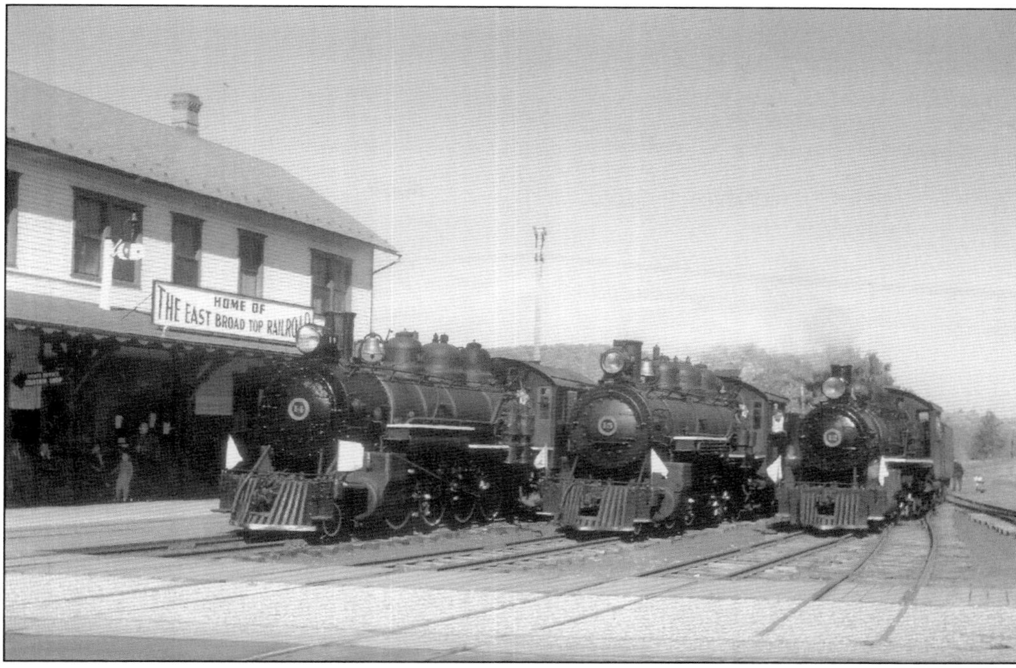

From left to right, locomotives No. 14, No. 15, and No. 12 are posing at the Meadow Street crossing with the Orbisonia station in the background on the East Broad Top Railroad on October 29, 1961. The Orbisonia station signs at each end of the building and sign on top of the roof were added in 1960. (Photograph by Louis J. G. Buehler, Rockhill Trolley Museum collection.)

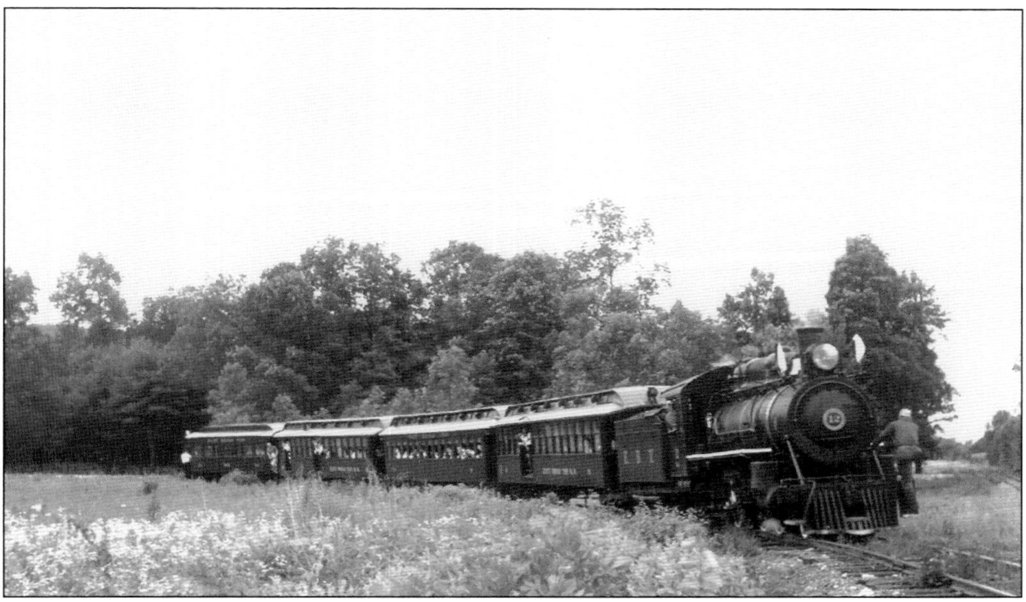

Locomotive No. 12 is pulling four passenger cars on the wye at the Colgate Grove picnic area on July 8, 1961. This is the current northern terminus of the restored line. The wye was built after tourist service began in 1960 and uses a portion of the former clay spur. (Photograph by Louis J. G. Buehler, Rockhill Trolley Museum collection.)

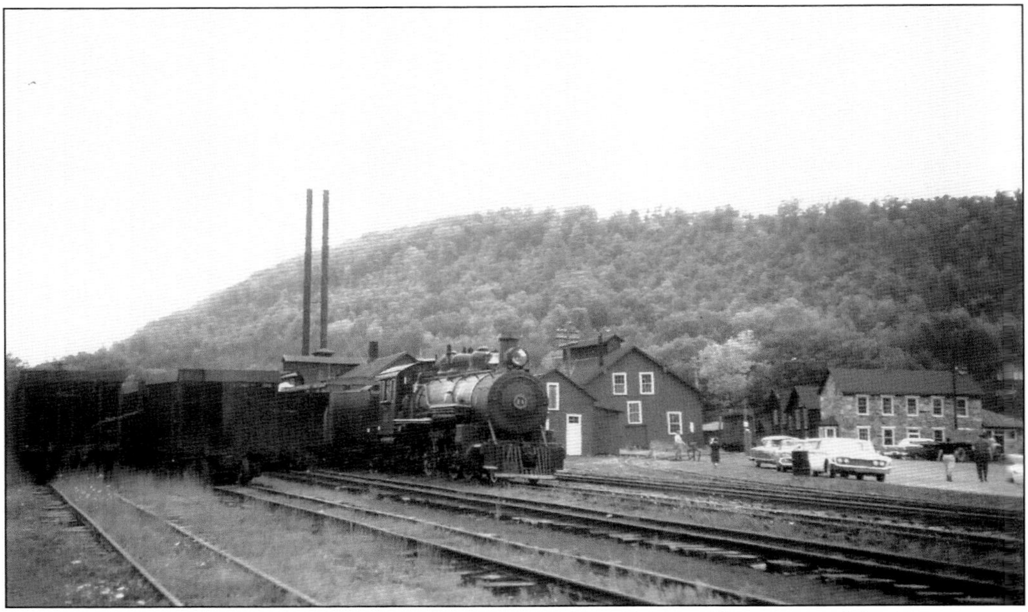

The Rockhill Furnace yard is the setting for East Broad Top Railroad locomotive No. 14, preparing for its next run on September 1, 1962. This railroad yard and associated shop complex is the most complete historic railroad yard in the United States. The stone building in the right-hand section of the picture was a farmhouse built in the 1800s. (Photograph by Kenneth C. Springirth.)

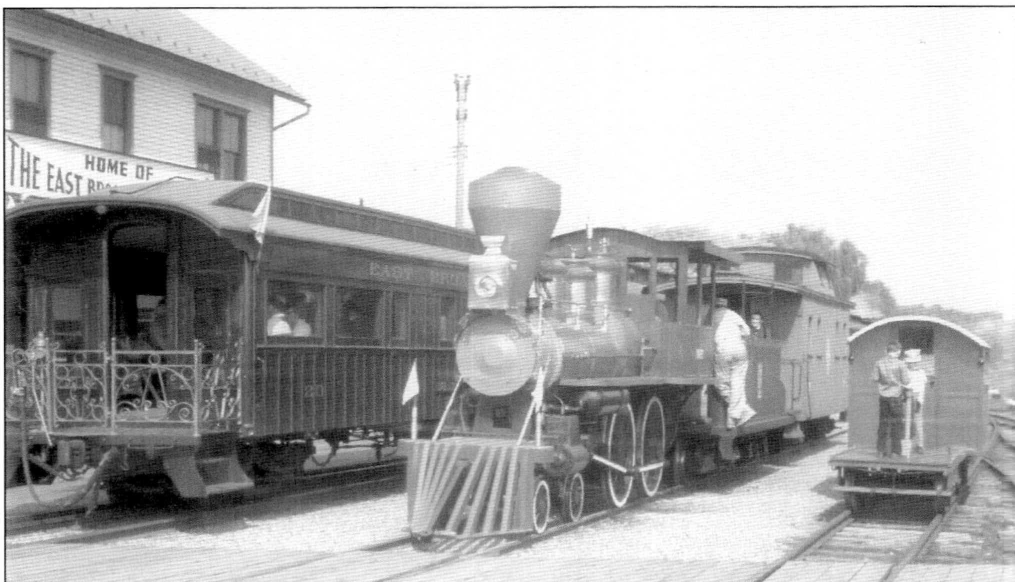

The Orbisonia station is busy on October 7, 1962, with, from left to right, parlor car No. 20 at the rear of the tourist train, Crown Locomotive Works 4-4-0 locomotive for testing purposes, and inspection vehicle M-3. The East Broad Top Railroad was an excellent place to test narrow-gauge locomotives. (Joel Salomon collection.)

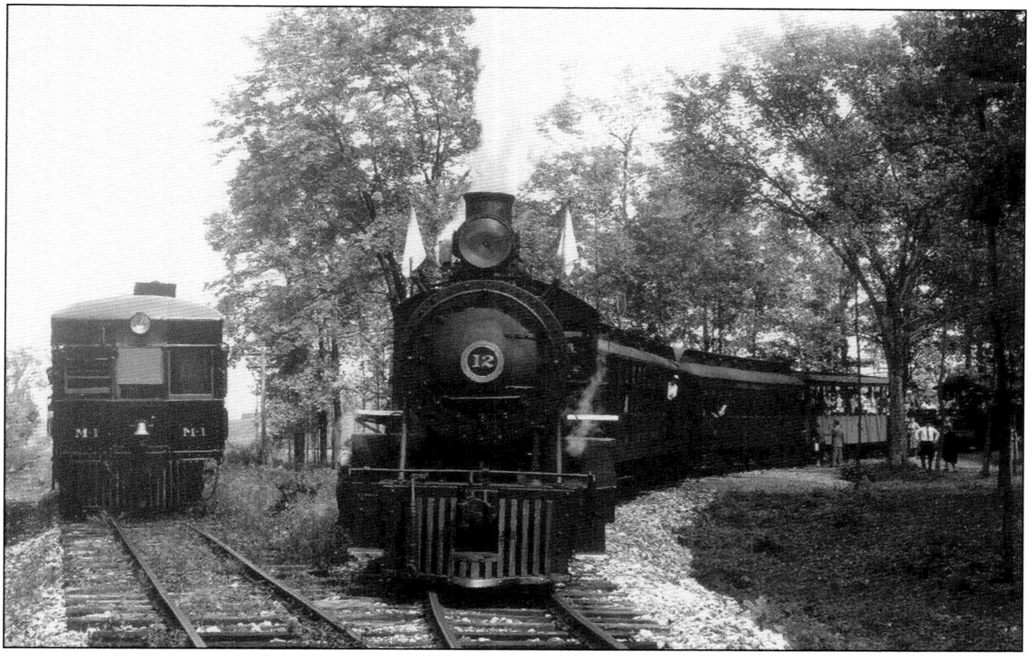

Gas-electric motor car M-1 is on the left while locomotive No. 12 is on the curved wye at Colgate Grove on October 8, 1961. When the East Broad Top Railroad reopened in 1960, the wye was built to reverse the train, which eliminated the need to have a steam locomotive at each end of the train. (Photograph by Louis J. G. Buehler, Rockhill Trolley Museum collection.)

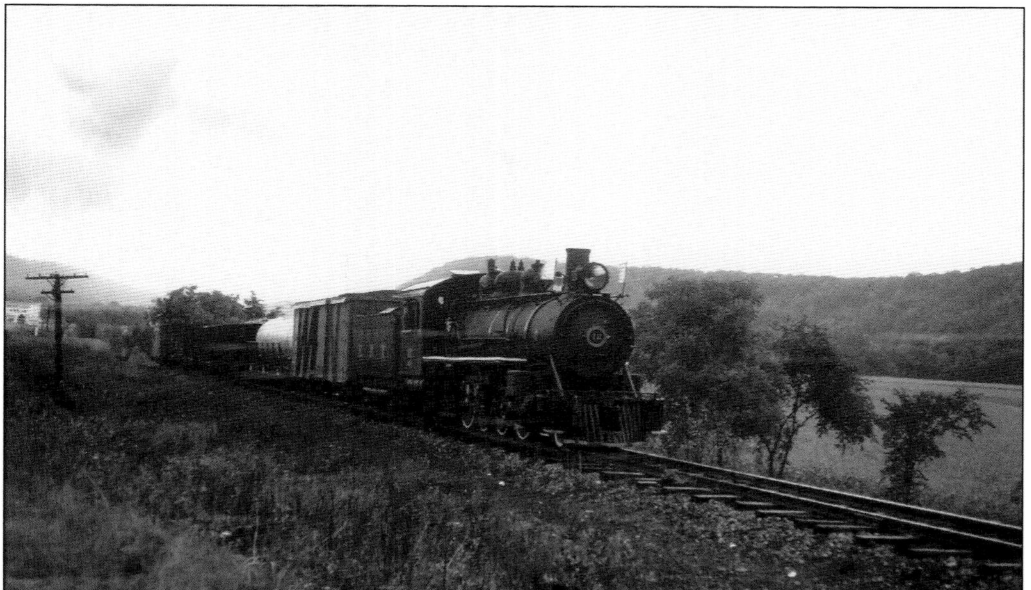

North of Orbisonia, East Broad Top Railroad steam locomotive No. 12 is heading a freight train on September 2, 1962. The railroad featured a wide well-maintained right-of-way that could handle heavy tonnage and, up to its 1956 closure, functioned like a main line railroad. (Photograph by Kenneth C. Springirth.)

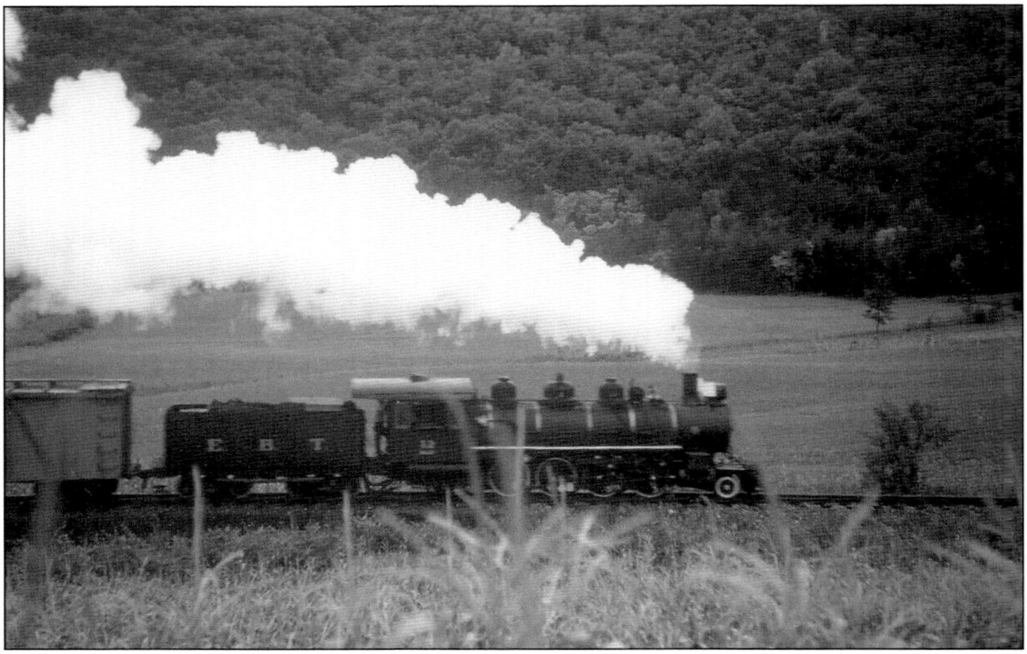

The oldest locomotive on the property, Mikado-type steam locomotive No. 12, with a 2-8-2 wheel arrangement, 48-inch-diameter drive wheels, and weighing 112,000 pounds, is northbound on September 2, 1962. Baldwin Locomotive Works built this locomotive in December 1911 for the East Broad Top Railroad. (Photograph by Kenneth C. Springirth.)

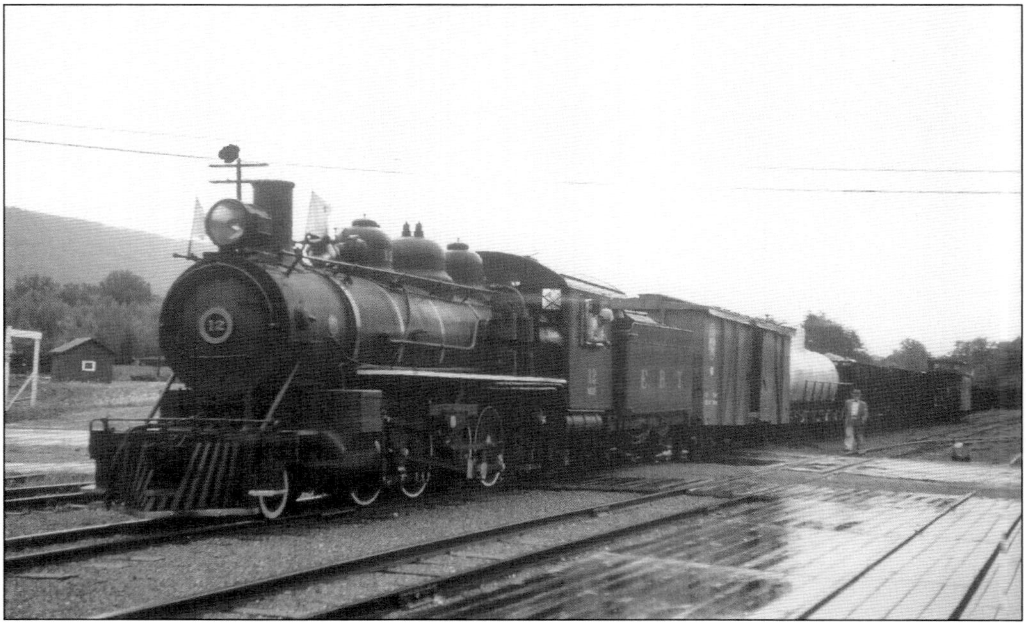

On a rainy September 2, 1962, East Broad Top Railroad locomotive No. 12 is backing the freight train in at the Rockhill Furnace yard. Over the years, the iron furnaces at the borough of Rockhill Furnace faded, but bituminous coal continued to be handled in large volumes until it declined and the railroad ended operations in 1956. (Photograph by Kenneth C. Springirth.)

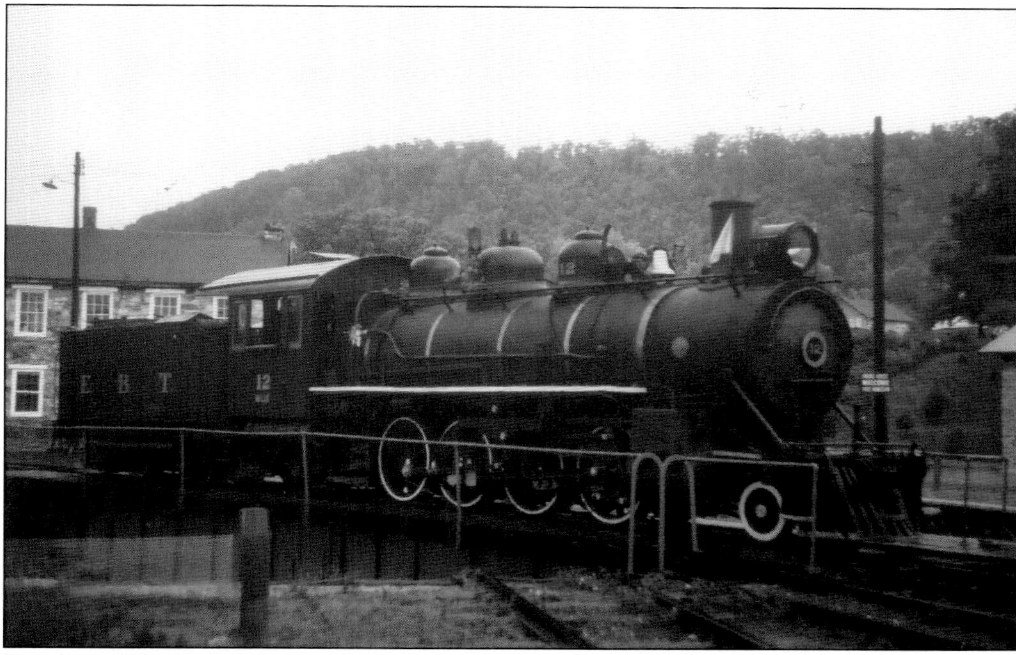

East Broad Top Railroad steam locomotive No. 12, affectionately known as *Millie* (named after Nick Kovalchick's daughter Millie), is on the turntable after a day's run on September 2, 1962. This locomotive made its first run in January 1912 and operated in tourist service from 1960 to 2001. It is stored inoperable in the roundhouse. (Photograph by Kenneth C. Springirth.)

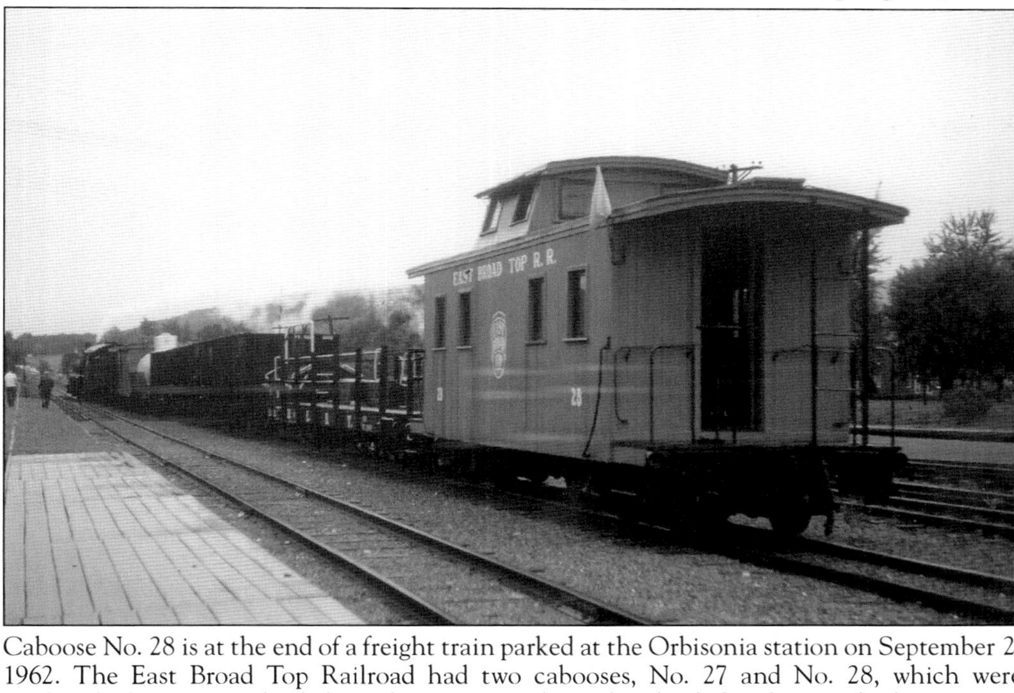

Caboose No. 28 is at the end of a freight train parked at the Orbisonia station on September 2, 1962. The East Broad Top Railroad had two cabooses, No. 27 and No. 28, which were steel-underframe, wood-sided, and center-cupola eight-wheeled cabooses built in 1920. (Photograph by Kenneth C. Springirth.)

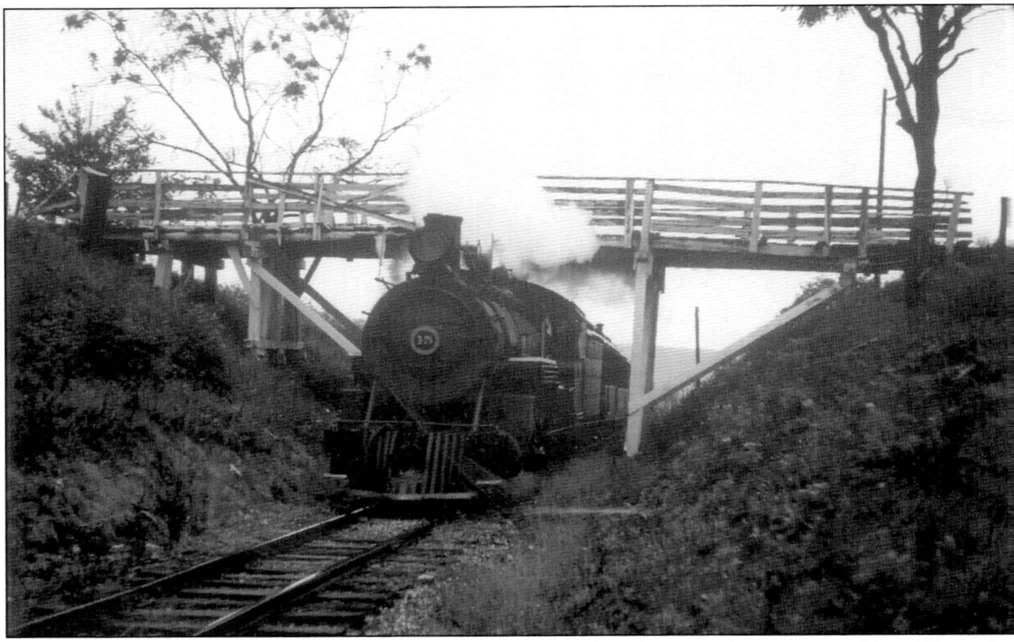

North of the Orbisonia station, East Broad Top Railroad steam locomotive No. 15, with a 2-8-2 wheel arrangement, crosses under the white wooden private driveway bridge on September 2, 1962. Baldwin Locomotive Works built this Mikado-type locomotive in February 1914, and it has 48-inch-diameter drive wheels and weighs 150,150 pounds. (Photograph by Kenneth C. Springirth.)

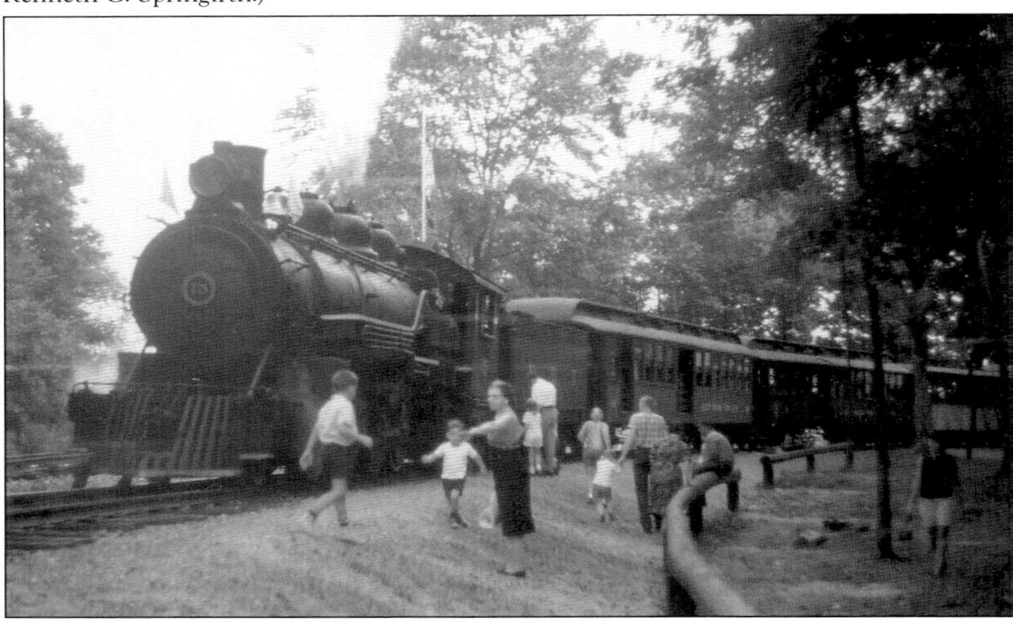

The Colgate Grove picnic grounds are popular for passengers to have a picnic lunch and take a later train back to Orbisonia, as seen in this view with East Broad Top Railroad steam locomotive No. 15 on September 2, 1962. During 2002, this locomotive was overhauled to meet new Federal Railway Administration safety standards. (Photograph by Kenneth C. Springirth.)

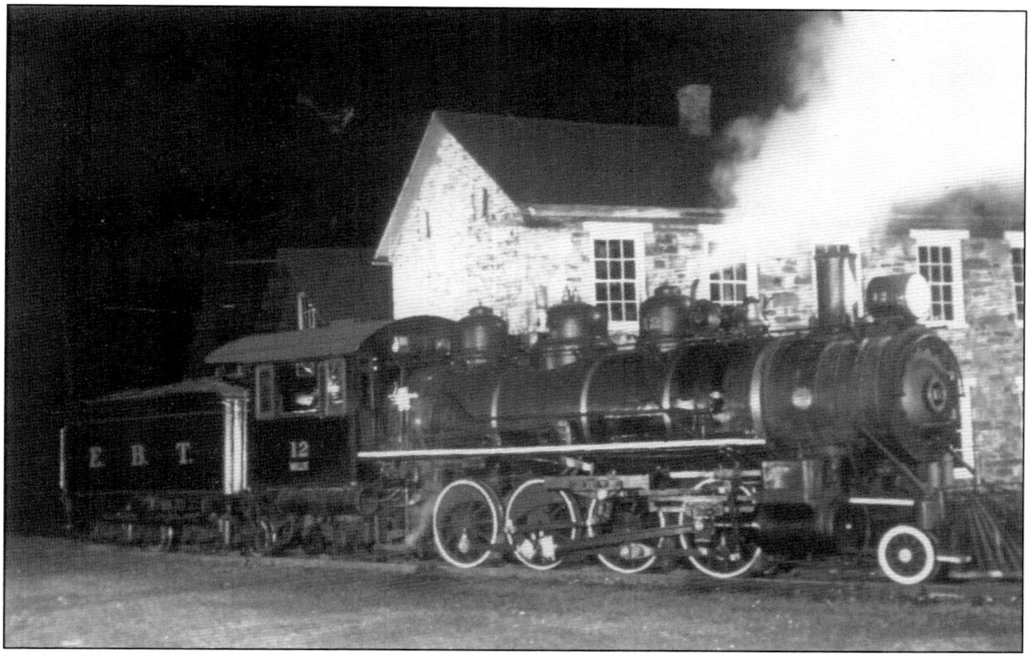

In this classic night scene of the 1960s, East Broad Top Railroad locomotive No. 12 is posing by the 1800s stone farmhouse at the Rockhill Furnace yard. This scene has remained virtually the same since the Baldwin Locomotive Works delivered this locomotive in December 1911. (East Broad Top Railroad photograph, Kenneth C. Springirth collection.)

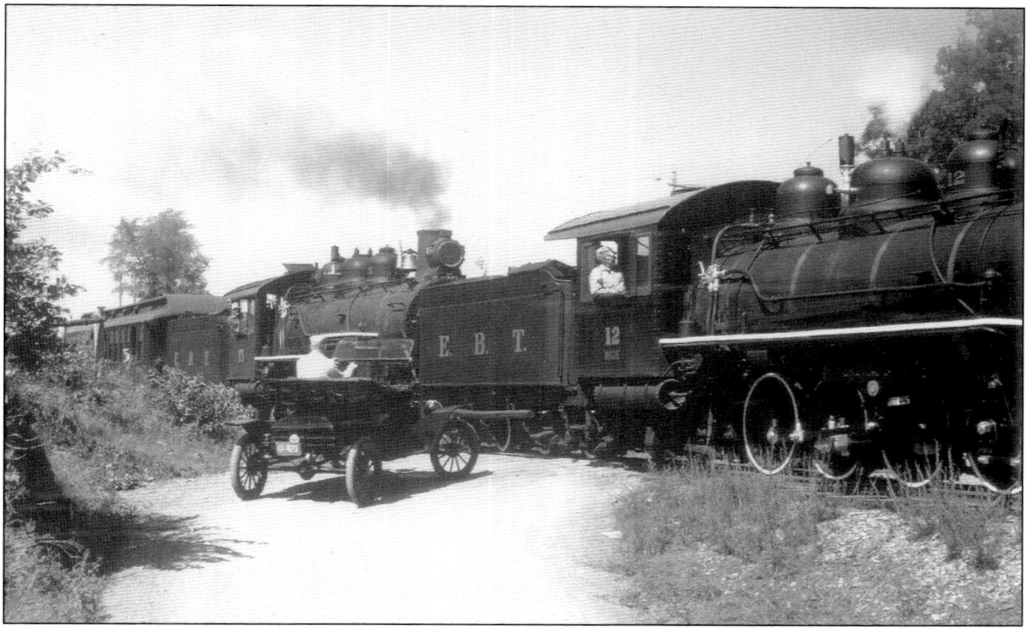

A 1913 Ford automobile is at the crossing waiting for a East Broad Top Railroad train pulled by locomotives No. 12 and No. 15 to pass on August 9, 1964. The 50-minute round-trip train ride passes through the scenic Aughwick Valley, much of which has remained unchanged over the last 100 years. (Photograph by Louis J. G. Buehler, Rockhill Trolley Museum collection.)

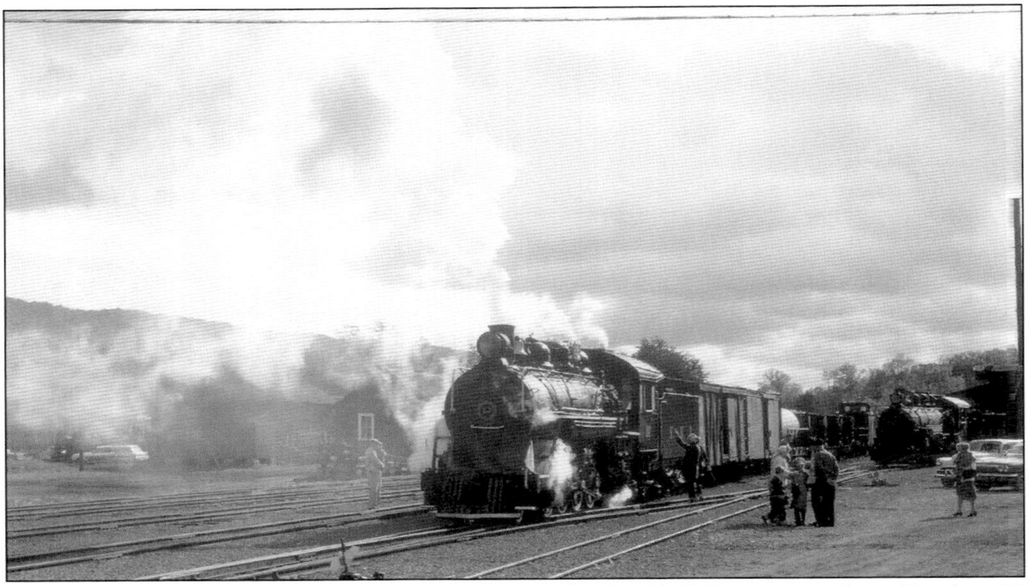

Locomotive No. 17 is powering a freight train at the Rockhill Furnace yard on October 17, 1965. The East Broad Top Railroad is the most authentic railroad site in North America and provides visitors with an appreciation of history and the contribution of workers who built about 290 freight cars during the years 1913 to 1930 of which about 240 were hopper cars. (Photograph by Louis J. G. Buehler, Rockhill Trolley Museum collection.)

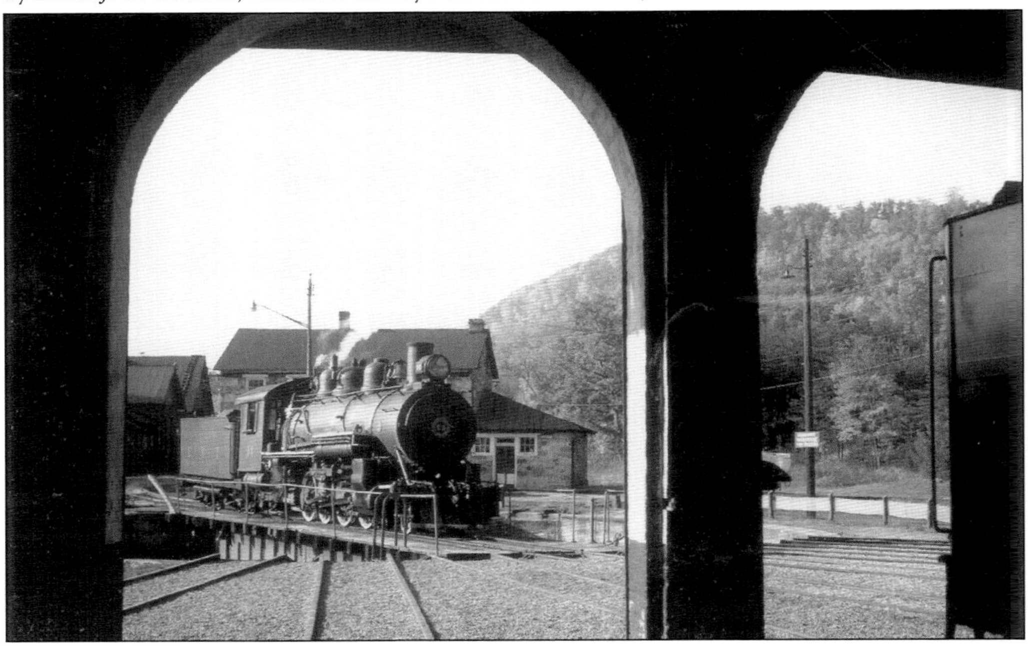

East Broad Top Railroad locomotive No. 14 is on the Rockhill Furnace turntable as viewed from inside the roundhouse on October 9, 1966. Behind the locomotive is the stone house that was built in the 1800s as a farmhouse that later became the East Broad Top Railroad general offices and still later the yard office. (Photograph by Louis J. G. Buehler, Rockhill Trolley Museum collection.)

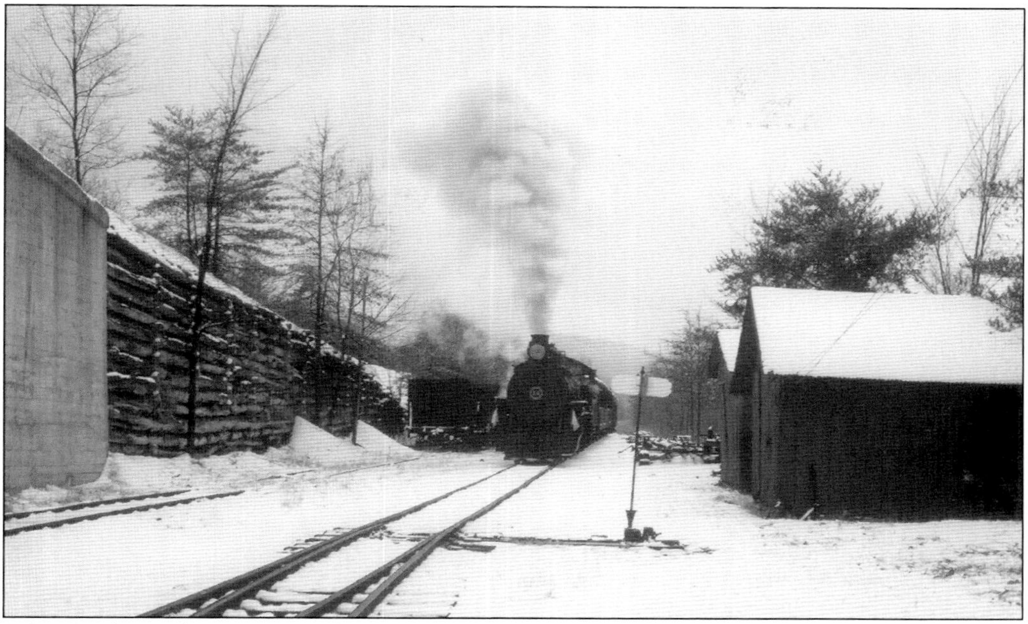

After backing the train south of the Rockhill Furnace yard, locomotive No. 14 is now heading northward as though it came from Robertsdale in the winter snow of February 18, 1967. This duplicated a view that was virtually unchanged since the East Broad Top Railroad line was opened to Robertsdale in 1874. (Photograph by Louis J. G. Buehler, Rockhill Trolley Museum collection.)

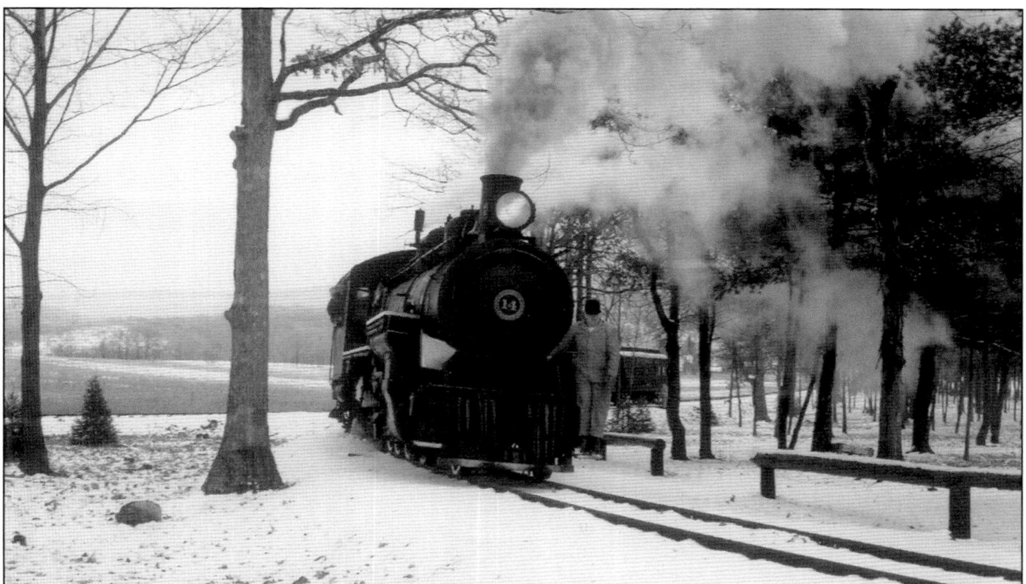

East Broad Top Railroad locomotive No. 14 is leading a train on the Colgate Grove wye during the Winter Spectacular of February 18, 1967. The other leg of the wye is just behind the trees on the left side of the picture. Winter Spectaculars were operated from 1966 through 1981 with a Spring Spectacular in 1982. (Photograph by Louis J. G. Buehler, Rockhill Trolley Museum collection.)

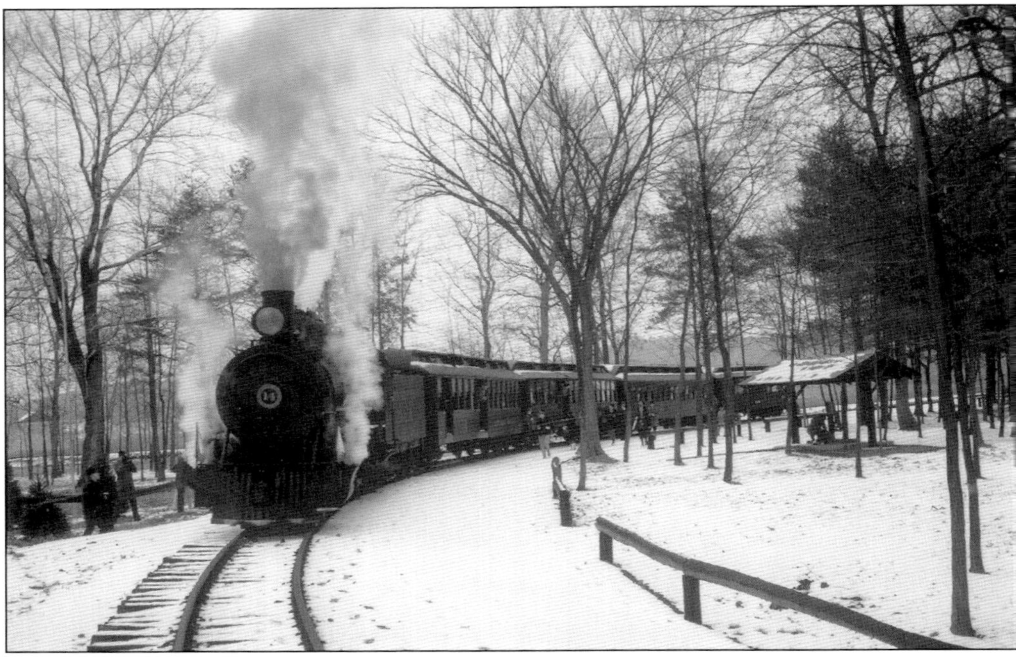

Locomotive No. 14 is at the snow-covered picnic area at the Colgate Grove wye on a February 18, 1967, winter excursion for a photograph stop. This northern end of the restored East Broad Top Railroad line was a popular stop for winter snow scenes and summer foliage views. (Photograph by Louis J. G. Buehler, Rockhill Trolley Museum collection.)

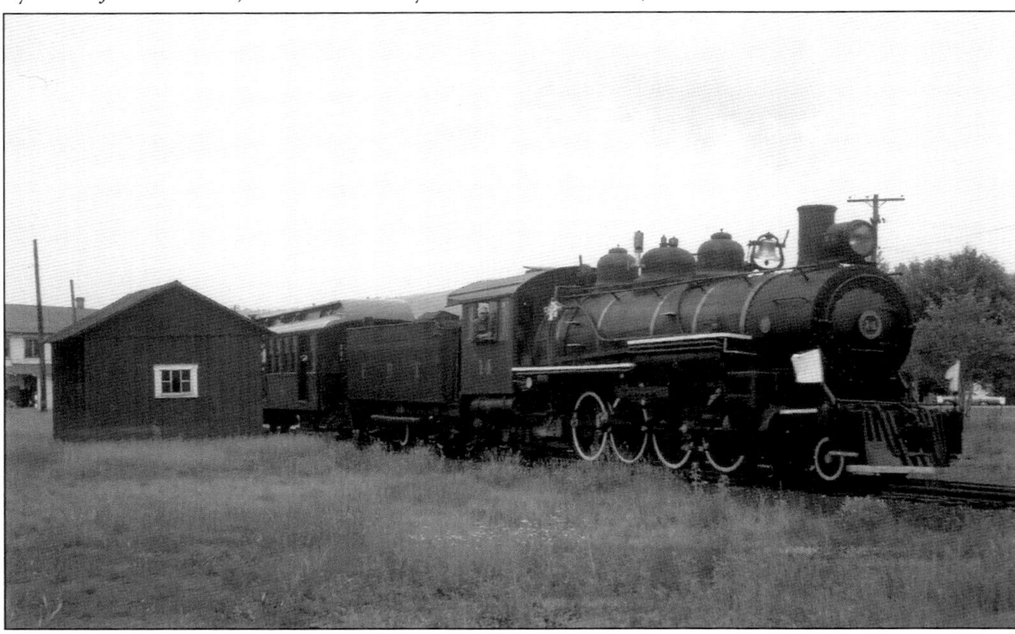

East Broad Top Railroad steam locomotive No. 14 is heading a passenger train on the Rockhill Furnace wye on June 2, 1968. This Mikado-type locomotive with a 2-8-2 wheel arrangement was delivered by Baldwin Locomotive Works in October 1912. Total locomotive weight is 147,150 pounds, and it has 48-inch-diameter drive wheels. (Photograph by Kenneth C. Springirth.)

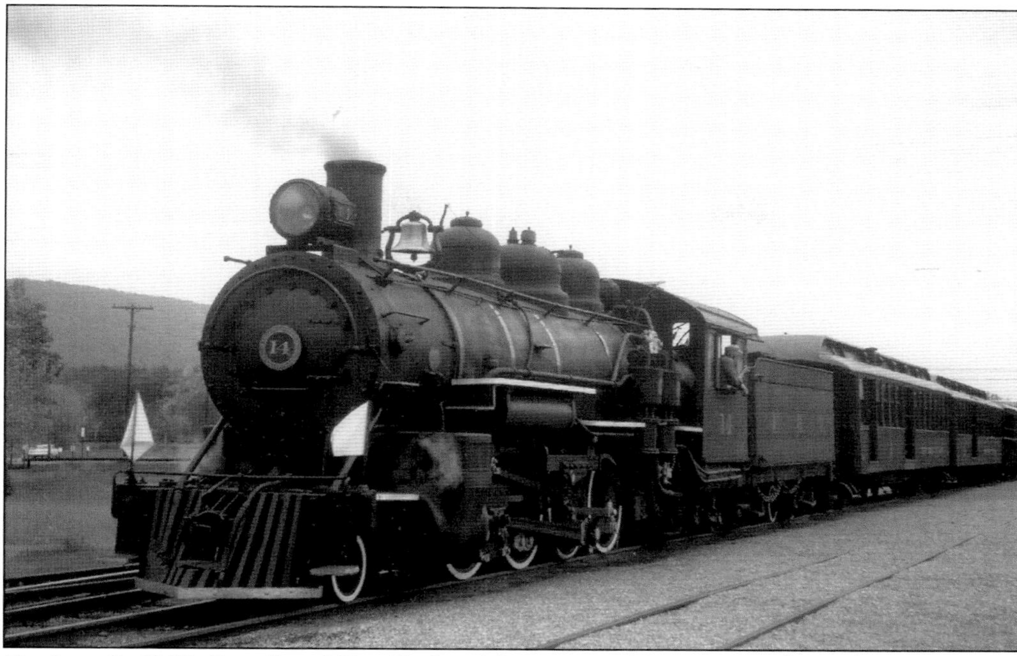

On June 2, 1968, East Broad Top Railroad locomotive No. 14 is at the Orbisonia station. Because of the success of locomotive No. 12, the railroad had Baldwin Locomotive Works build No. 14, which was larger and more powerful. As the railroad worked to increase the volume of coal handled per freight train, it needed more powerful locomotives. (Photograph by Kenneth C. Springirth.)

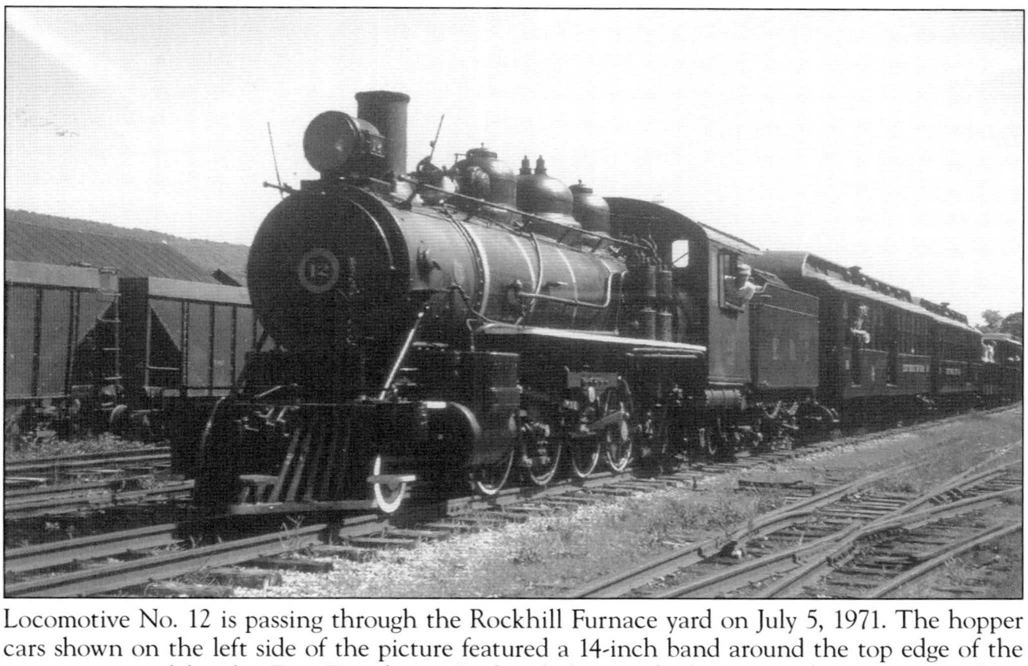

Locomotive No. 12 is passing through the Rockhill Furnace yard on July 5, 1971. The hopper cars shown on the left side of the picture featured a 14-inch band around the top edge of the car constructed by the East Broad Top Railroad shops, which increased car capacity from 70,000 pounds to 80,000 pounds. (Photograph by Kenneth C. Springirth.)

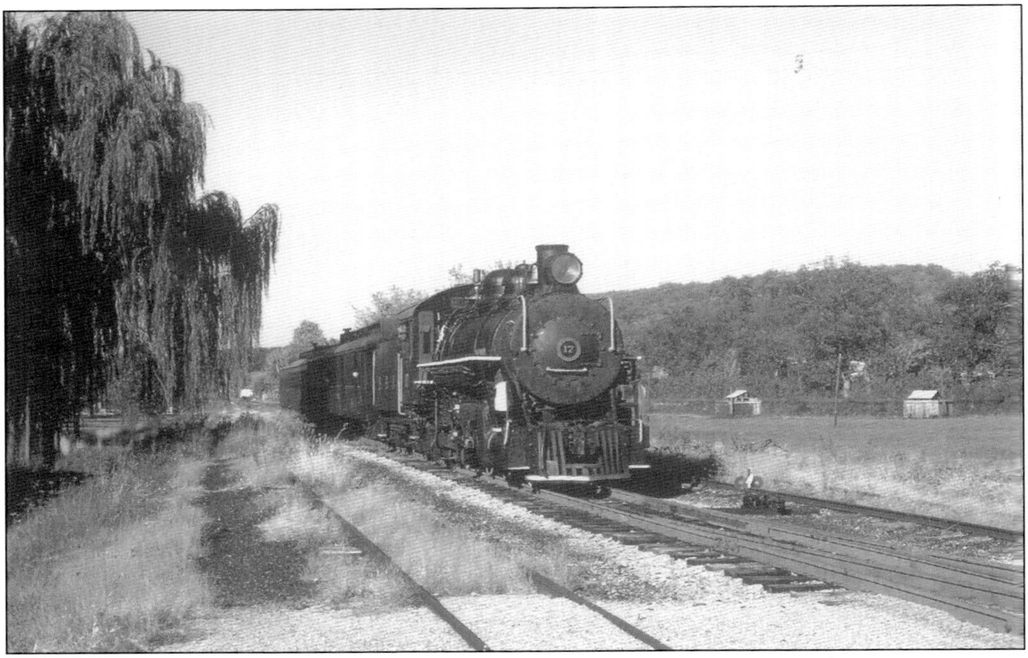

On October 18, 1970, East Broad Top Railroad steam locomotive No. 17 is bringing a vintage passenger train to the Orbisonia station. This afternoon scene of a local passenger train coming to town was once a common event in the United States. (Photograph by Louis J. G. Buehler Rockhill Trolley Museum collection.)

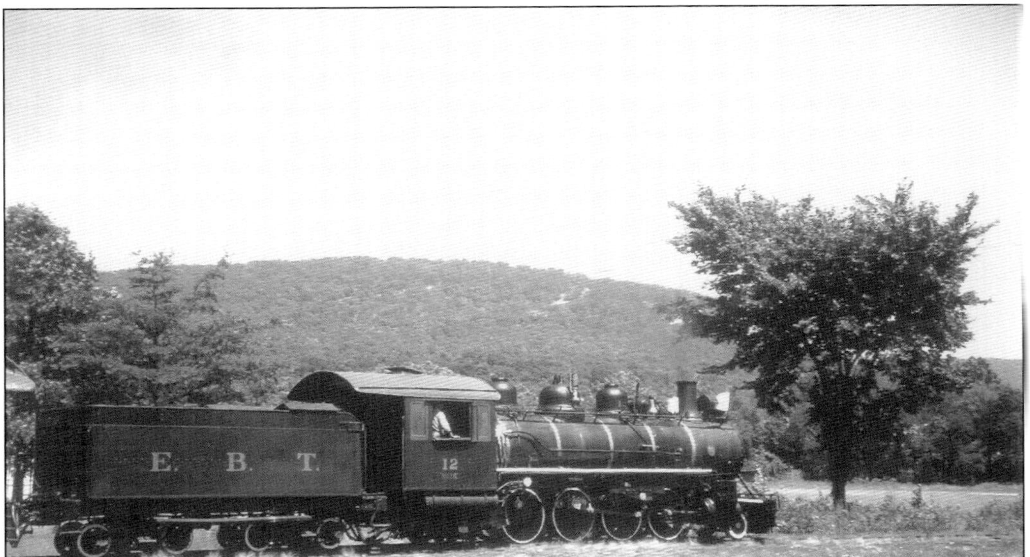

Locomotive No. 12 is at the Orbisonia station in the beautiful Aughwick Valley on July 5, 1971. The East Broad Top Railroad overcame the disadvantages of narrow gauge by maximizing tonnage hauled per train with its higher capacity hopper cars and by transferring standard-gauge freight cars to narrow-gauge trucks to deliver freight directly to customers on the line. (Photograph by Kenneth C. Springirth.)

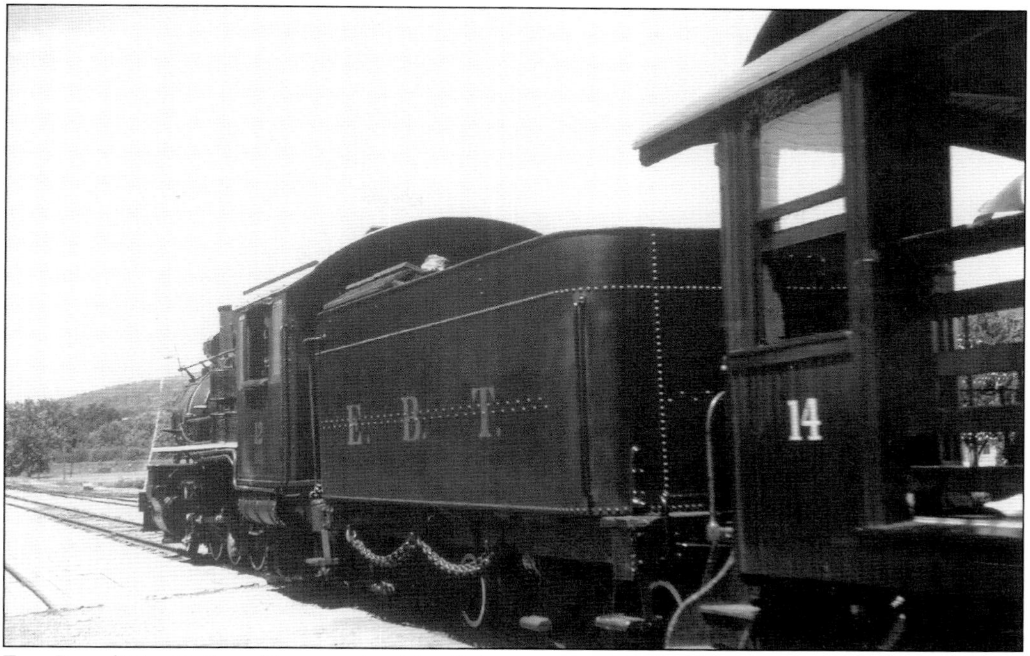

East Broad Top Railroad locomotive No. 12 is crossing Meadow Street to stop at the Orbisonia station on July 5, 1971. Combination passenger-baggage car No. 14, shown in this picture, was built by Laconia Car Company in 1882 and was purchased from the Boston, Revere Beach and Lynn Railroad in 1916. (Photograph by Kenneth C. Springirth.)

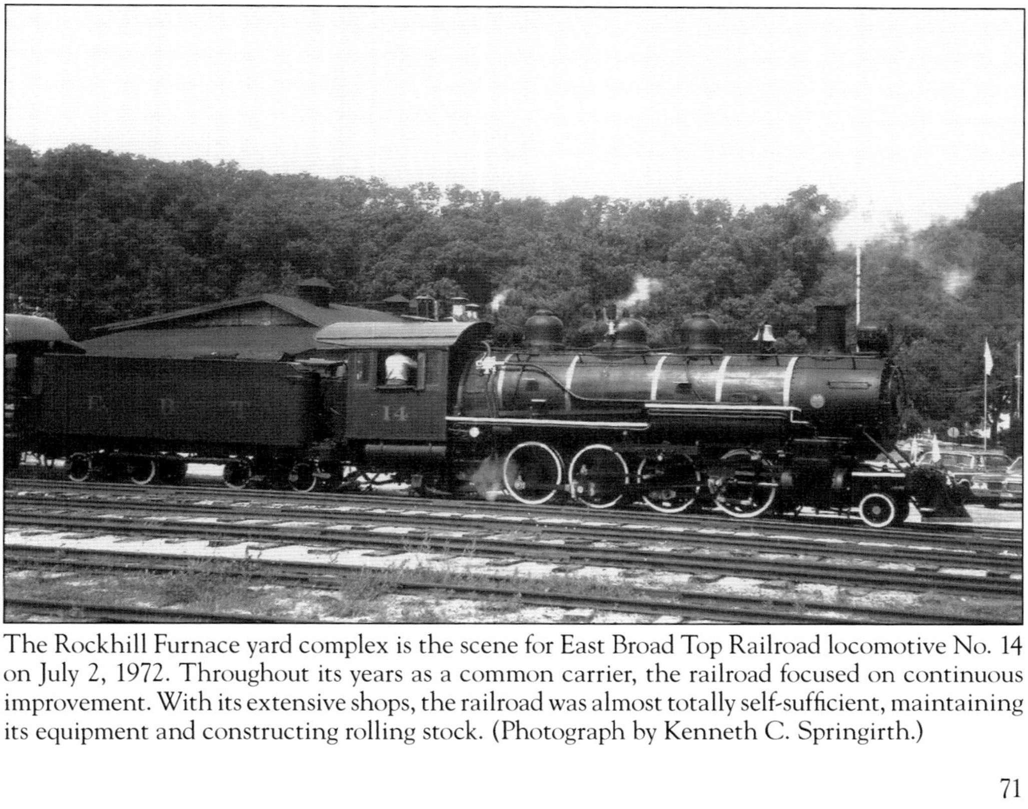

The Rockhill Furnace yard complex is the scene for East Broad Top Railroad locomotive No. 14 on July 2, 1972. Throughout its years as a common carrier, the railroad focused on continuous improvement. With its extensive shops, the railroad was almost totally self-sufficient, maintaining its equipment and constructing rolling stock. (Photograph by Kenneth C. Springirth.)

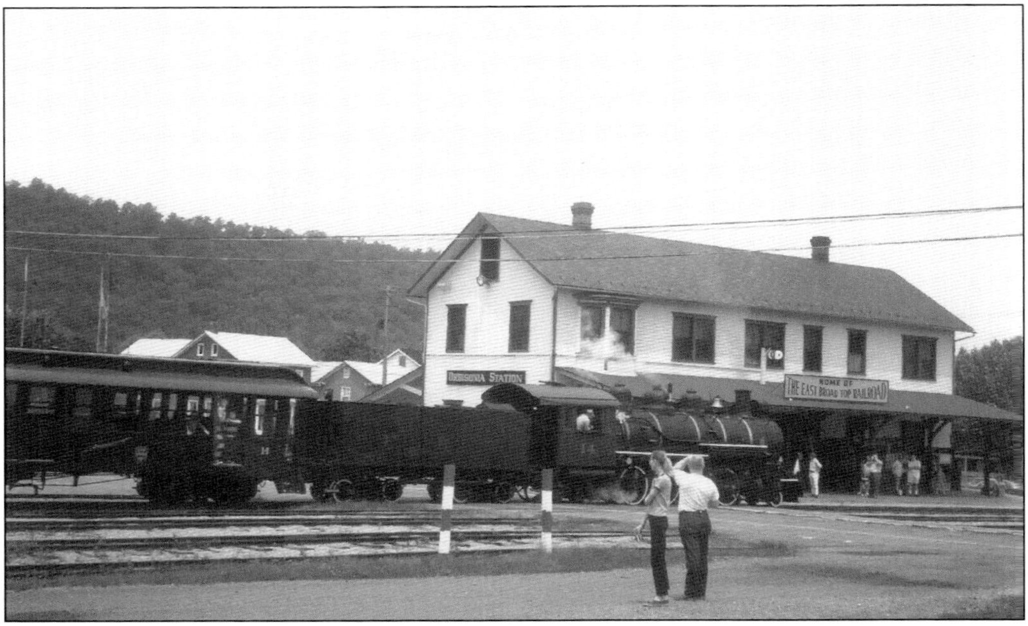

Passengers at the Orbisonia station of the East Broad Top Railroad are ready to board the arriving passenger train pulled by locomotive No. 14 on July 2, 1972. The current station was built in 1906. The original station was known as Rockhill Furnace Station, but since freight was often mistakenly taken to other Rockhill locations in Pennsylvania, the name was changed to Orbisonia in 1905. (Photograph by Kenneth C. Springirth.)

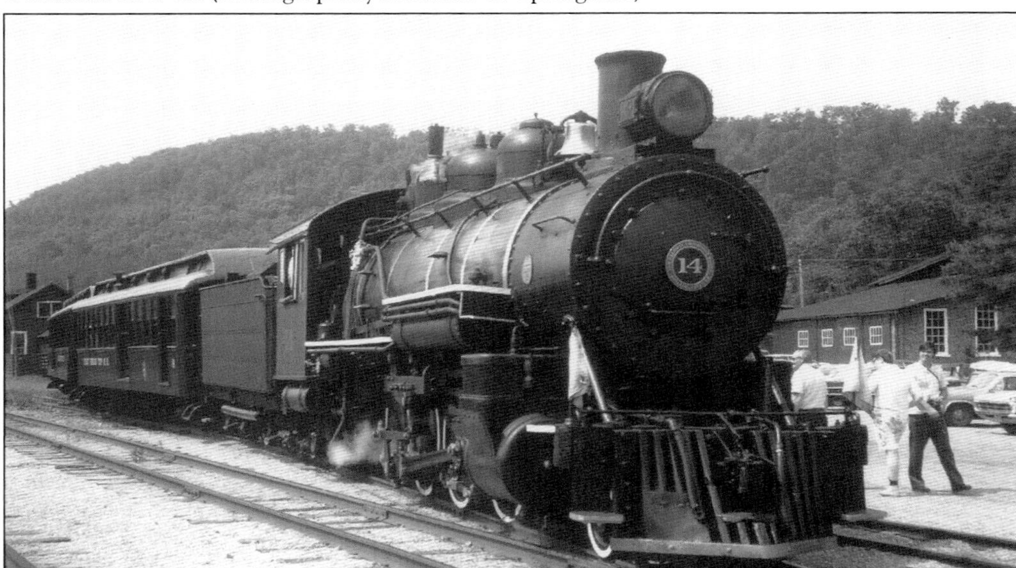

On July 2, 1972, East Broad Top Railroad locomotive No. 14 is at the Rockhill Furnace yard. On the right side of the picture is the former East Broad Top Transit Company bus garage, which was actually an addition to the roundhouse. When the railroad was completed from Mount Union to Rockhill Furnace on August 30, 1873, farmland was transformed into the railroad yard. (Photograph by Kenneth C. Springirth.)

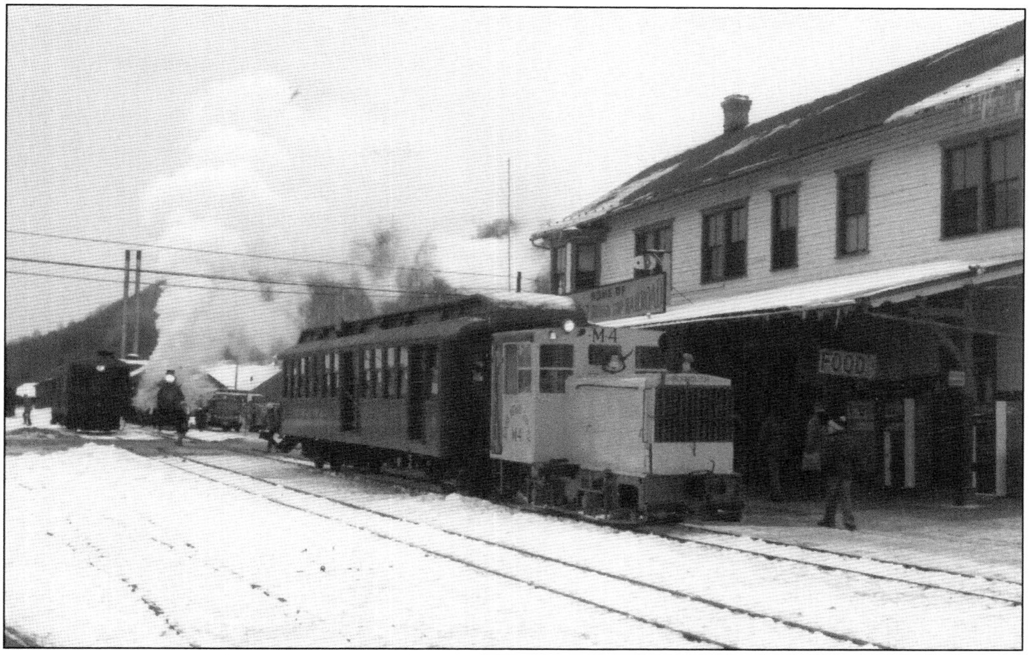

In the winter snow of February 1979, Plymouth Locomotive Works diesel mechanical locomotive M-4 with combination passenger-baggage car No. 14 is at the Orbisonia station. The East Broad Top Railroad purchased this locomotive to perform switching duties when it was not cost-effective or practical to use a steam locomotive. (Photograph by James A. Gillin.)

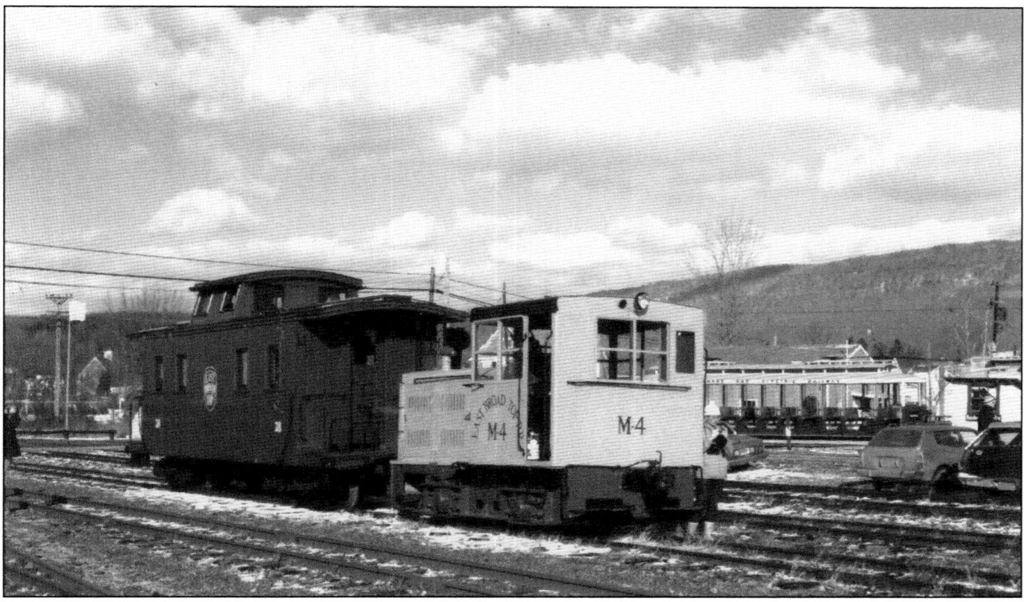

The Rockhill Furnace yard, just south of the Meadow Street crossing, is the scene for 1947-built Plymouth Locomotive Works diesel M-4 pulling East Broad Top Railroad caboose No. 28 for the February 1980 Winter Spectacular. In the background is the Rockhill Trolley Museum open trolley car from Companhia de Transportes Colectivos of Rio de Janeiro, Brazil. (Photograph by James A. Gillin.)

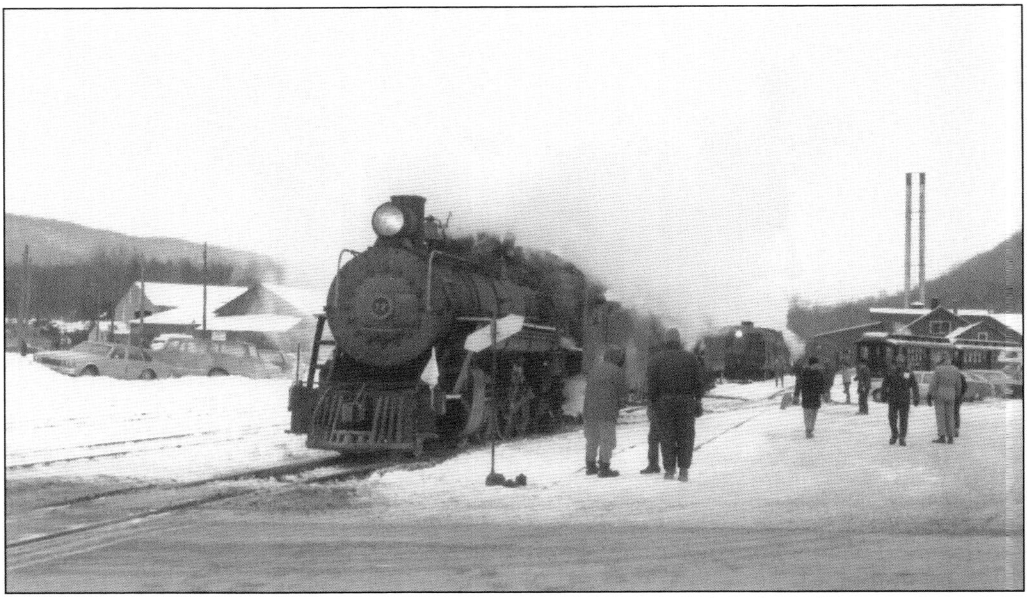

Hardy rail enthusiasts are in the snow at the Rockhill Furnace yard on the February 1979 Winter Spectacular with East Broad Top Railroad locomotive No. 17 ready to cross Meadow Street. No. 17 was the fifth Mikado-type locomotive built for the railroad by the Baldwin Locomotive Works. (Photograph by James A. Gillin.)

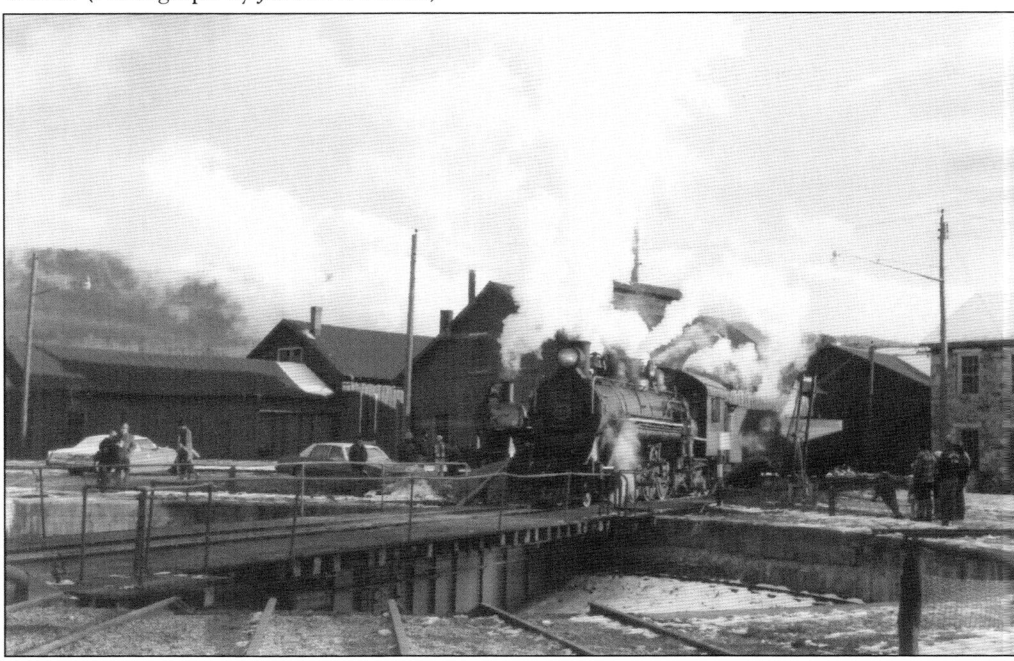

East Broad Top Railroad locomotive No. 17 is at the Rockhill Furnace roundhouse turntable with a slight dusting of snow on the February 1980 Winter Spectacular. The skilled workers using steam-generated, belt-driven machinery produced most of the rolling stock and over the years implemented the railroad's goal of maximizing the hauling capacity of its freight cars. (Photograph by James A. Gillin.)

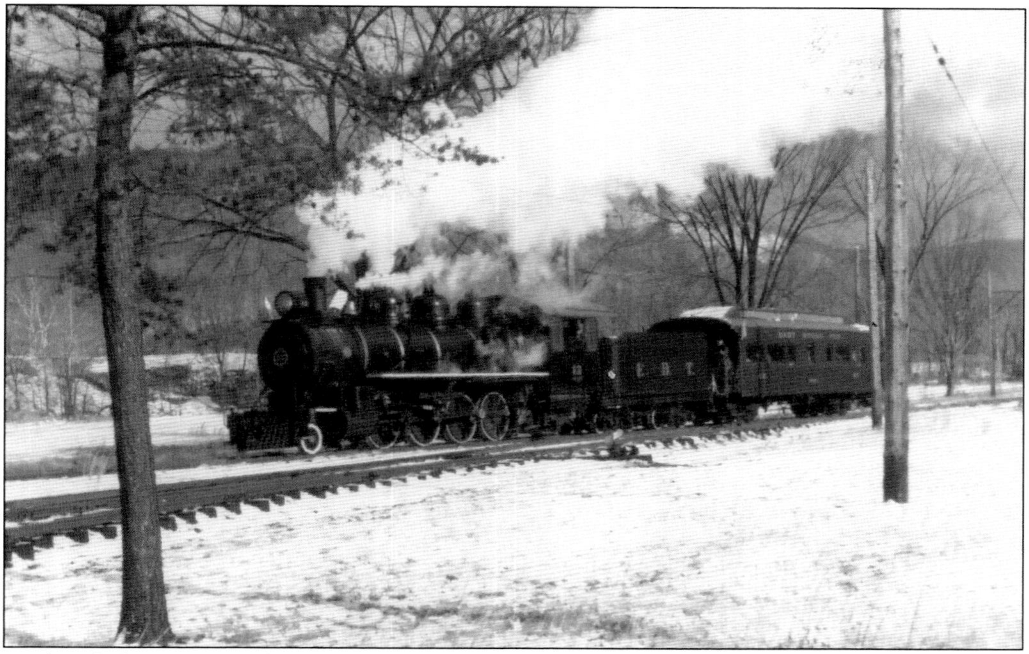

With a light coating of snow, East Broad Top Railroad locomotive No. 12 with parlor car No. 20 is at the Rockhill Furnace wye during the February 1980 Winter Spectacular. When Baldwin Locomotive Works delivered No. 12 in December 1911, it was so successful that over a period of time the railroad purchased five more locomotives with the same wheel arrangement. (Photograph by James A. Gillin.)

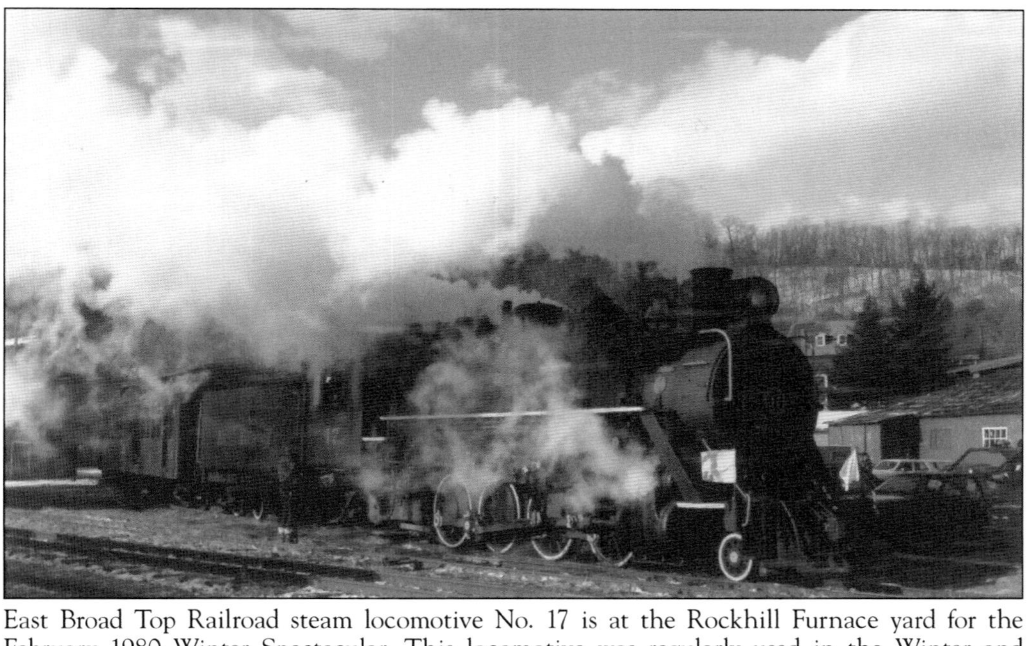

East Broad Top Railroad steam locomotive No. 17 is at the Rockhill Furnace yard for the February 1980 Winter Spectacular. This locomotive was regularly used in the Winter and Fall Spectaculars for many years and since 2002 has been stored out of service at the Rockhill Furnace roundhouse. (Photograph by James A. Gillin.)

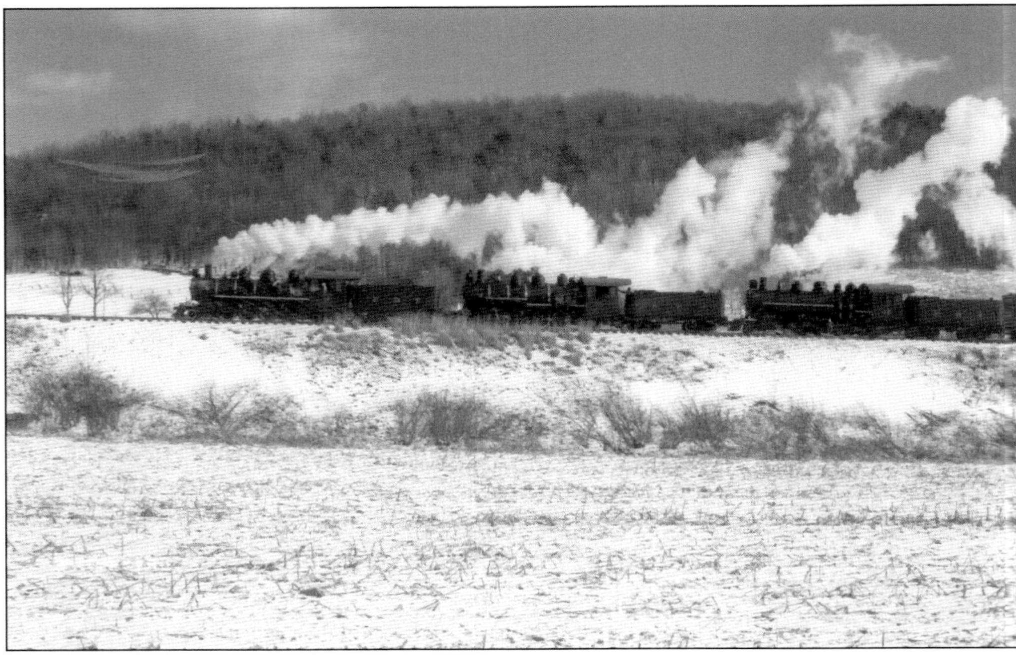

East Broad Top Railroad locomotives No. 12, No. 15, and No. 17 are northbound in the snow near the Runk Road Bridge for the February 1980 Winter Spectacular. Over the last 100 years, this location has kept its rural charm and has been an excellent location for photograph runs. (Photograph by James A. Gillin.)

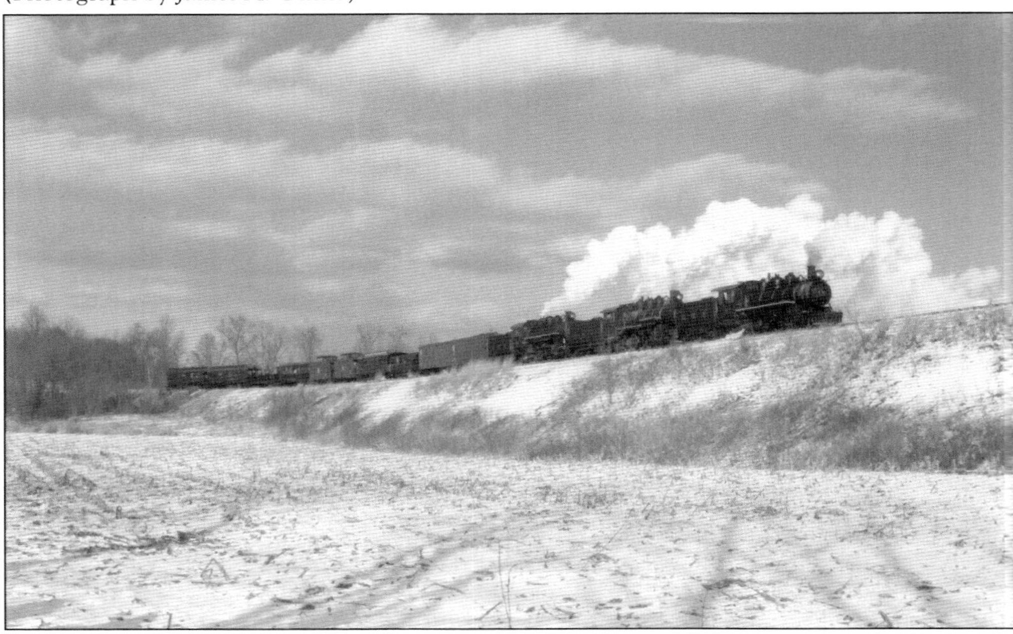

Southbound East Broad Top Railroad locomotives No. 12, No. 15, and No. 17 are nearing the Runk Road Bridge during February 1980. Tractive effort, which is a calculated ability of the locomotive to start a train, was 22,100 pounds for No. 12, a larger 27,600 pounds for No. 15, and an even larger 30,600 pounds for No. 17. (Photograph by James A. Gillin.)

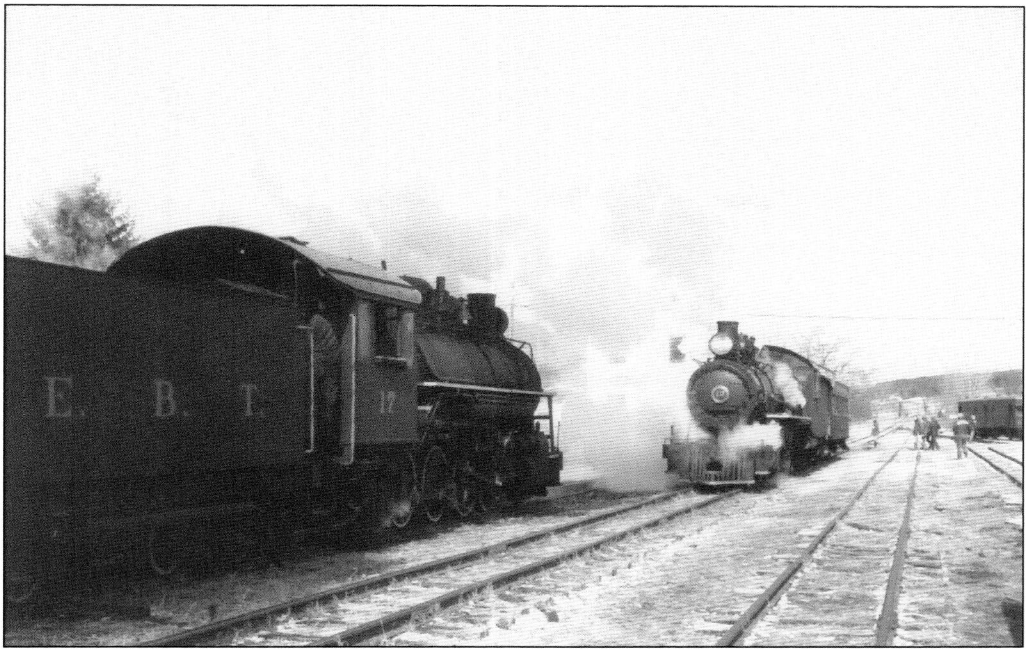

Northbound East Broad Top Railroad locomotive No. 17 looks like a giant compared to southbound locomotive No. 12 at the Rockhill Furnace yard during the February 1980 Winter Spectacular. With a total weight of 163,500 pounds, locomotive No. 17 was larger and more powerful than locomotive No. 12, which weighed 112,000 pounds. (Photograph by James A. Gillin.)

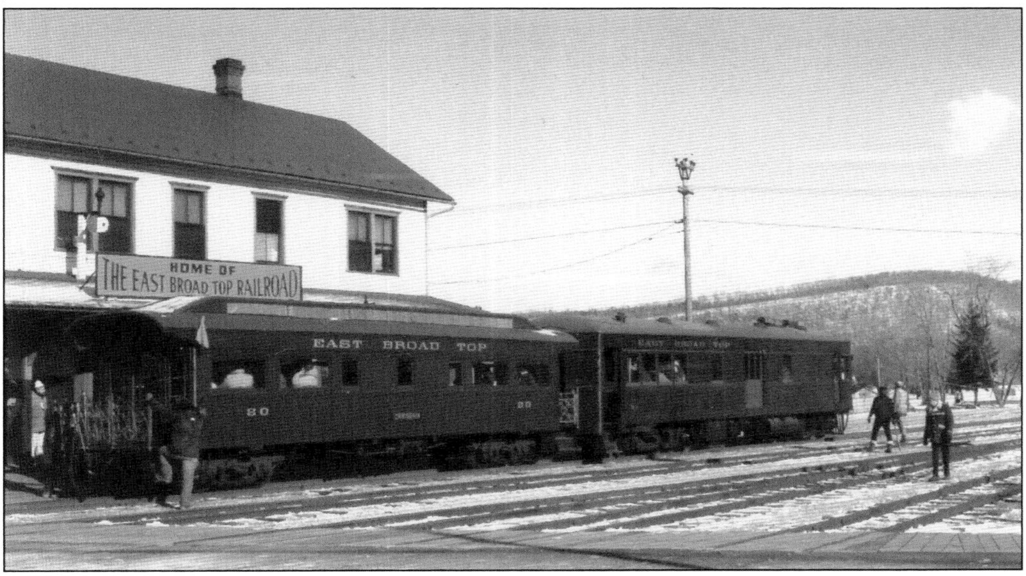

The unique East Broad Top Railroad gas-electric motor car M-1 pulling parlor car No. 20 is shown at the Orbisonia station during the February 1980 Winter Spectacular. Using parts supplied by J. G. Brill Car Company and Westinghouse Electric Company, this motor car is the only narrow-gauge gas-electric car operating on its original right-of-way with original major component parts in North America. (Photograph by James A. Gillin.)

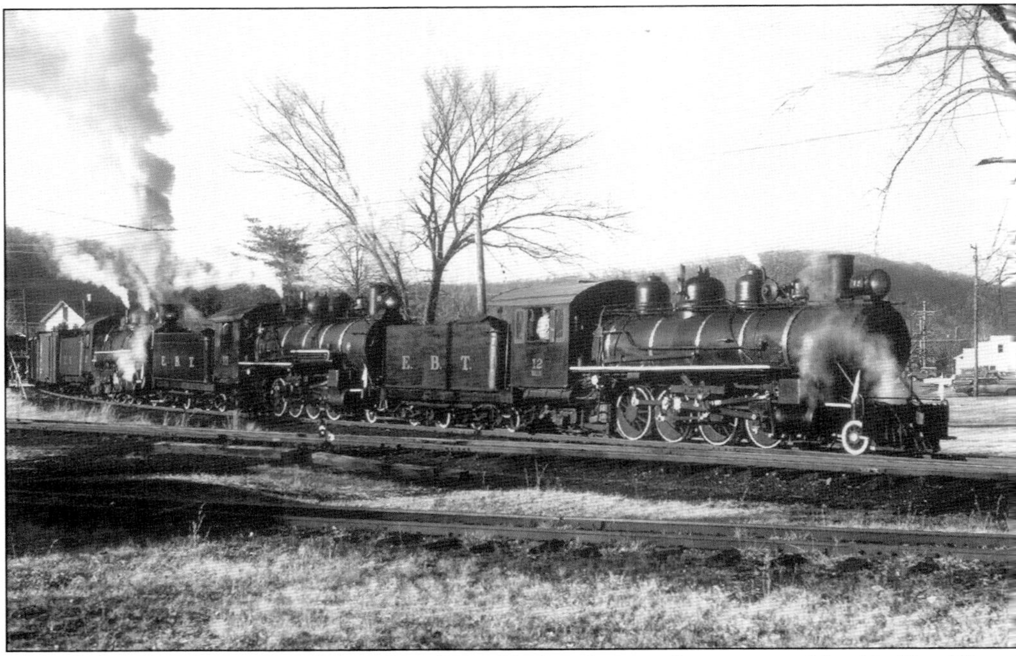

A triple header consisting of East Broad Top Railroad steam locomotives No. 12, No. 15, and No. 17 is on the Rockhill Furnace wye pulling a freight train on February 14, 1981. Special runs were made during this Winter Spectacular to accommodate the students of rail transportation with unique photograph opportunities. (Photograph by Joel Salomon.)

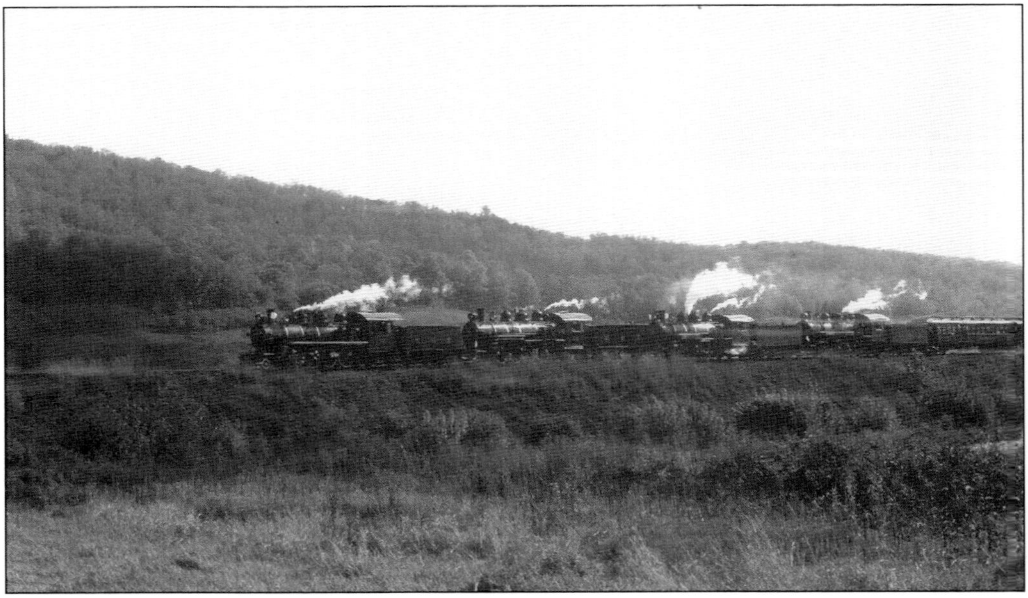

Four Mikado-type steam locomotives are leading a train through historic Aughwick Valley on the Fall Spectacular of October 10, 1987, which was the only time a quadruple header was ever operated on the East Broad Top Railroad. With its convenient yet remote location, the railroad is a nice one-day outing from areas such as Pittsburgh, Philadelphia, Baltimore, and Washington, D.C. (Photograph by Joel Salomon.)

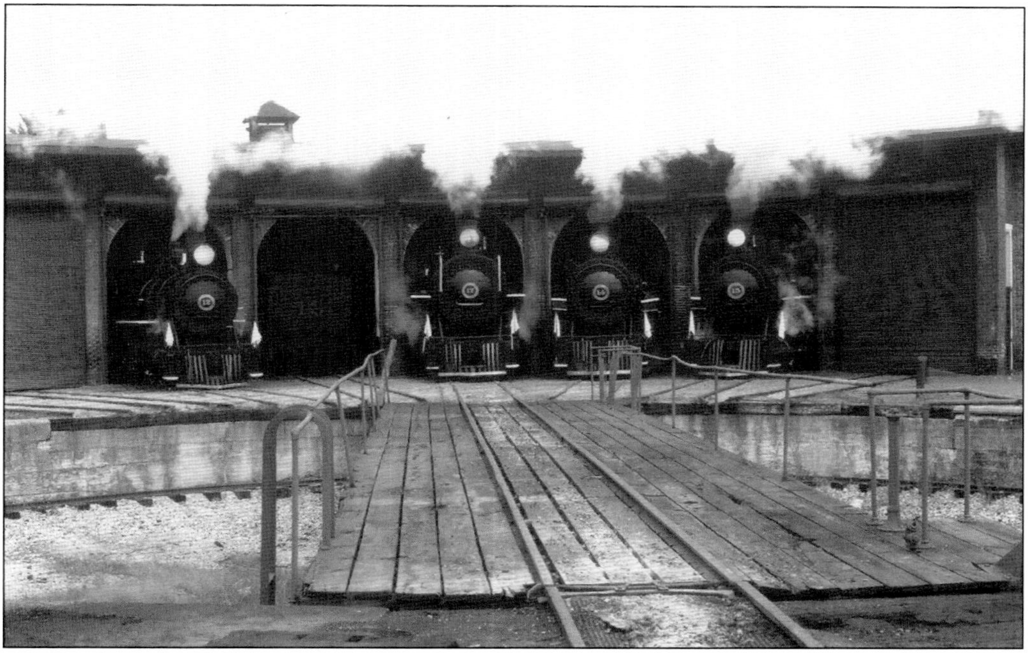

The brick Rockhill Furnace roundhouse finds East Broad Top Railroad locomotives No. 12, No. 17, No. 14, and No. 15 preparing to go into service during October 1988. In 1917, two stalls were added, making it an eight-stall roundhouse. A bus garage addition was added in 1933 for East Broad Top Transit Company buses to replace a garage previously lost in a fire. (Photograph by Joel Salomon.)

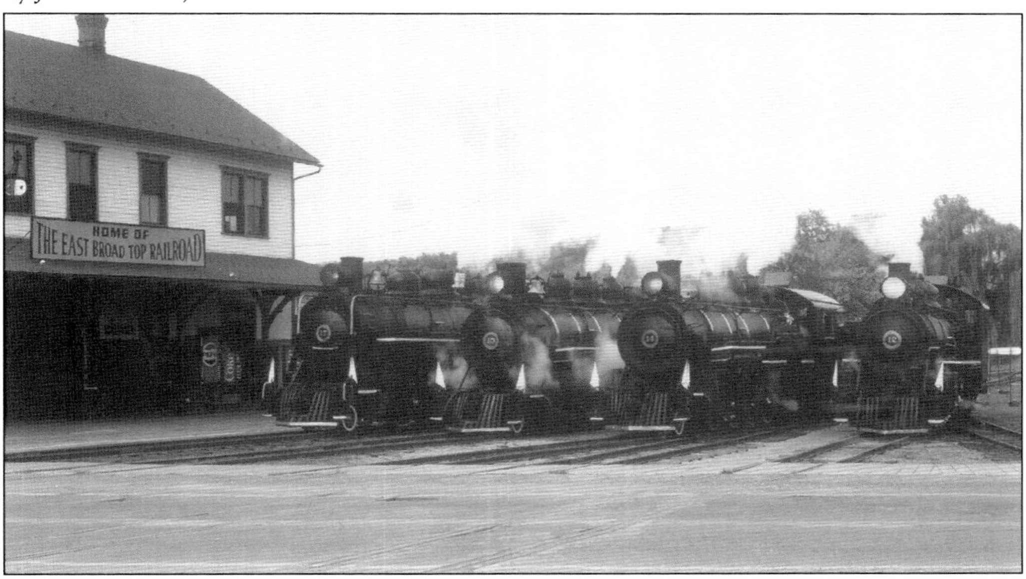

From left to right, East Broad Top Railroad locomotives No. 17, No. 15, No. 14, and No. 12 are positioned at the Orbisonia station during October 1988. Baldwin Locomotive Works built all of these Mikado-type locomotives. Scenes like this intensified interest in the railroad and attracted visitors from throughout the United States and around the world. (Photograph by Joel Salomon.)

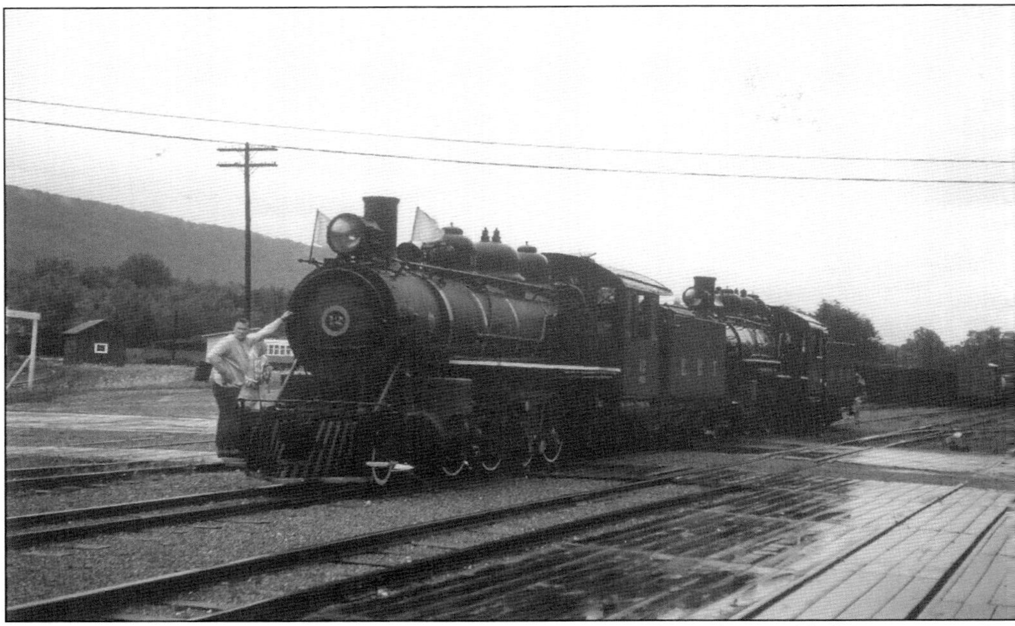

Locomotives No. 12 and No. 14 are crossing Meadow Street from the Rockhill Furnace yard on September 2, 1962. Both of these locomotives were successful, with No. 12 the first and smallest Mikado-type to enter service on the East Broad Top Railroad followed by the more powerful No. 14. (Photograph by Kenneth C. Springirth.)

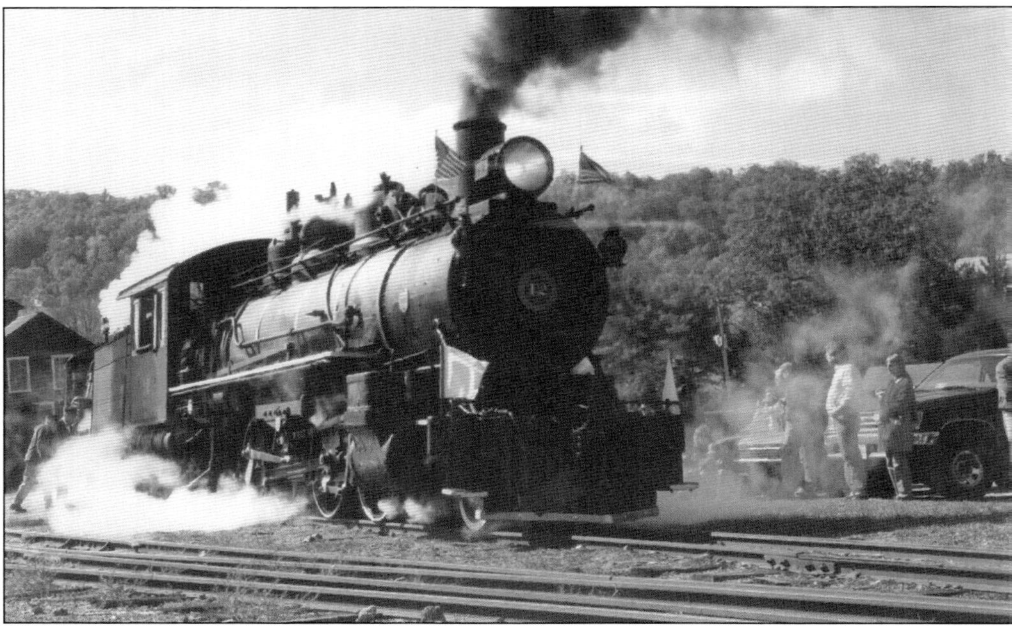

At the October 12, 1996, Fall Spectacular with the leaves turning color, East Broad Top Railroad locomotive No. 12 thrills visitors at the Rockhill Furnace yard. This locomotive, delivered in December 1911, marked the continuation of a modernization program that included heavier track and, over a period of time, five additional larger narrow-gauge locomotives. (Photograph by Kenneth C. Springirth.)

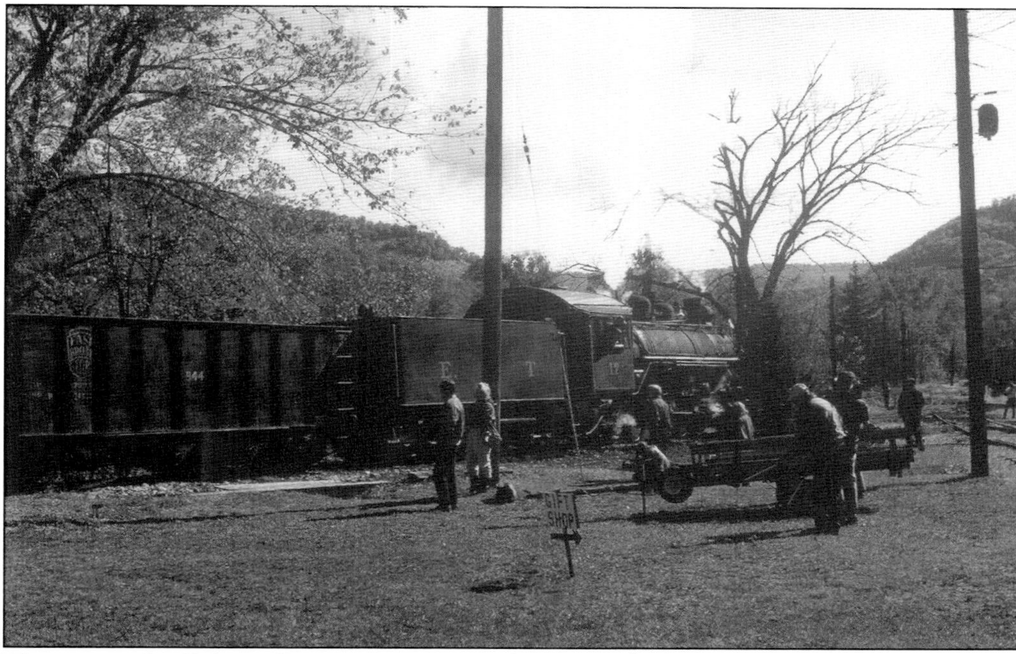

The wye at the Colgate Grove picnic area is the setting for locomotive No. 17 with a special freight train during the October 12, 1996, Fall Spectacular. Three-bay steel hopper car No. 944 in the train was built at the East Broad Top Railroad shops in 1916. (Photograph by Kenneth C. Springirth.)

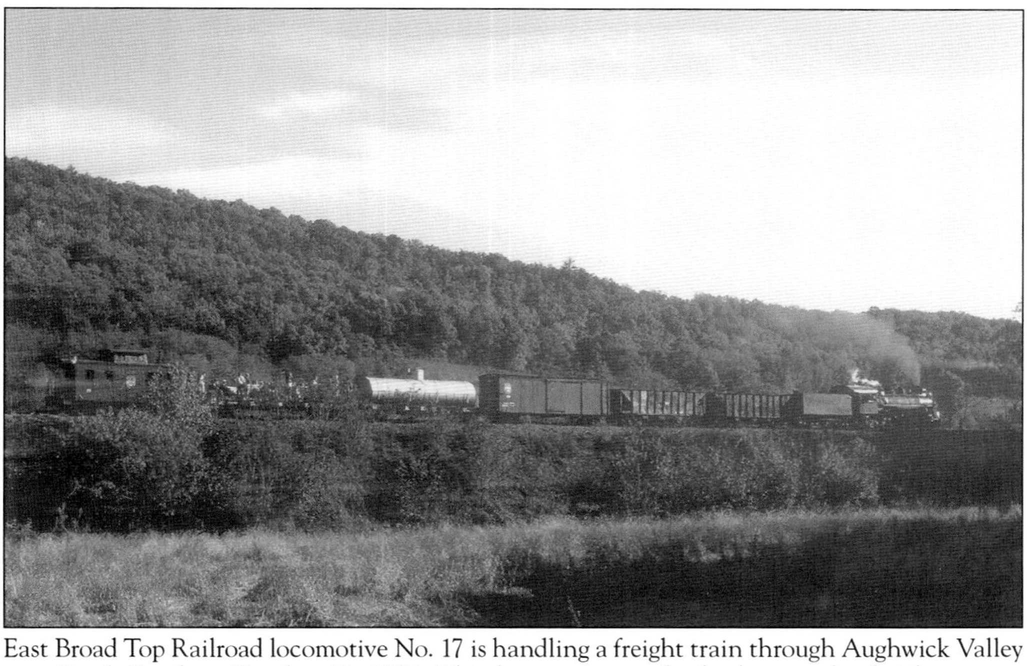

East Broad Top Railroad locomotive No. 17 is handling a freight train through Aughwick Valley near Runk Road on October 12, 1996. This locomotive made the last regular freight run on the East Broad Top Railroad on April 6, 1956. Except for the growth of foliage, this area has remained virtually unchanged since that last run. (Photograph by Kenneth C. Springirth.)

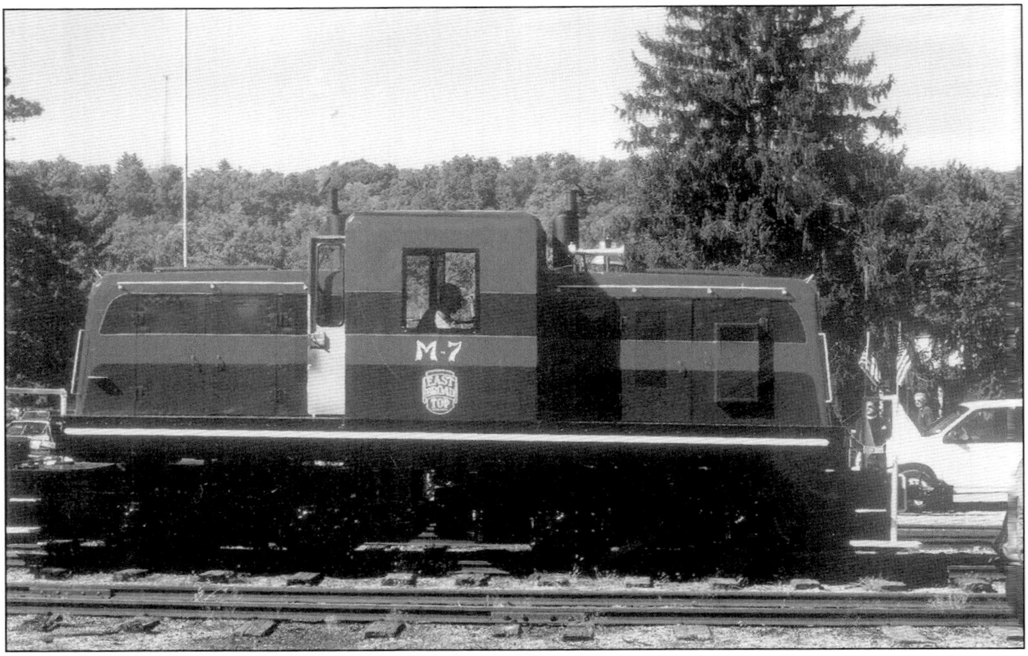

Diesel-electric center-cab switcher M-7 is pictured at the Rockhill Furnace yard on October 12, 1996. This 55-ton heavy-duty yard switcher built in 1964 by General Electric Company was purchased by the East Broad Top Railroad in 1993. It has been used on passenger runs during the Fall Spectacular weekends that have been held in October. (Photograph by Kenneth C. Springirth.)

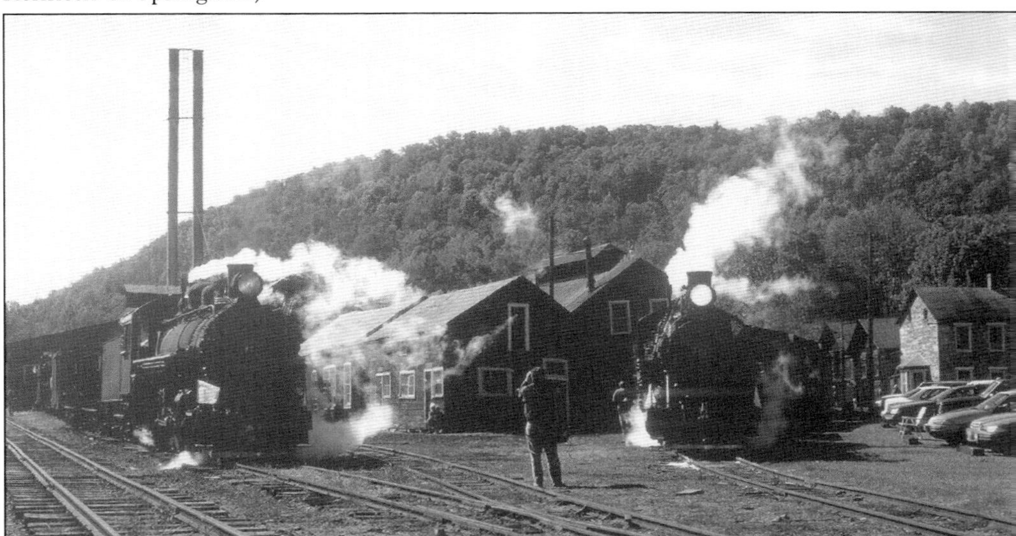

From left to right, East Broad Top Railroad locomotives No. 17 and No. 14 are preparing to depart from the Rockhill Furnace yard during the Fall Spectacular of October 12, 1996. Locomotive No. 17, with a 2-8-2 wheel arrangement, weight of 163,500 pounds, and having 48-inch-diameter drive wheels, made the last run of the railroad's common carrier era on April 6, 1956. (Photograph by Kenneth C. Springirth.)

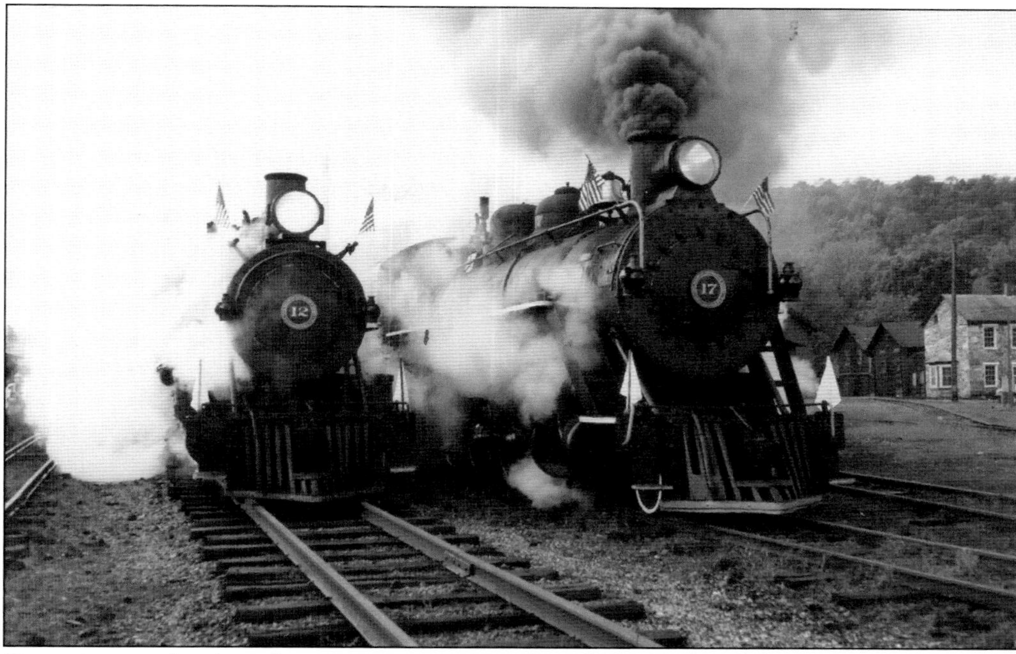

Operating on the three-foot narrow-gauge East Broad Top Railroad, locomotives No. 12 and No. 17 are shown at the Rockhill Furnace yard on October 10, 1998. As of 2002, both locomotives have been stored inoperable. This picture could have been taken 70 years earlier with almost the exact same scene. (Photograph by Kenneth C. Springirth.)

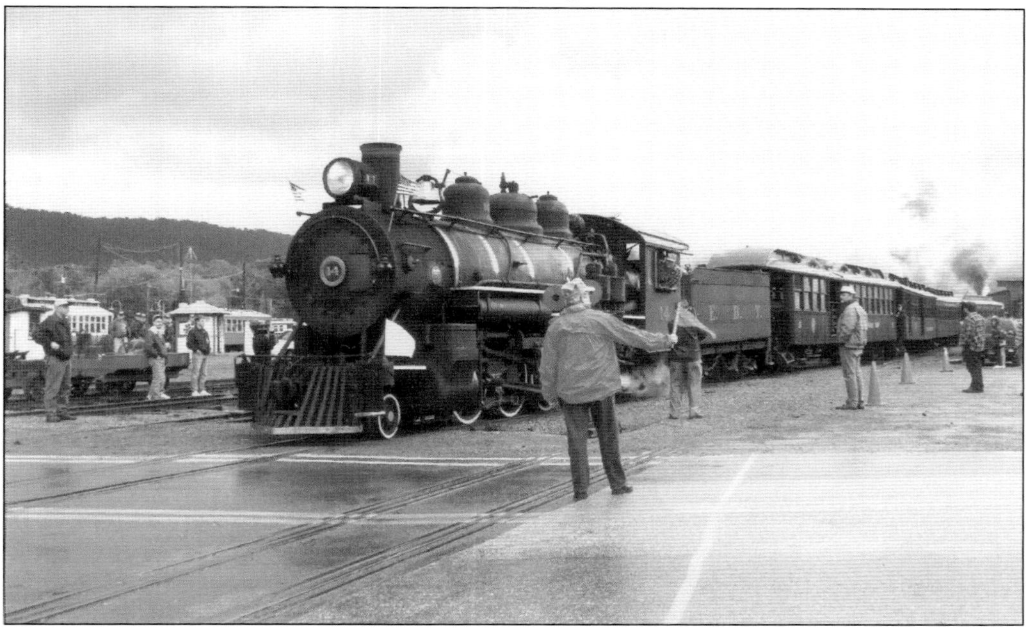

On a rainy October 10, 1998, Mikado-type steam locomotive No. 14, with a 2-8-2 wheel arrangement, prepares to cross Pennsylvania State Highway 994 at the borough of Rockhill Furnace for its next round-trip through the historic Aughwick Valley. On the left of the locomotive are the trolleys of the Rockhill Trolley Museum. (Photograph by Kenneth C. Springirth.)

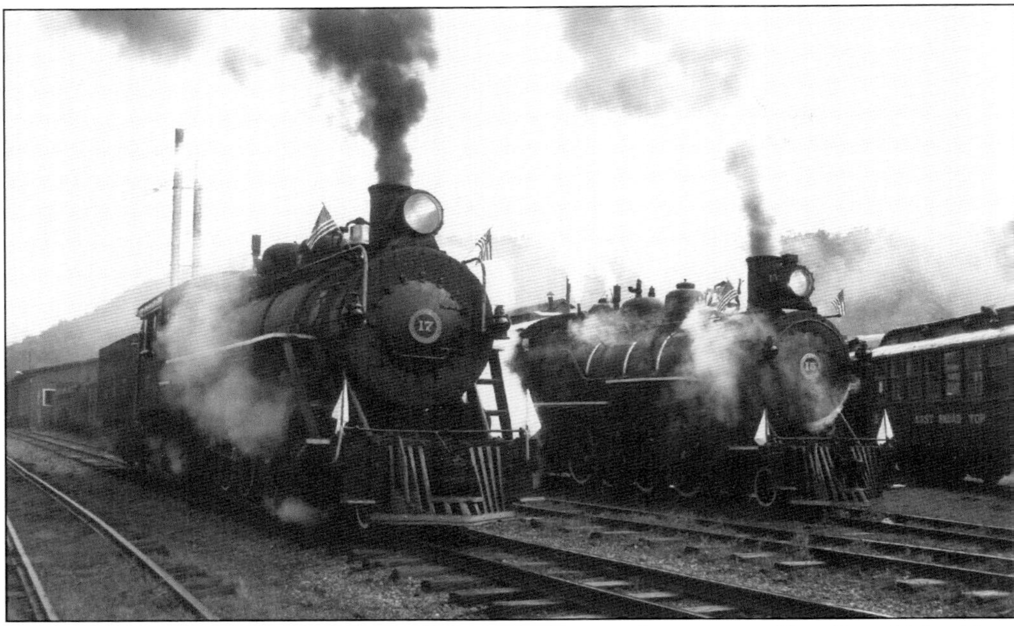

Preparing for their next assignments, Mikado-type steam locomotives No. 17 and No. 15 are at the Rockhill Furnace yard on October 10, 1998. Baldwin Locomotive Works built both locomotives with No. 17 in March 1918 and No. 15 in February 1914. No. 17 has been stored inoperable while No. 15 was overhauled during 2002 to 2005 to meet new Federal Railway Administration safety standards. (Photograph by Kenneth C. Springirth.)

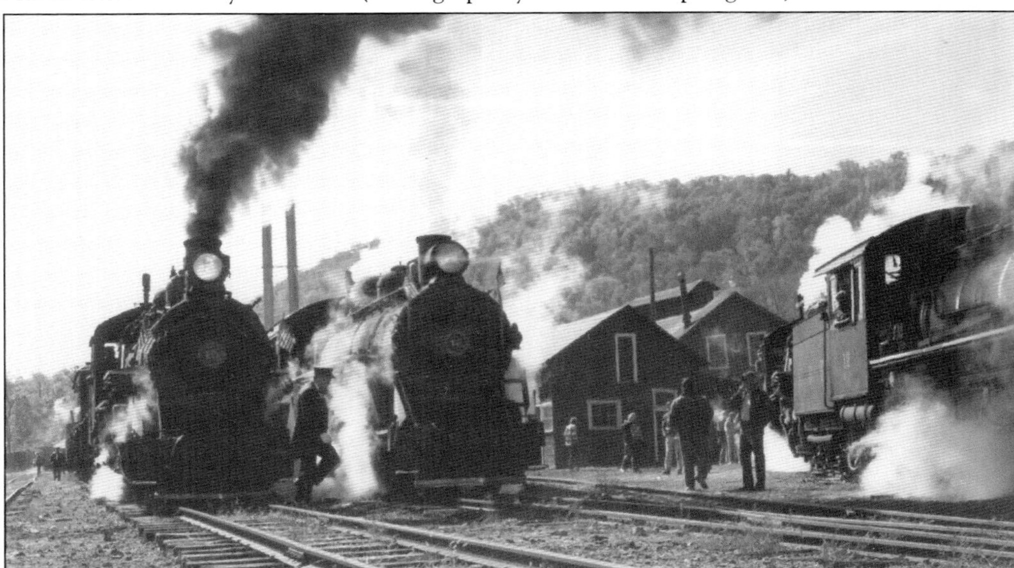

From left to right, East Broad Top Railroad steam locomotives No. 15, No. 17, and No. 12 are getting ready to do a whistle salute at the October 12, 1996, Fall Spectacular. After the railroad ended service on April 13, 1956, Nick Kovalchick of Kovalchick Salvage Company purchased the line and restored service over a portion of the line for the Orbisonia bicentennial in 1960. (Photograph by Kenneth C. Springirth.)

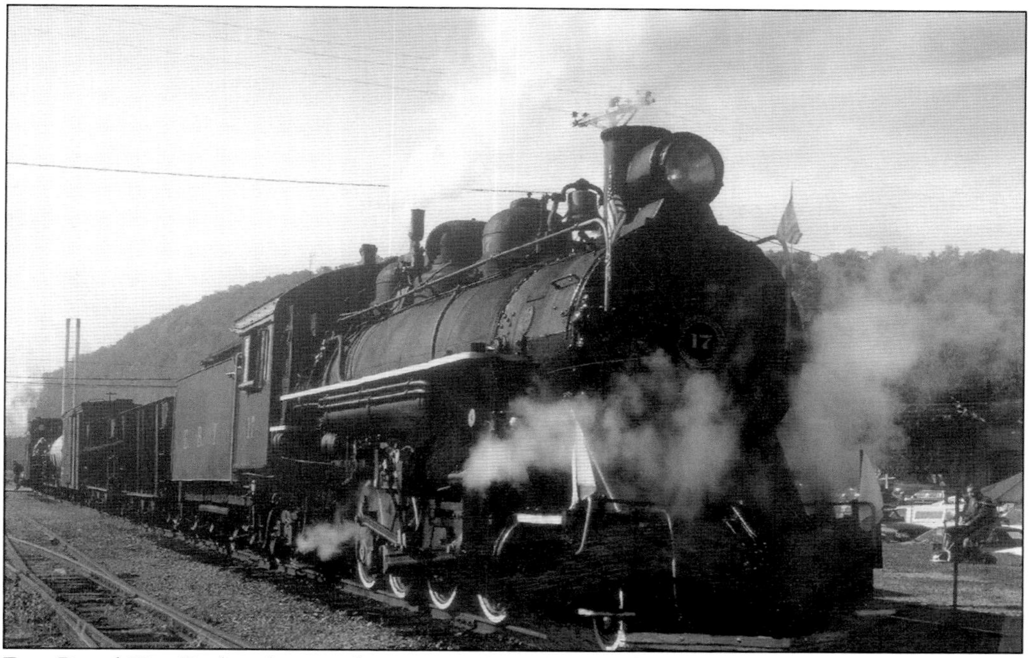

East Broad Top Railroad steam locomotive No. 17 is ready to haul out a freight train at the Rockhill Furnace yard on October 12, 1996. Built by Baldwin Locomotive Works in March 1918, this locomotive scene could have been taken 50 years earlier and, except for the motor vehicles in the parking lot on the right, the picture could have been remarkably similar. (Photograph by Kenneth C. Springirth.)

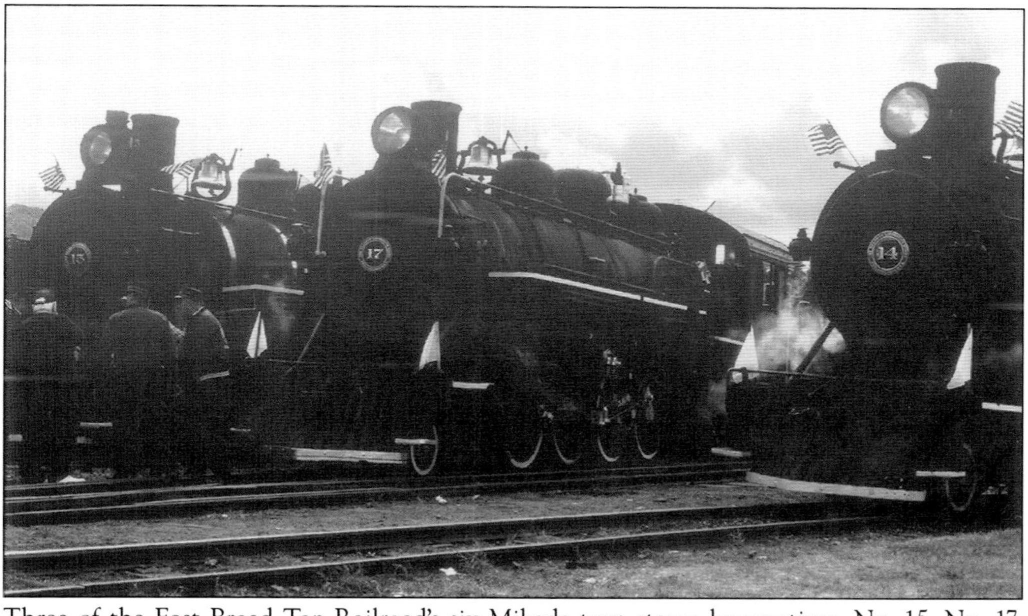

Three of the East Broad Top Railroad's six Mikado-type steam locomotives, No. 15, No. 17, and No. 14, are shown in this whistle salute in the Fall Spectacular of October 6, 2001, at the Rockhill Furnace yard. Hundreds of visitors came to this event from all parts of the United States and from other countries. (Photograph by Kenneth C. Springirth.)

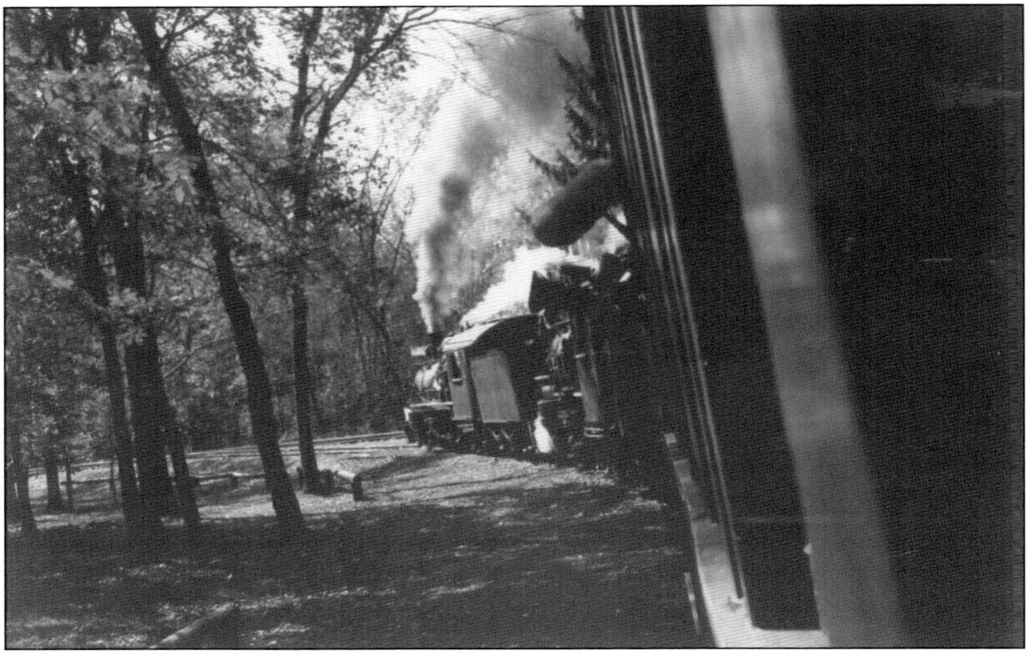

A doubleheader steam excursion is at Colgate Grove during the East Broad Top Railroad Fall Spectacular of October 12, 1996. This annual event attracted hundreds of rail enthusiasts from around the country to savor the beautiful autumn scenery and a narrow-gauge steam railroad where time has stood still. (Photograph by Kenneth C. Springirth.)

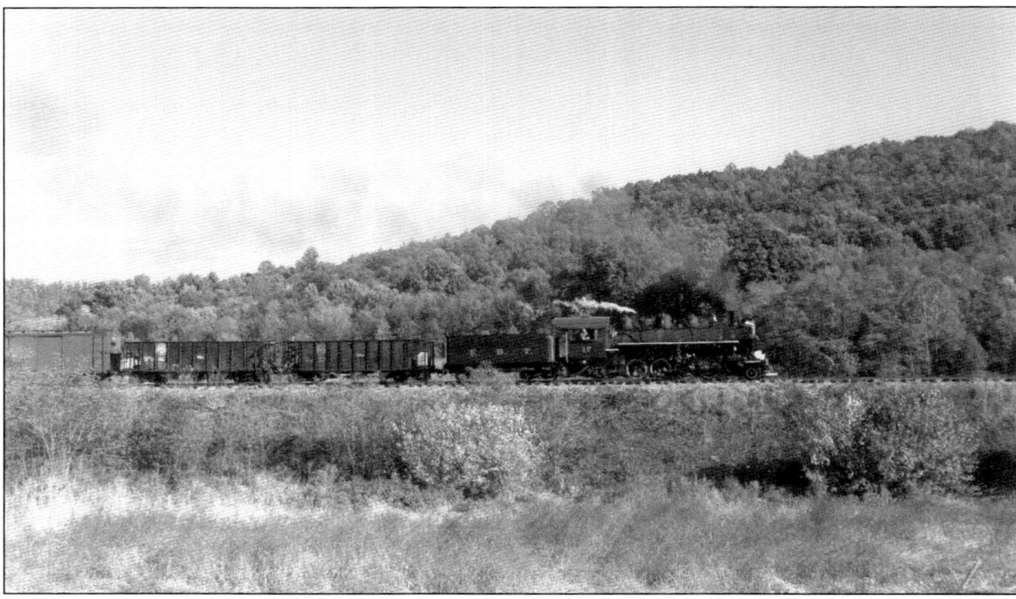

Southbound for the Orbisonia station finds Mikado-type locomotive No. 17 on October 12, 1996, just south of Runk Road on the elevated fill in the picturesque Aughwick Valley. Scenes like this were commonplace in regular service on the East Broad Top Railroad before closure in 1956. This is the last authentic narrow-gauge steam railroad east of the Rocky Mountains. (Photograph by Kenneth C. Springirth.)

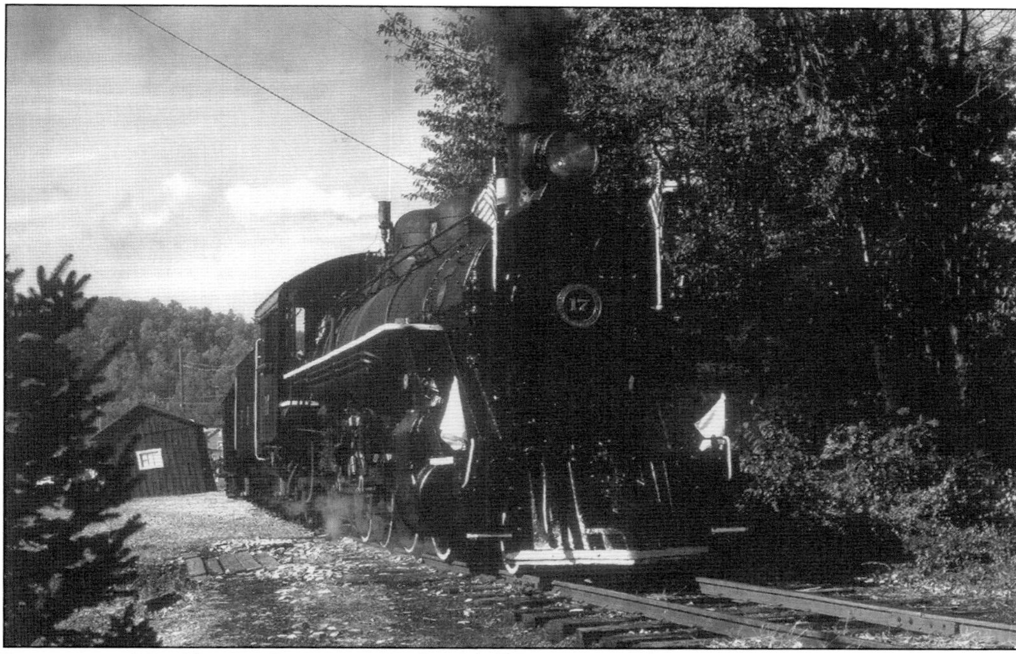

Locomotive No. 17 is on the wye at the Rockhill Furnace yard on October 12, 1996. As a result of the successful operation of this locomotive, the East Broad Top Railroad ordered No. 18, which was the largest, most powerful, and final narrow-gauge locomotive purchased by the railroad. (Photograph by Kenneth C. Springirth.)

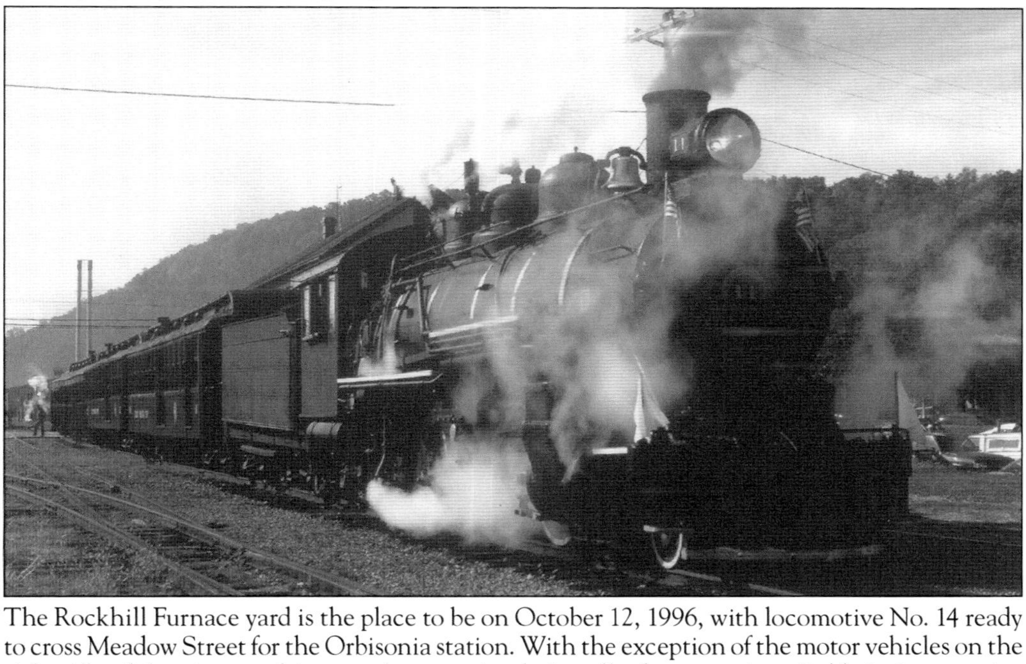

The Rockhill Furnace yard is the place to be on October 12, 1996, with locomotive No. 14 ready to cross Meadow Street for the Orbisonia station. With the exception of the motor vehicles on the right side of the picture, this scene has remained virtually the same since Baldwin Locomotive Works delivered No. 14 to the East Broad Top Railroad during October 1912. (Photograph by Kenneth C. Springirth.)

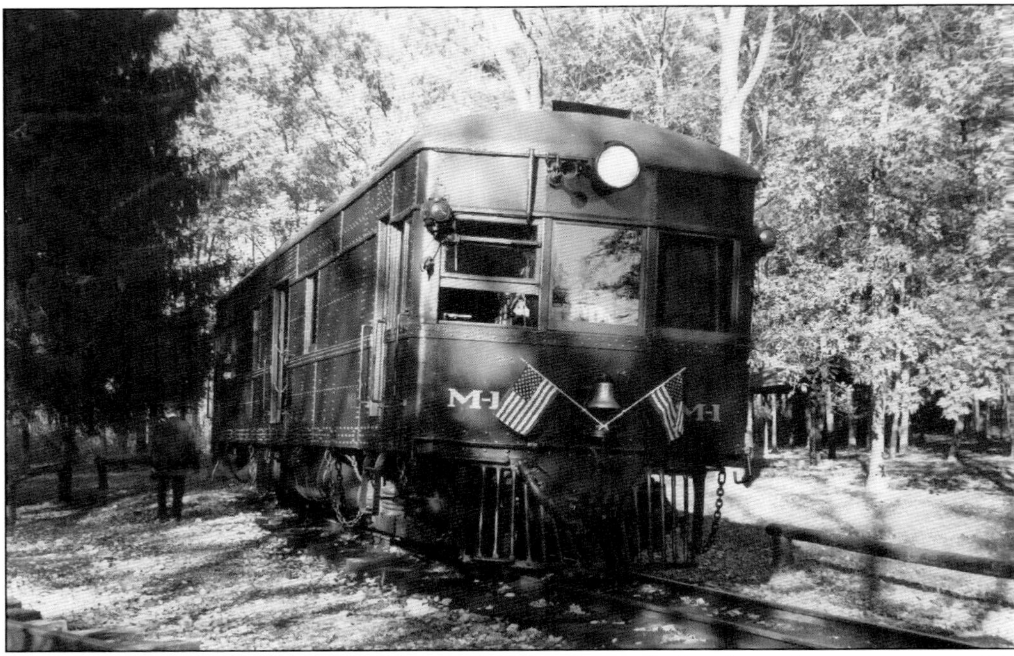

Amid the fall foliage of October 12, 1996, East Broad Top Railroad gas-electric motor car M-1 is at Colgate Grove for the return trip to Orbisonia. J. G. Brill Car Company and Westinghouse Electric Company supplied the parts for this motor car. It is the only gas-electric car to survive in the United States with its original machinery intact. (Photograph by Kenneth C. Springirth.)

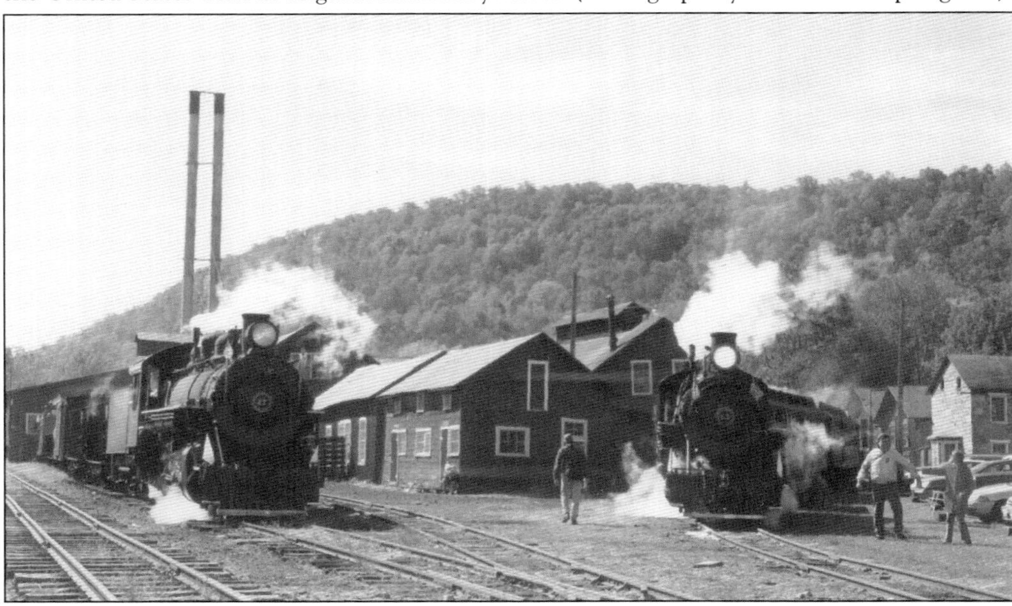

From left to right, locomotive No. 17 with a freight train and locomotive No. 14 with a passenger train are at the Rockhill Furnace yard on October 12, 1996. In the 1980s, locomotive No. 14 was overhauled in the East Broad Top Railroad shops. Locomotive No. 17, which made the last revenue run on the railroad on April 6, 1956, has been stored inoperable since 2002. (Photograph by Kenneth C. Springirth.)

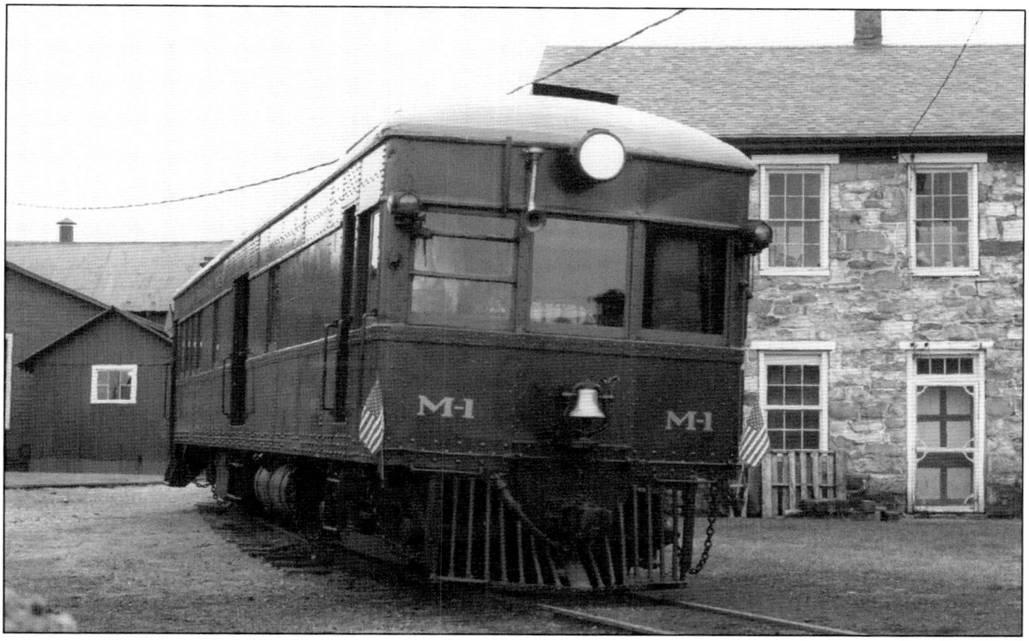

Gas-electric motor car M-1 is at the Rockhill Furnace yard on October 7, 2006. This car was built to narrow-gauge proportions by East Broad Top Railroad engineers and craftsmen based on standard-gauge drawings and parts provided by J. G. Brill Car Company and Westinghouse Electric Company. In the background is the 1800s farmhouse that is now a storehouse. (Photograph by Kenneth C. Springirth.)

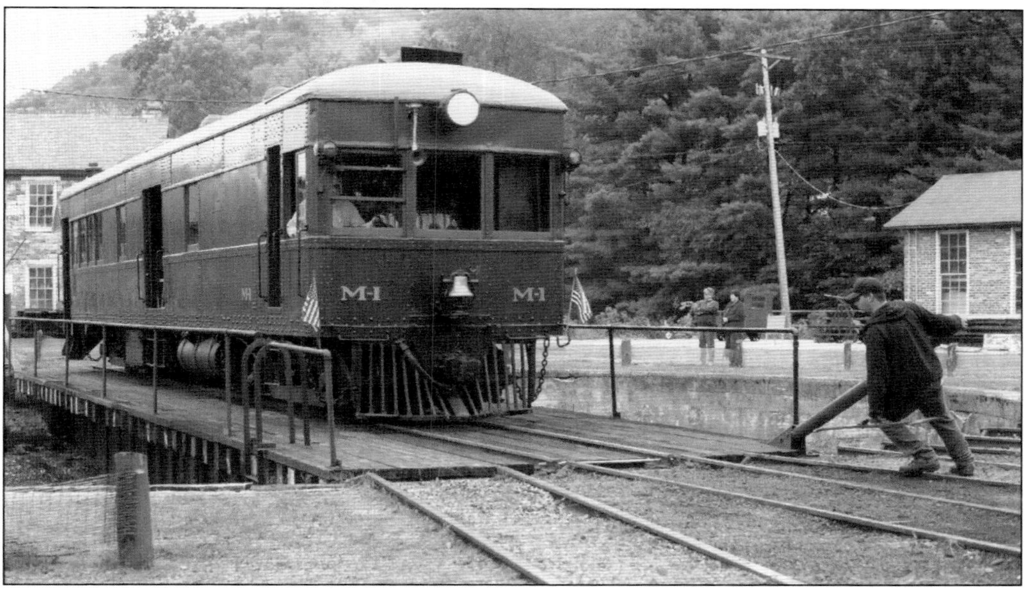

Gas-electric motor car M-1 is properly positioned on the Rockhill Furnace turntable on October 7, 2006, ready to be turned. On the right side of the photograph is the paint shop, which was built to replace the paint shop that, along with the East Broad Top Transit Company bus garage, burned on July 8, 1933. The bus garage was rebuilt as an addition to the roundhouse. (Photograph by Kenneth C. Springirth.)

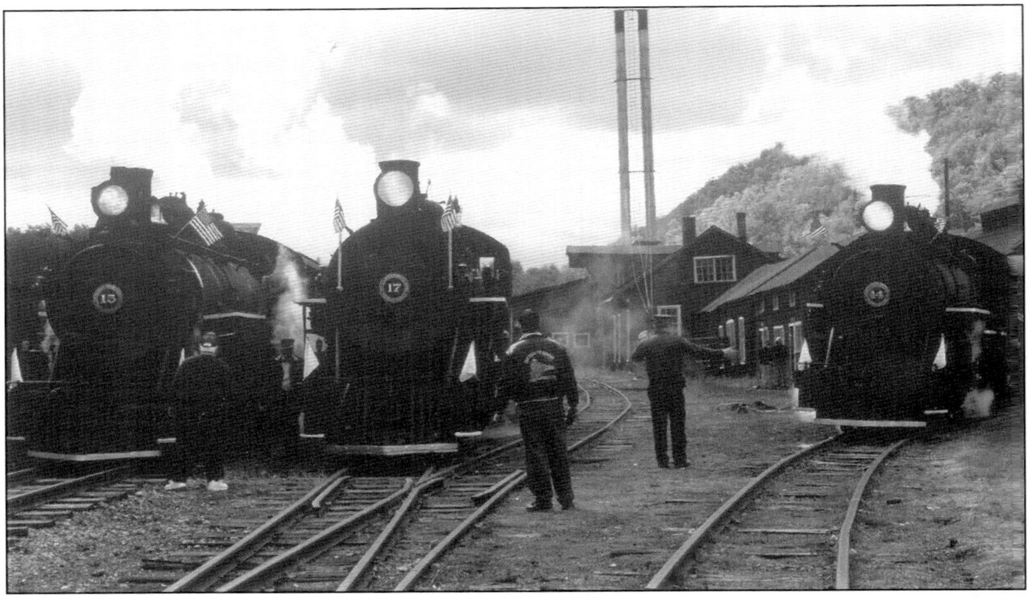

From left to right, East Broad Top Railroad locomotives No. 15, No. 17, and No. 14 have lined up at the Rockhill Furnace yard on October 6, 2001, for a whistle salute. Looking at tractive effort (the force that a locomotive can apply to its coupler to pull a train), No. 14 and No. 15 are identical at 27,600 pounds, while No. 17 was more powerful at 30,600 pounds. (Photograph by Kenneth C. Springirth.)

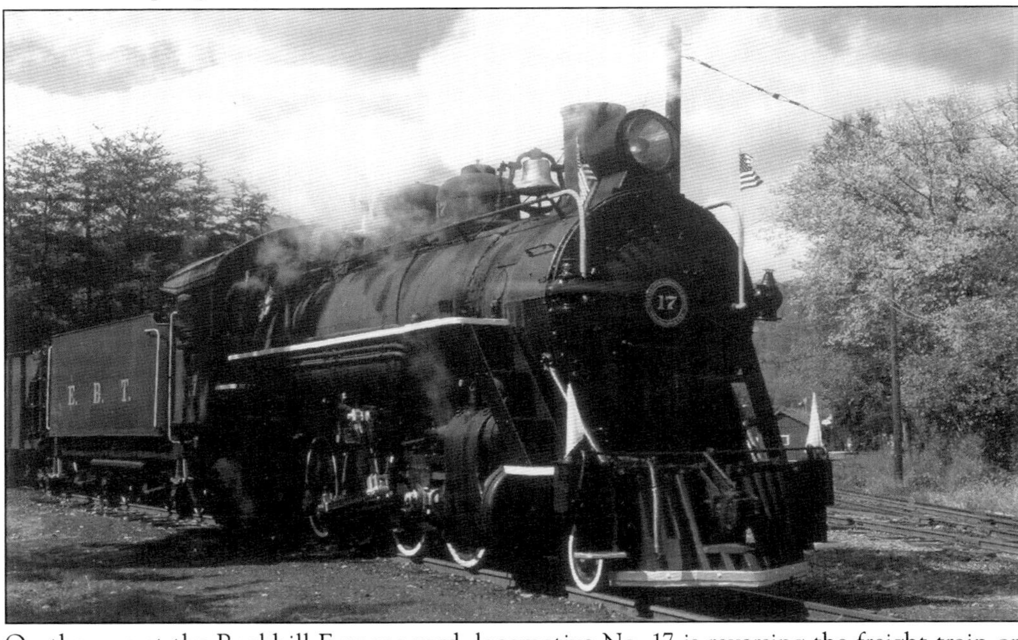

On the wye at the Rockhill Furnace yard, locomotive No. 17 is reversing the freight train on October 6, 2001. Because of the success with this locomotive, the East Broad Top Railroad went back to Baldwin Locomotive Works for an even larger locomotive, No. 18, which was delivered in 1920. Each new Mikado-type locomotive purchased represented an improvement over earlier locomotives. (Photograph by Kenneth C. Springirth.)

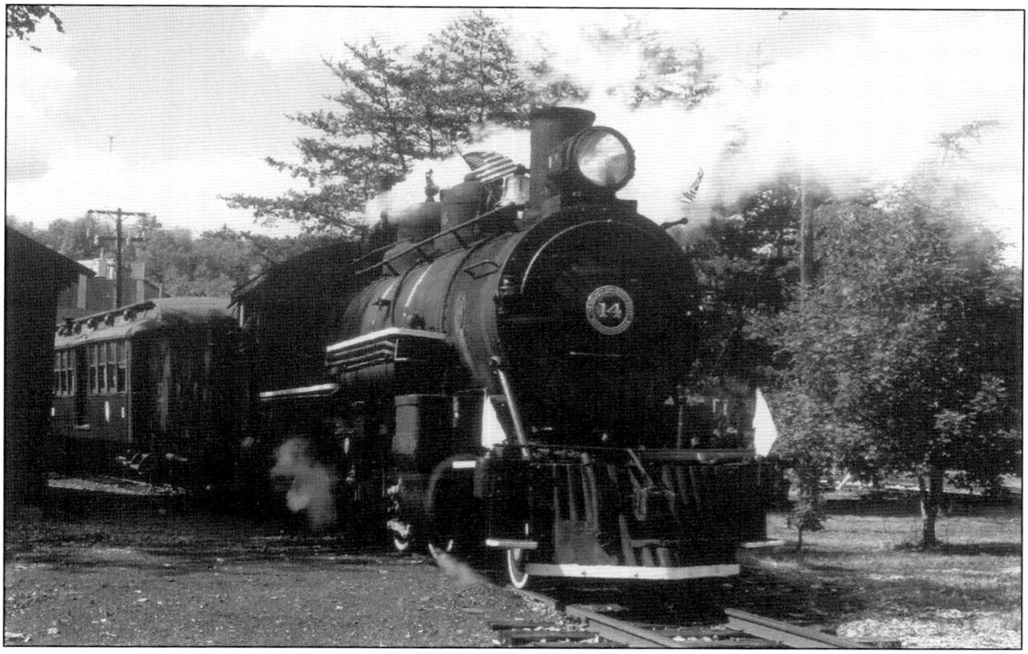

Locomotive No. 14 is on the Rockhill Furnace wye on October 6, 2001. The well-run East Broad Top Railroad had the management skill to work with its locomotive supplier Baldwin Locomotive Works to achieve improvements in each new locomotive purchased. This contributed to the longevity of the railroad. (Photograph by Kenneth C. Springirth.)

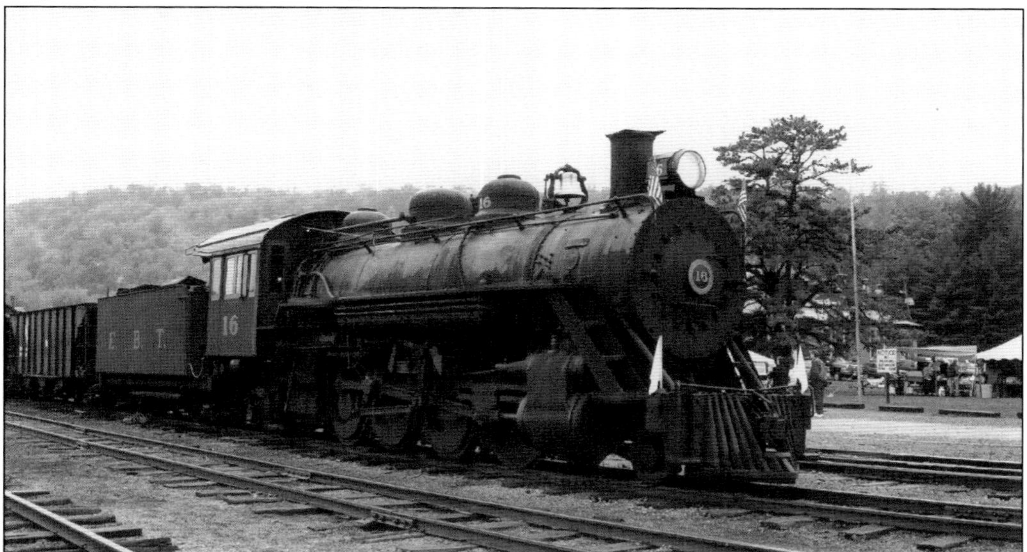

East Broad Top Railroad locomotive No. 16, built by Baldwin Locomotive Works in June 1916, is at the Rockhill Furnace yard on October 12, 2002, with a group of narrow-gauge hopper cars behind it. Currently inoperable, the locomotive was equipped with superheaters, piston valves, and a Southern valve gear (first used on the Southern Railroad in 1913), which is the mechanism that operates the inlet and exhaust valves on a steam locomotive. (Photograph by Kenneth C. Springirth.)

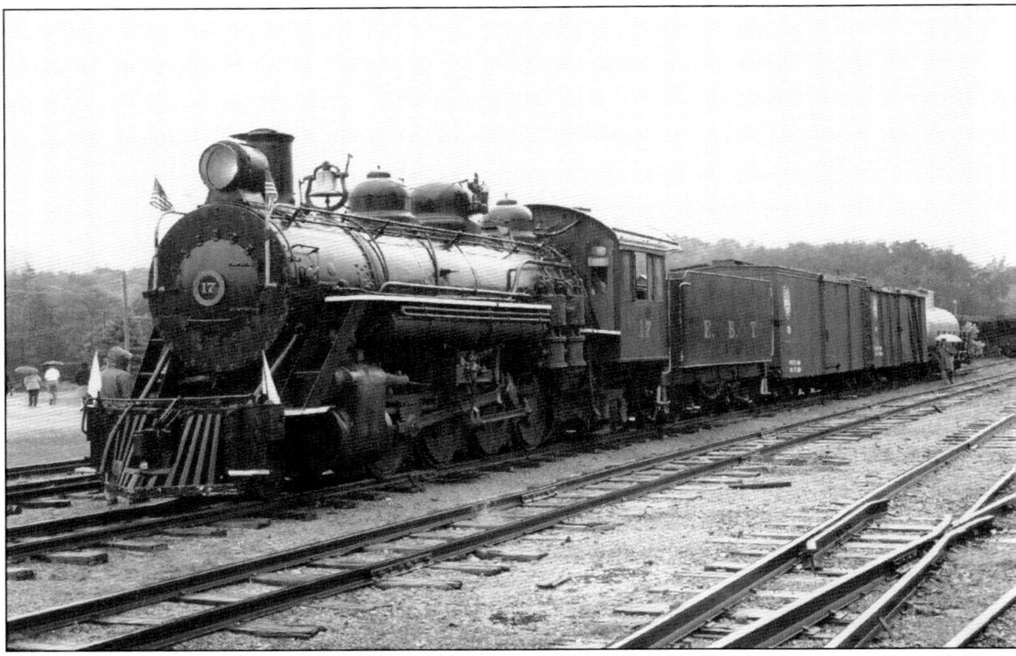

As a narrow-gauge common carrier, the East Broad Top Railroad had a large number of freight cars, and two of the restored boxcars plus a tank car with locomotive No. 17 were on show for display purposes at the Rockhill Furnace yard on October 8, 2005. Since the line closed in 1956, most of the cars have remained at this site and the Mount Union yard. (Photograph by Kenneth C. Springirth.)

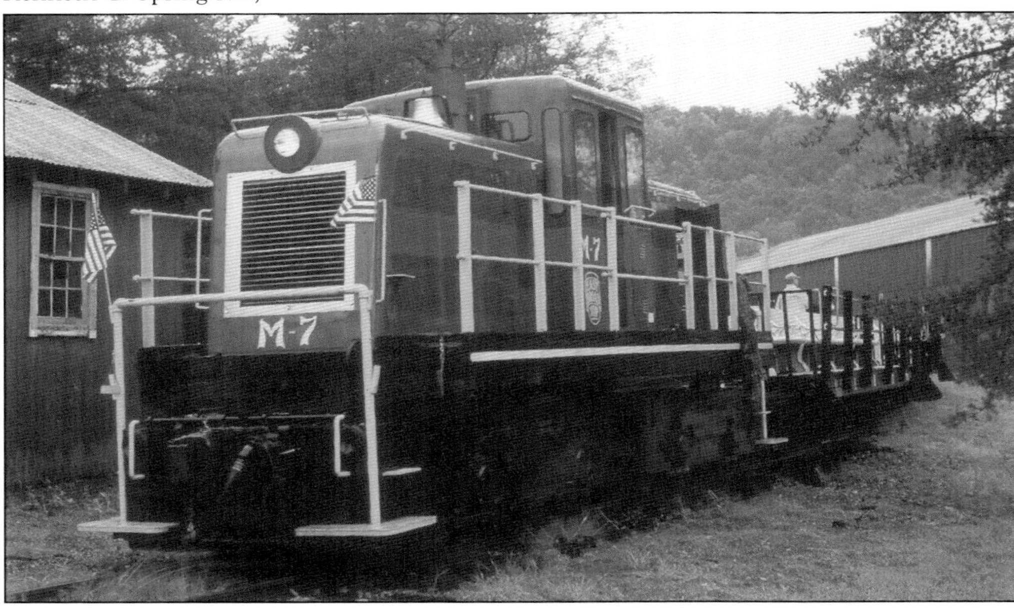

On the Rockhill Furnace wye, center-cab diesel switcher M-7, built in 1964 by the General Electric Company, is powering a picnic train on the October 8, 2005, Fall Spectacular. This locomotive also handles yard-switching duties. Extra trains provided excellent service for the large crowds in attendance for this event. (Photograph by Kenneth C. Springirth.)

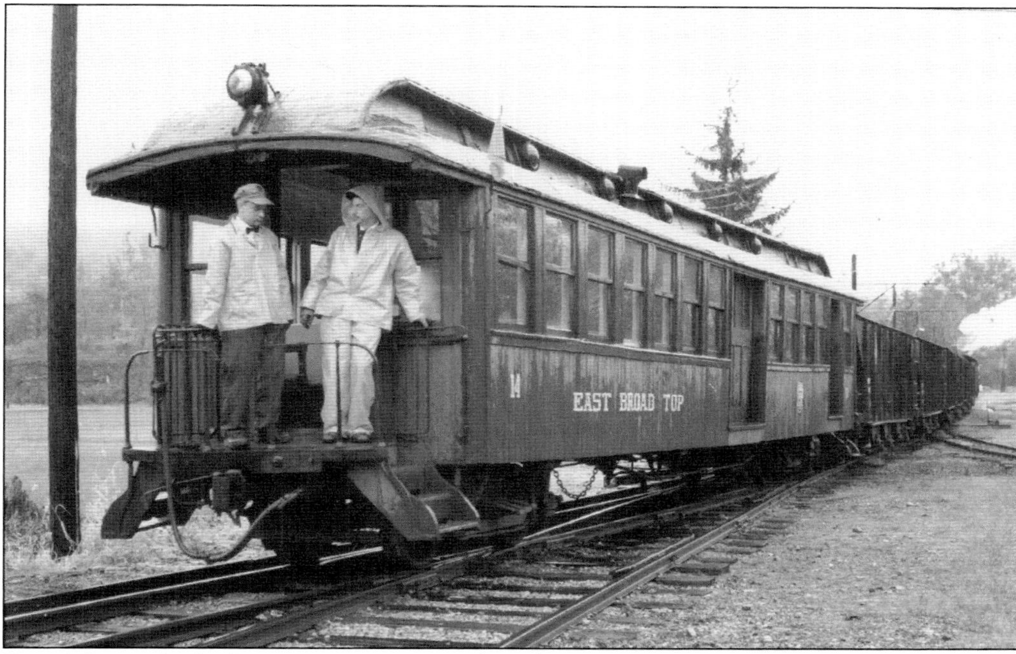

From left to right, brakeman Henry Long and conductor Stanley Hall Jr. are on the rear platform of combination baggage-passenger coach No. 14 behind a group of hopper cars at Rockhill Furnace wye on October 8, 2005. Laconia Car Company built this coach in 1882. The East Broad Top Railroad purchased this coach from the Boston, Revere Beach and Lynn Railroad in 1916. (Photograph by Kenneth C. Springirth.)

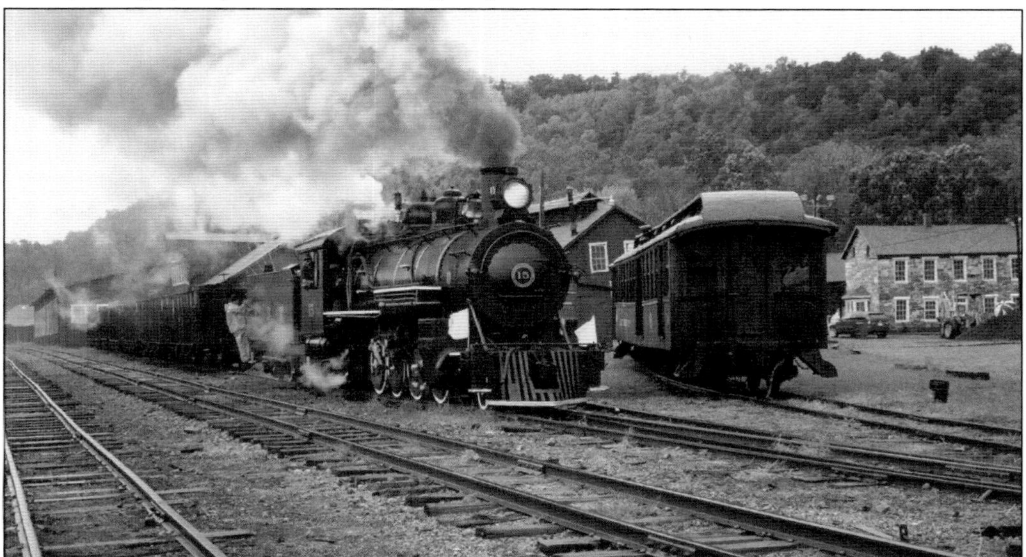

East Broad Top Railroad locomotive No. 15 is backing up to pull a group of restored hopper cars at the Rockhill Furnace shops on October 8, 2005. This locomotive had received an overhaul and was returned to service during September 2005. When the railroad closed in 1956, the track, motive power, rolling stock, and buildings in this scene remained intact. (Photograph by Kenneth C. Springirth.)

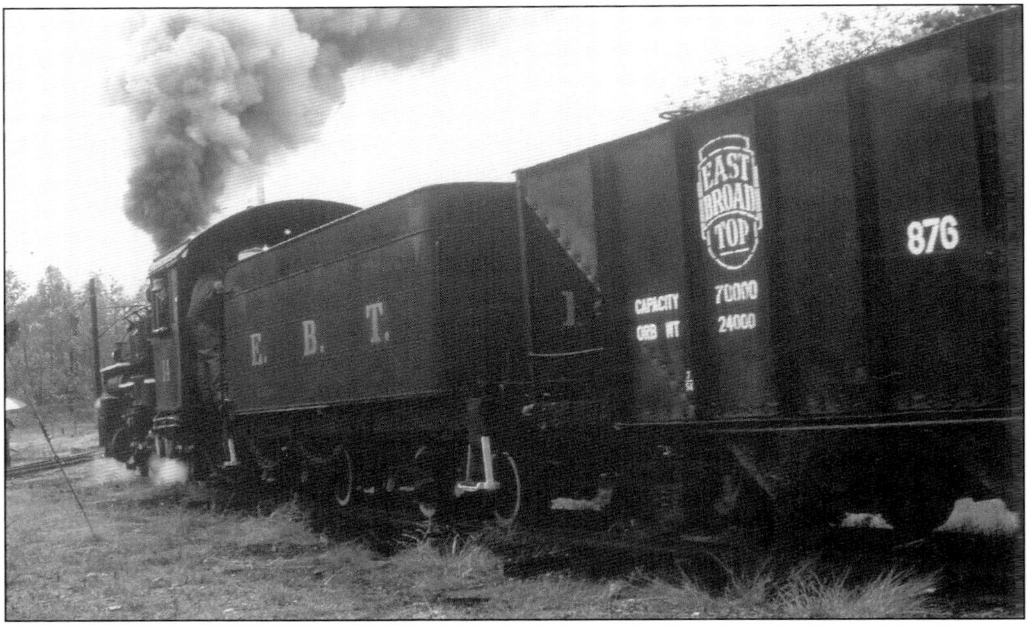

During the October 8, 2005, Fall Spectacular, locomotive No. 14 is leading a freight train through the Rockhill Furnace wye. Steel hopper car No. 876, built during 1915, was one of about 240 hopper cars built by the East Broad Top Railroad shops during the years 1914 to 1930. A number of these hopper cars have been restored and are at the Rockhill Furnace yard (Photograph by Kenneth C. Springirth.)

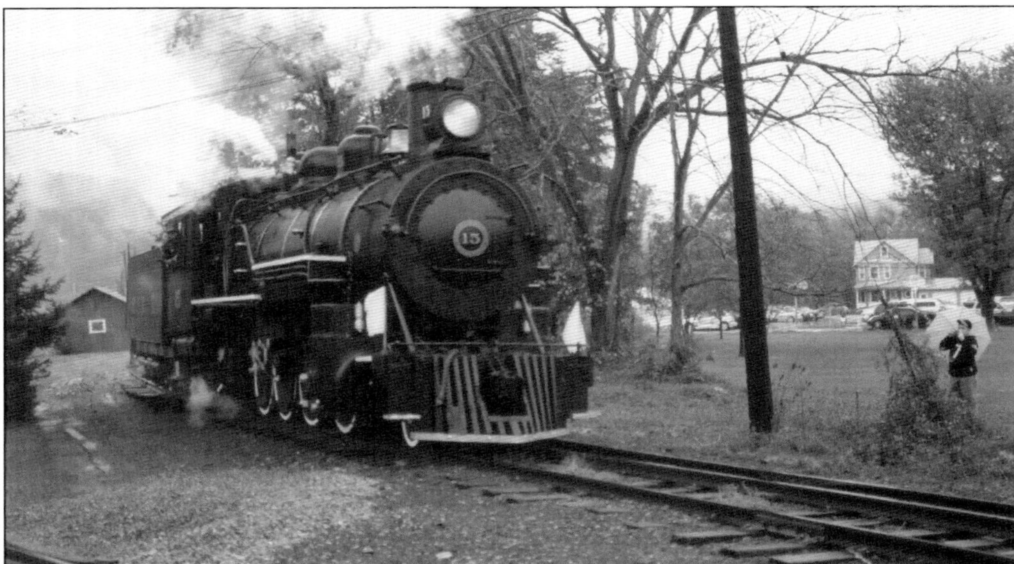

East Broad Top Railroad steam locomotive No. 15 is at the Rockhill Furnace wye on October 8, 2005. From 1873 to 1956, this narrow-gauge railroad carried coal from the remote Broad Top Mountain area of south-central Pennsylvania to the Pennsylvania Railroad at Mount Union. Its infrastructure has remained in place with excursion service over a five-mile portion of the 32.54-mile main line. (Photograph by Kenneth C. Springirth.)

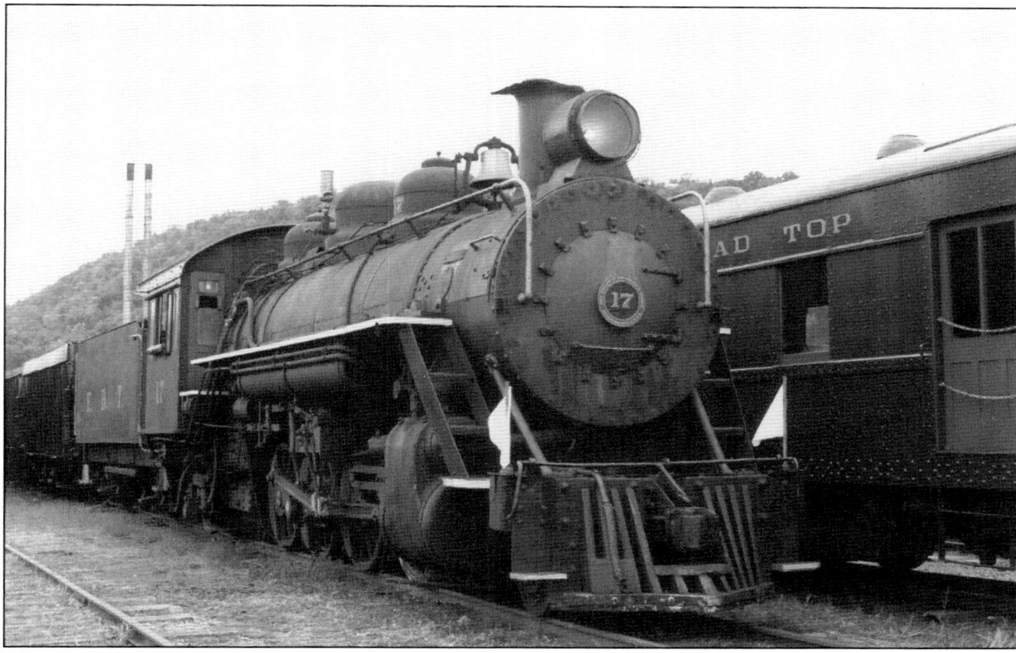

The Rockhill Furnace yard is the setting for East Broad Top Railroad locomotive No. 17 on the October 7, 2006, Fall Spectacular. This locomotive was on display with the large number of hopper cars in the yard, which has virtually remained unchanged over the last 70 years. (Photograph by Kenneth C. Springirth.)

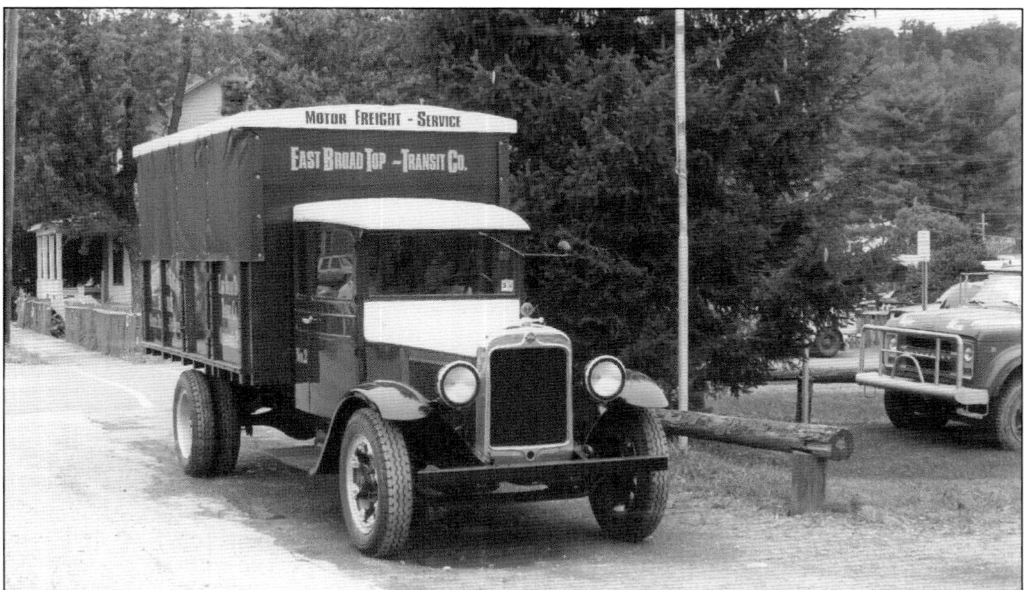

This is a restored East Broad Top Transit Company truck No. 2 at the borough of Rockhill Furnace on October 7, 2006. The original two-ton truck was built by Dodge Brothers and was acquired in 1931. It was destroyed in the July 8, 1933, Orbisonia bus garage fire. (Photograph by Kenneth C. Springirth.)

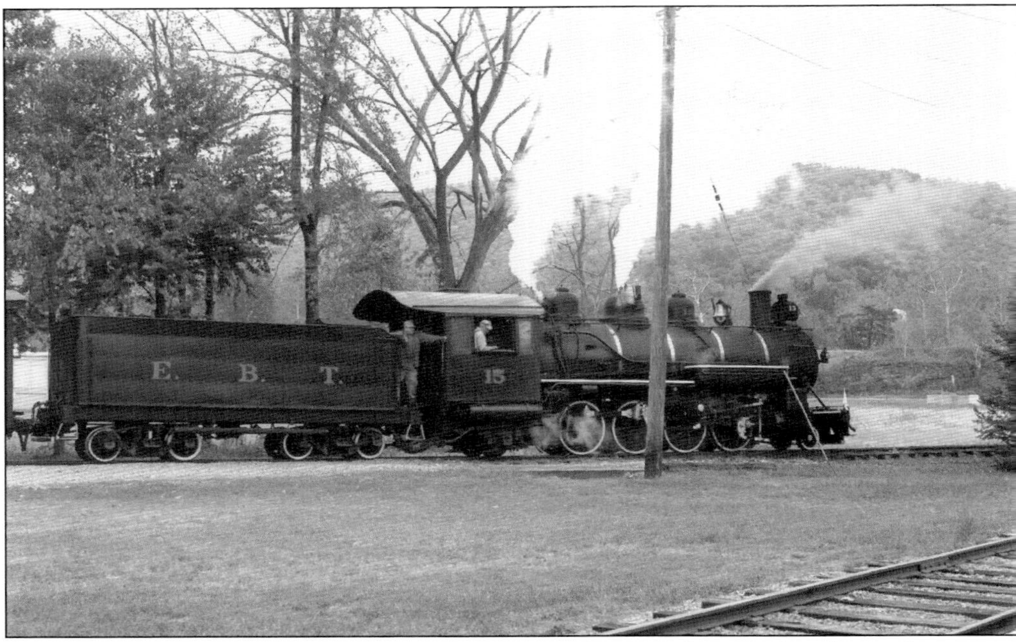

Built by Baldwin Locomotive Works in February 1914, East Broad Top Railroad steam locomotive No. 15 is south of the Orbisonia station on October 7, 2006. This was the third Mikado-type locomotive purchased by the railroad. The trackage in the right front of the picture is for the standard-gauge Rockhill Trolley Museum. (Photograph by Kenneth C. Springirth.)

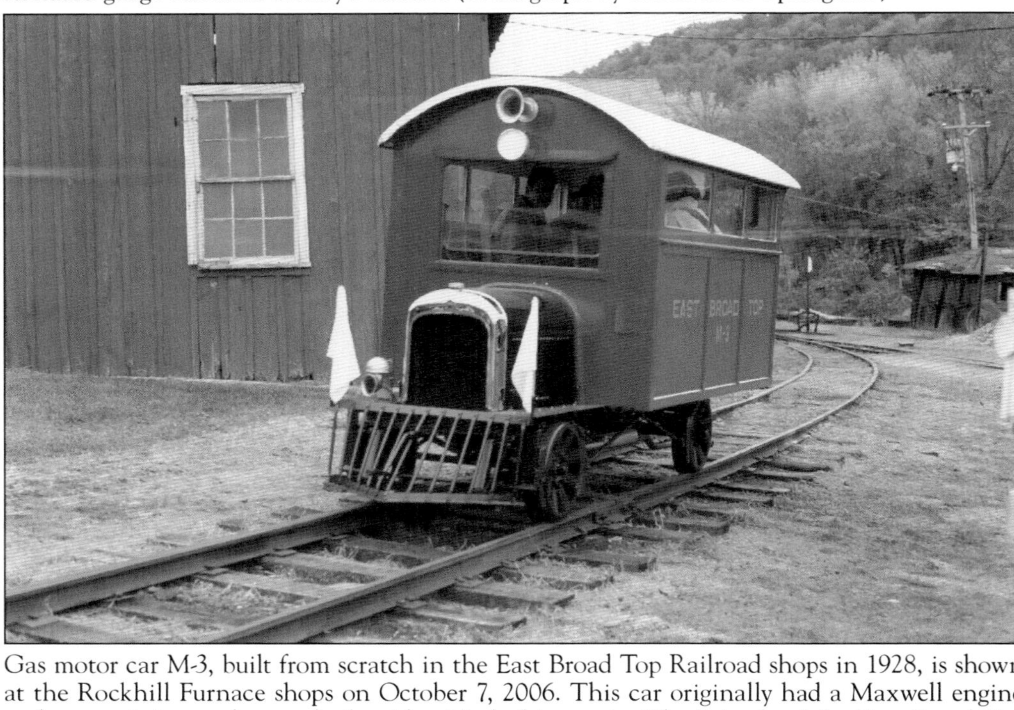

Gas motor car M-3, built from scratch in the East Broad Top Railroad shops in 1928, is shown at the Rockhill Furnace shops on October 7, 2006. This car originally had a Maxwell engine and transmission and was rebuilt with a Nash drive train. The Friends of the East Broad Top extensively restored this car during 2006. (Photograph by Kenneth C. Springirth.)

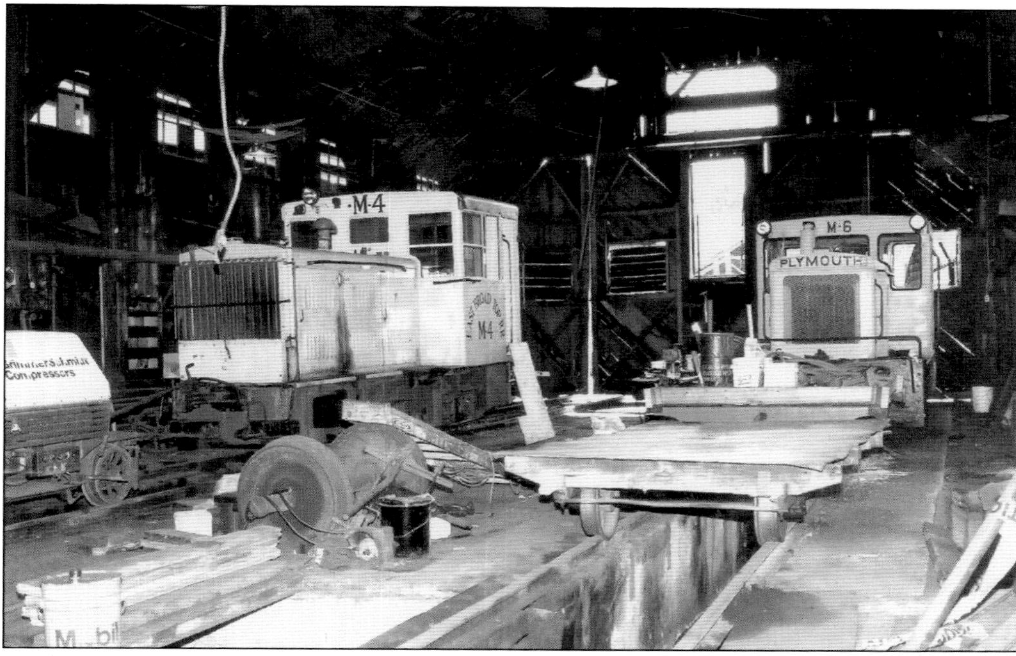

Inside the Rockhill Furnace shops of the East Broad Top Railroad on August 18, 2007, are Plymouth Locomotive Works diesel switcher locomotive M-4, built in 1947 weighing 12 tons, and M-6, built in 1969 weighing 16 tons. Both of these locomotives have been used for moving freight cars and other switching assignments. (Photograph by Kenneth C. Springirth.)

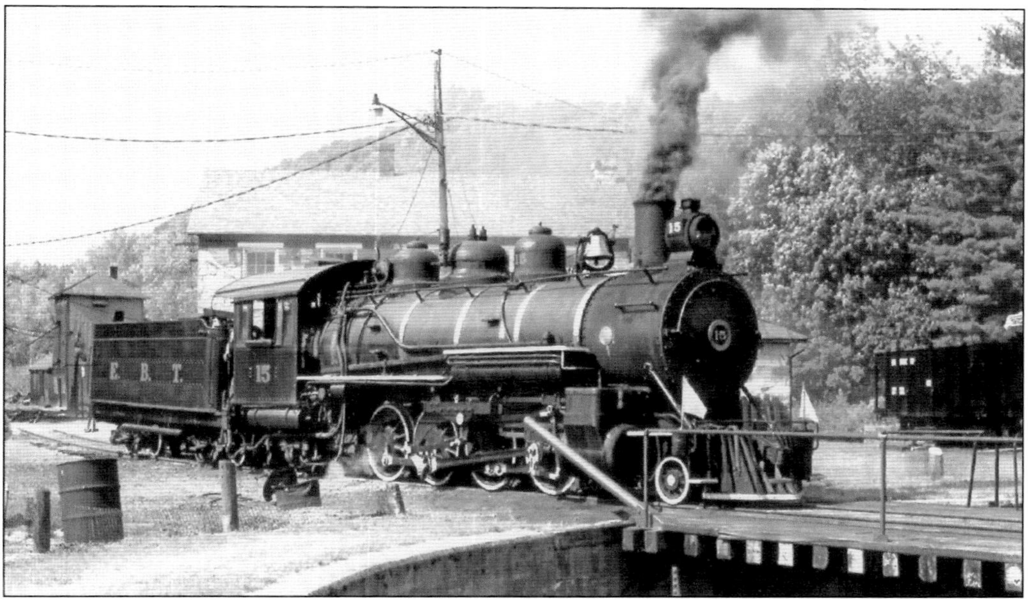

With the stone facade of the vintage superintendent's office in the background, Mikado-type locomotive No. 15 has just come off the turntable at the Rockhill Furnace shops of the East Broad Top Railroad on June 9, 2007. The stone building was originally a farmhouse that became the superintendent's office and later a storehouse after the railroad reached the borough of Rockhill Furnace on August 30, 1873. (Photograph by Kenneth C. Springirth.)

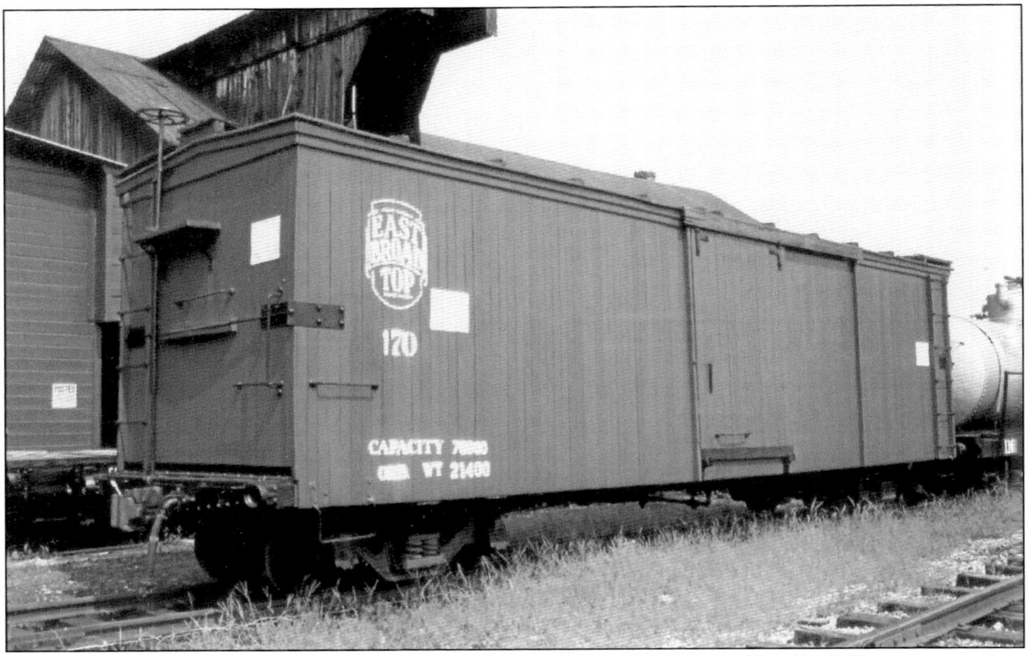

Boxcar No. 170, with a 70,000-pound capacity, is on the siding at the Rockhill Furnace yard on August 5, 2007. It is an example of a wooden-body, steel-frame transition boxcar built by the East Broad Top Railroad in 1913. This is the oldest freight car still on the property and the only car of its type on the railroad. (Photograph by Kenneth C. Springirth.)

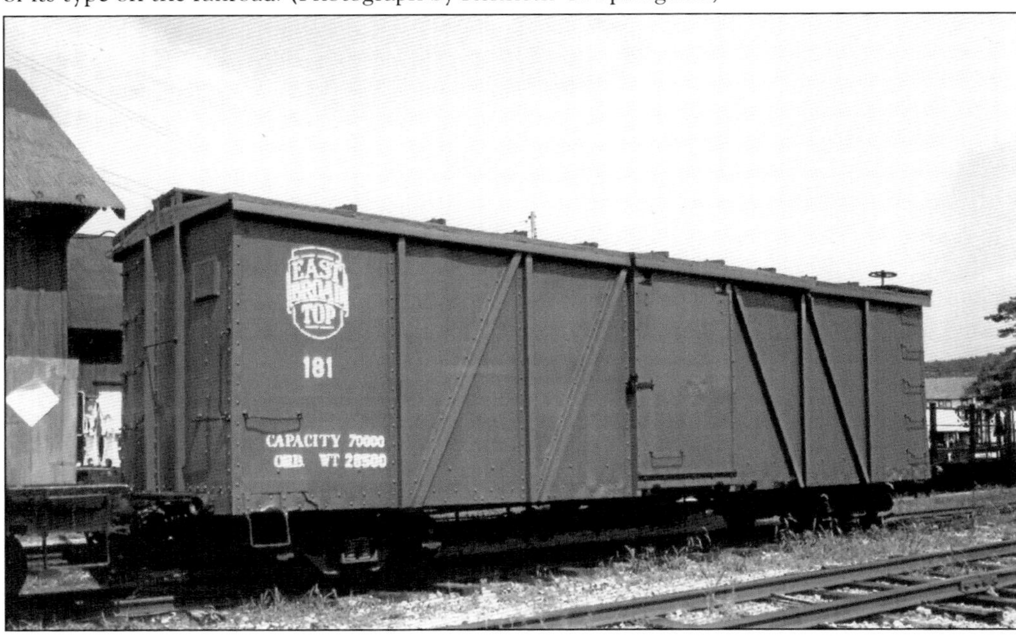

Boxcar No. 181 with a 70,000-pound capacity is pictured at the Rockhill Furnace yard on August 5, 2007. It is an all-steel boxcar built by the East Broad Top Railroad in 1920. The Rockhill Furnace shops built about 20 boxcars during 1913 to 1920 for the railroad. (Photograph by Kenneth C. Springirth.)

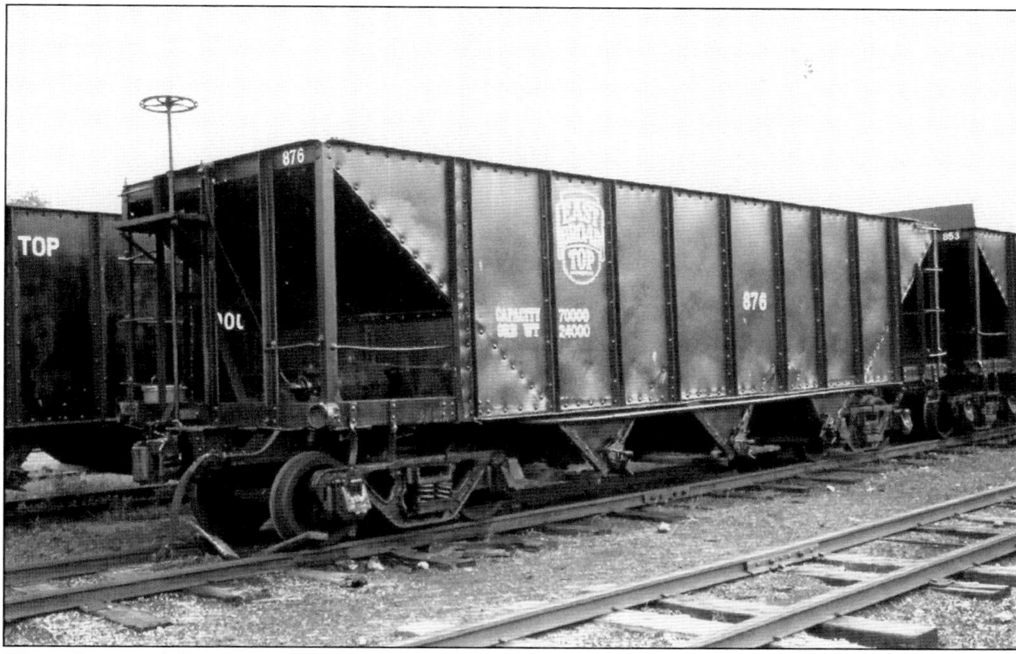

Three-bay steel hopper car No. 876 is at the Rockhill Furnace yard on July 7, 2007. This car was built by the East Broad Top Railroad shops in 1915 and has a capacity of 70,000 pounds. A number of these hopper cars have been repainted and are on display at the yard. (Photograph by Kenneth C. Springirth.)

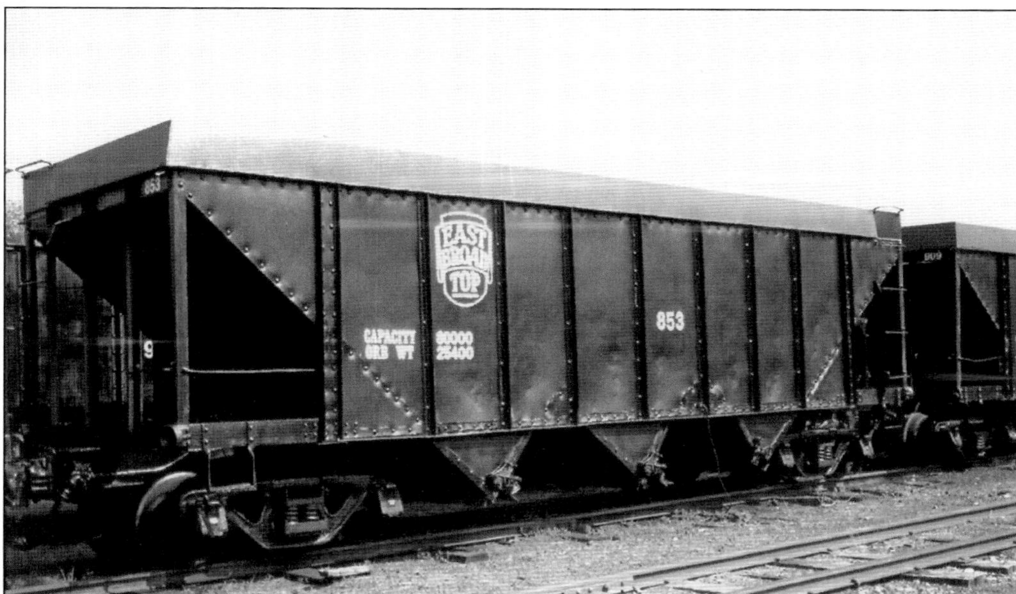

An example of a higher-capacity steel hopper car is No. 853 at the Rockhill Furnace yard on July 7, 2007. This car was built by the East Broad Top Railroad in 1914 and was modified sometime after 1943. The addition of a 14-inch steel band on the top increased the car's hauling capacity from 70,000 to 80,000 pounds. (Photograph by Kenneth C. Springirth.)

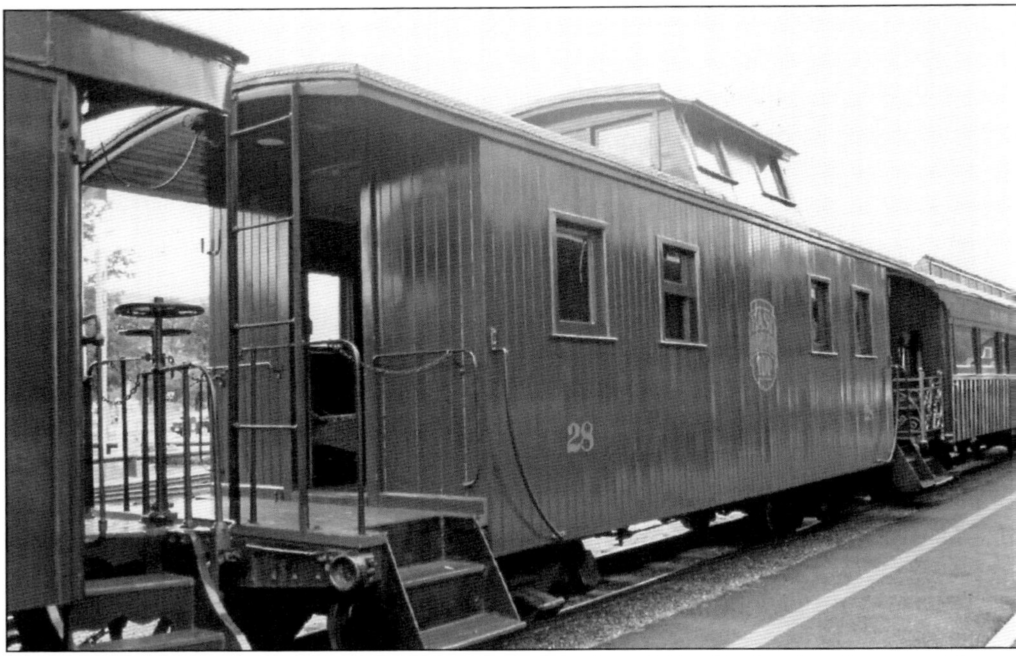

Green painted caboose No. 28 is used on regular East Broad Top Railroad trains, as evidenced by this view at the Orbisonia station on August 5, 2007. It was built in 1920 by the railroad at the Rockhill Furnace shops and was overhauled in 2004 at the same shops by the Friends of the East Broad Top. (Photograph by Kenneth C. Springirth.)

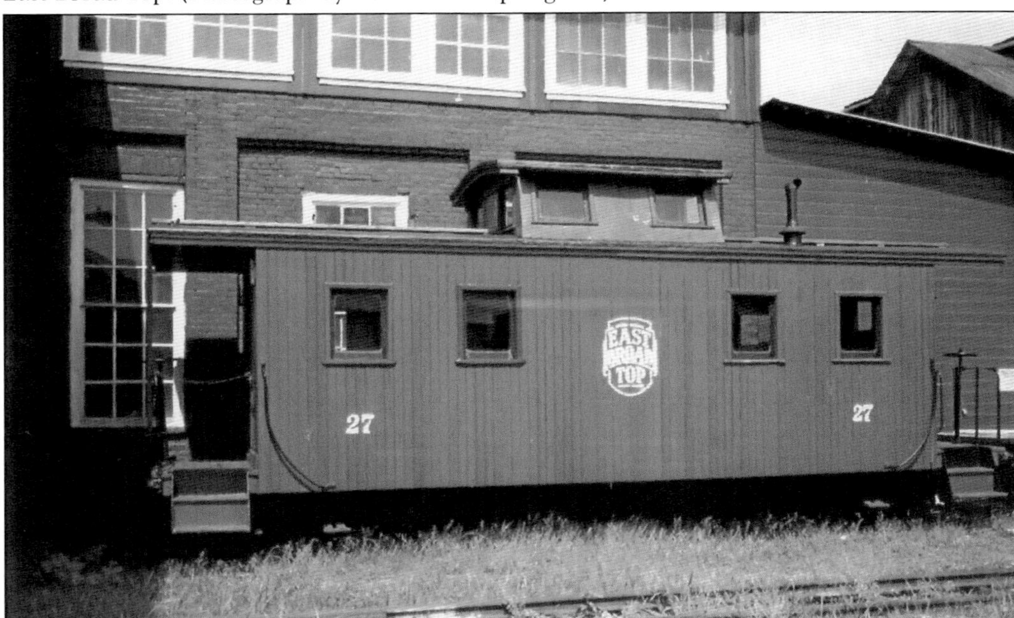

Red painted caboose No. 27 is pictured at the Rockhill Furnace yard on August 5, 2007. This was built by the East Broad Top Railroad shop in 1920. It has been used for Fall Spectaculars and special occasions. Cabooses No. 27 and No. 28 are examples of properly designed, well-proportioned rolling stock. (Photograph by Kenneth C. Springirth.)

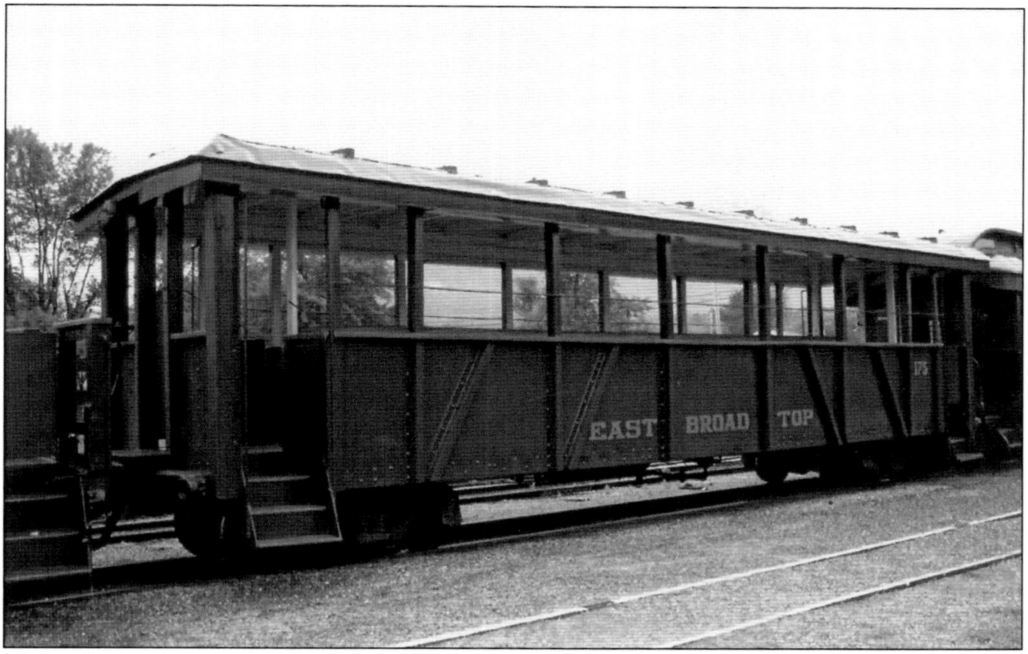

This is boxcar No. 175 on August 5, 2007, at the Rockhill Furnace yard. Built in 1916 by the East Broad Top Railroad, it was modified for passenger service in 1960. It is another example of skilled people making the necessary changes to adapt to tourist service. (Photograph by Kenneth C. Springirth.)

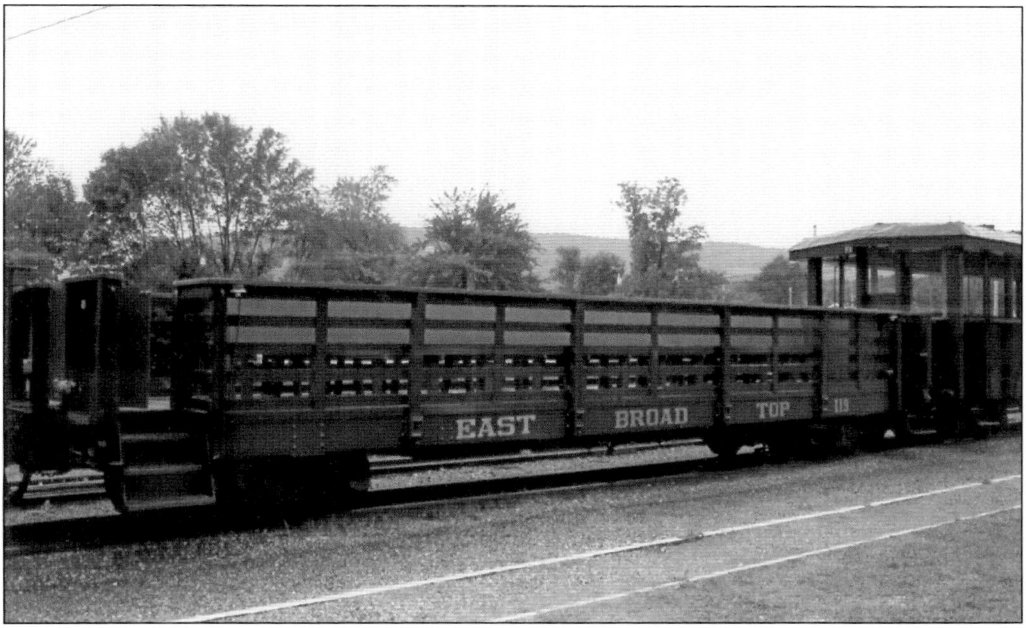

Open passenger car No. 119 is at the Rockhill Furnace yard on August 5, 2007. Built by the East Broad Top Railroad in 1925, this was a flatcar that was modified for passenger service in 1960. During the recent Fall Spectaculars held in October, this car is used to handle the extra passengers on the additional trains that are operated. (Photograph by Kenneth C. Springirth.)

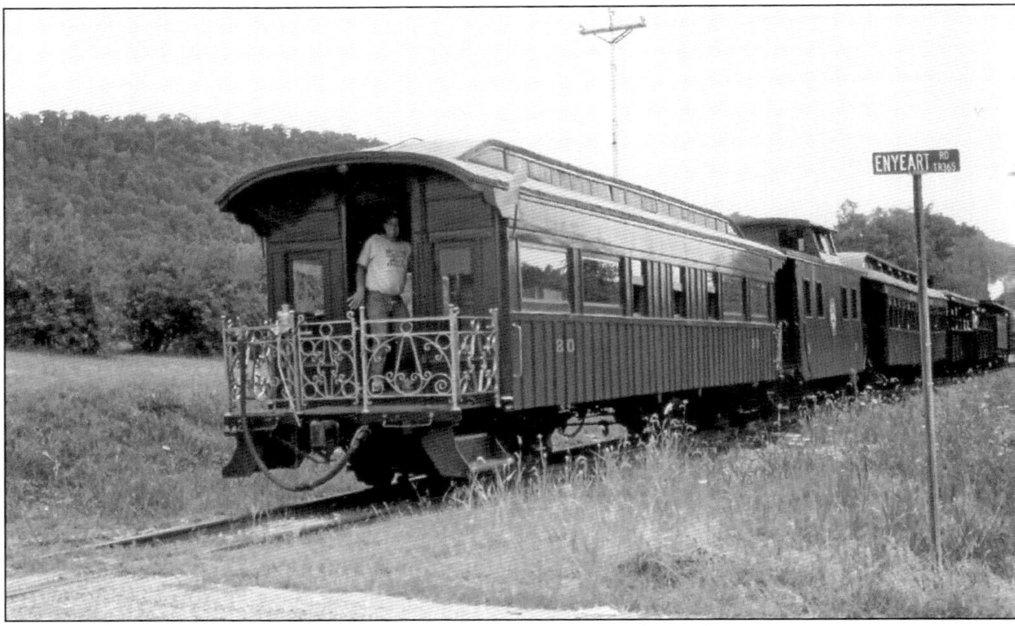

The northbound East Broad Top Railroad train, which left the Orbisonia station at 3:00 p.m. on August 5, 2007, has crossed Enyeart Road. Locomotive No. 15 is pulling cars No. 119, No. 175, No. 8, No. 28, and parlor car No. 20. With the exception of the street sign and paved road this Aughwick Valley scene has remained unchanged over the last 50 years. (Photograph by Kenneth C. Springirth.)

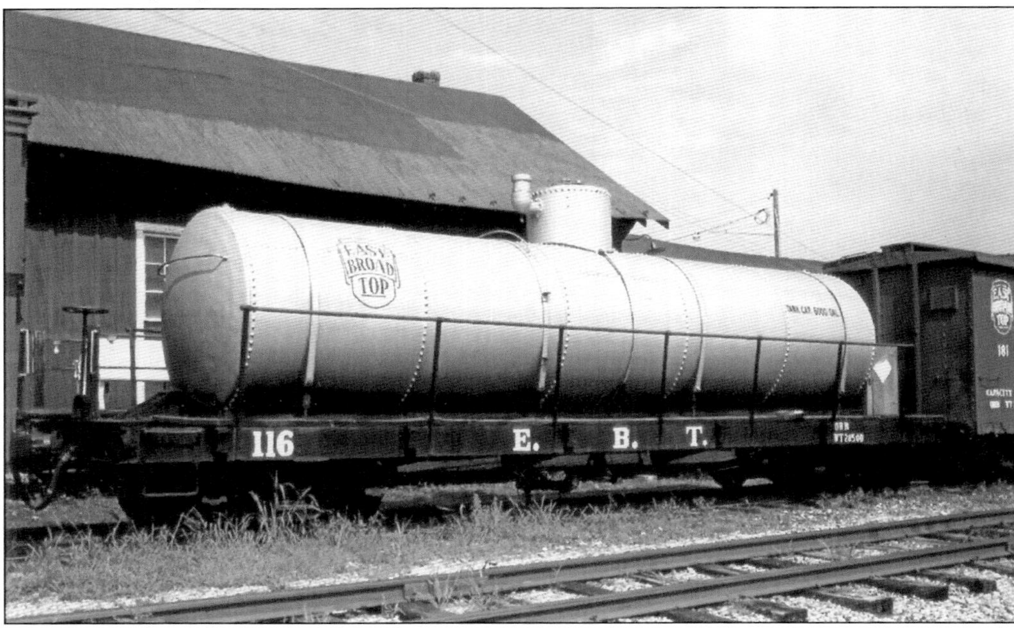

Tank car No. 116 with a 6,000-gallon capacity is shown at the Rockhill Furnace yard on August 5, 2007. This car was originally built as a flatcar in the East Broad Top Railroad shops in 1925, and after 1936, the tank was installed. It is the only narrow-gauge tank car on the railroad. (Photograph by Kenneth C. Springirth.)

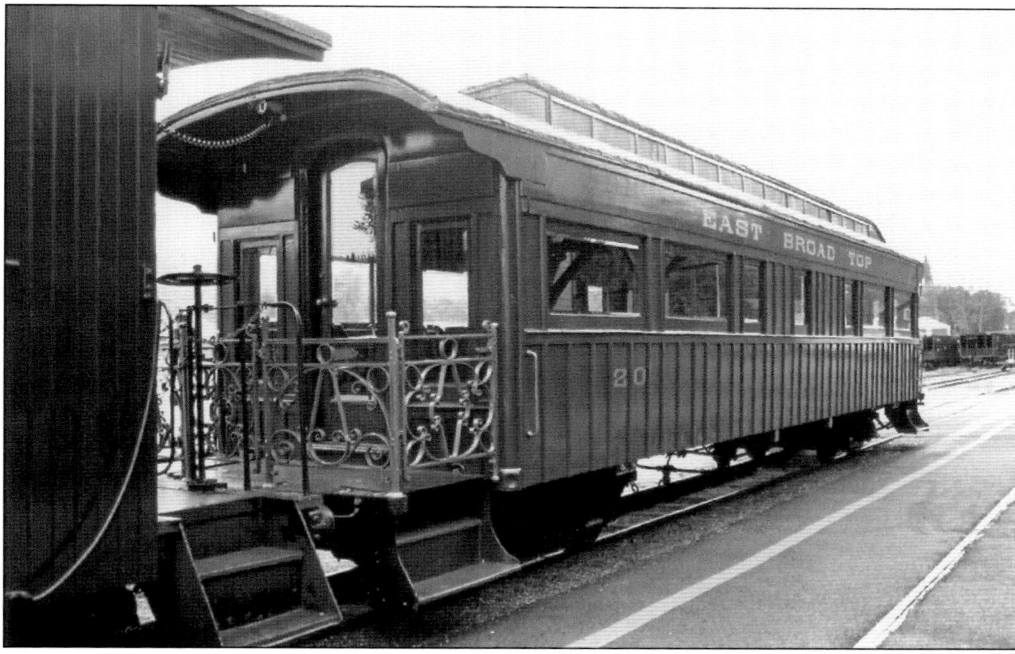

Parlor car No. 20 is the first-class car on the East Broad Top Railroad and is used in the rear of regularly scheduled trains. Billmeyer and Small Car Works built it in 1882. Purchased secondhand from the Big Level and Kinzua Railroad in 1907, it is in excellent condition as noted on August 5, 2007, at the Orbisonia station. (Photograph by Kenneth C. Springirth.)

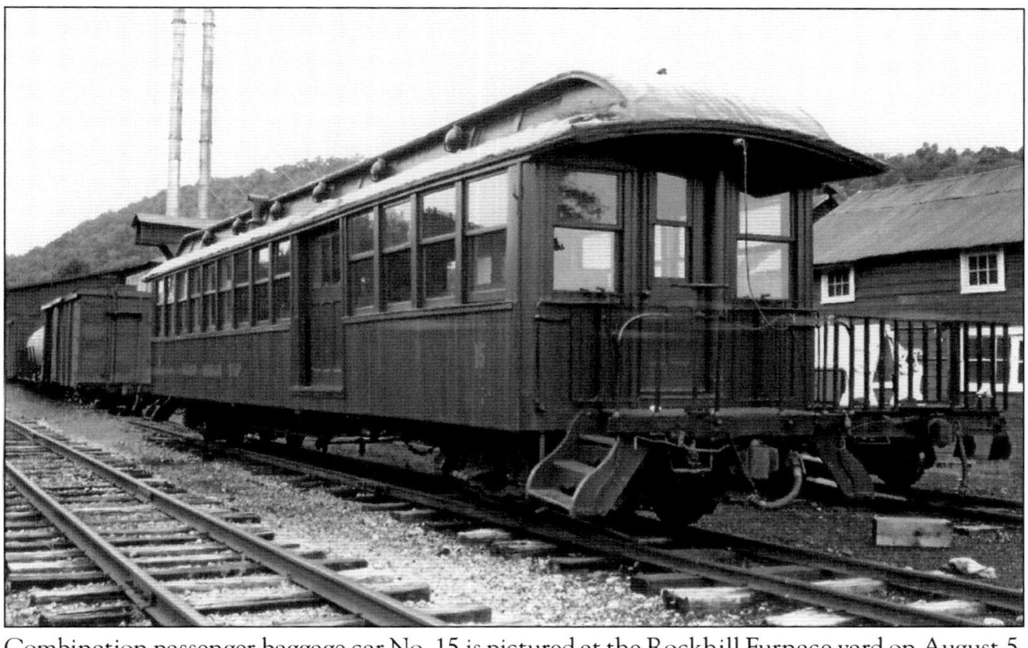

Combination passenger-baggage car No. 15 is pictured at the Rockhill Furnace yard on August 5, 2007. Laconia Car Company built this car in 1882, and 125 years later, it is in regular service in 2007 on the East Broad Top Railroad. It was purchased in 1916 from the Boston, Revere Beach and Lynn Railroad. (Photograph by Kenneth C. Springirth.)

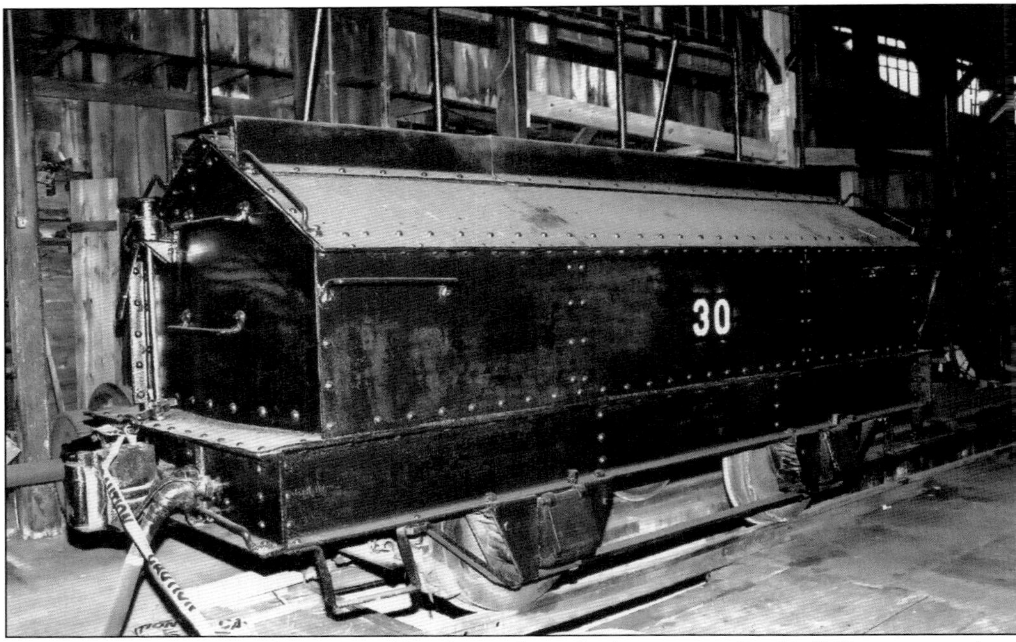

On August 18, 2007, scale car No. 30 is housed inside the vintage Rockhill Furnace machine shop, which has not changed since the shops closed in June 1956. Built in 1916 at the Rockhill Furnace shops of the East Broad Top Railroad, the scale car was used to calibrate three narrow-gauge scales on the railroad. (Photograph by Kenneth C. Springirth.)

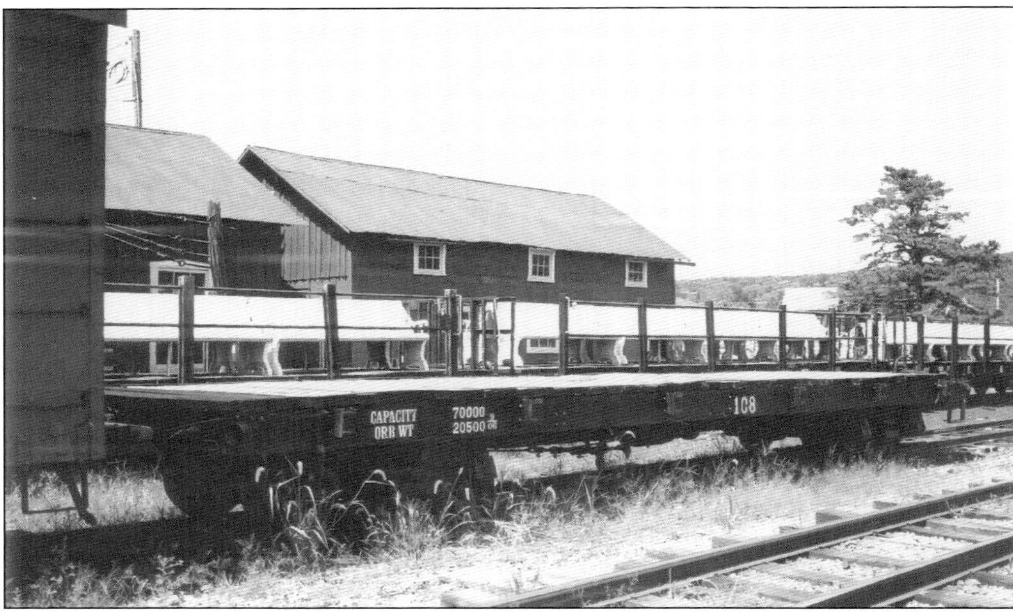

Flatcar No. 108 (the only true flatcar left on the railroad as remaining flatcars have been converted to passenger service) is at the Rockhill Furnace yard on August 18, 2007. This car, built in 1923 at the Rockhill Furnace shops of the East Broad Top Railroad (which built about 22 flatcars during 1923 to 1925), was restored for operation in July 2006. (Photograph by Kenneth C. Springirth.)

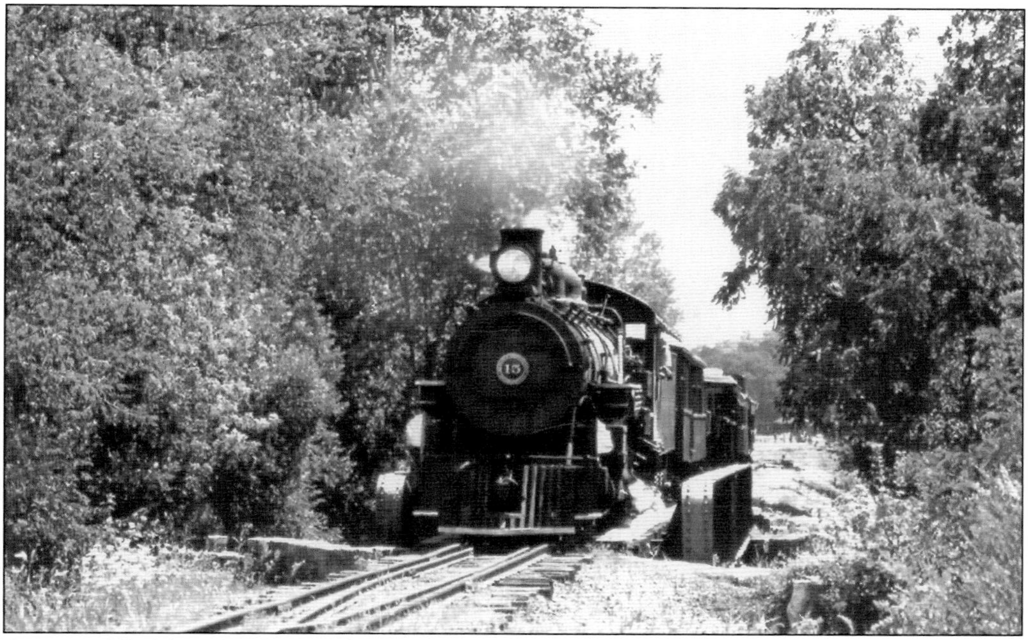

Crossing Blacklog Creek on July 21, 2007, is East Broad Top locomotive No. 15 heading a southbound passenger train into the borough of Rockhill Furnace. This steel plate girder bridge built in 1900 has two spans with a total length of 90 feet and is located north of the Orbisonia depot. (Photograph by Kenneth C. Springirth.)

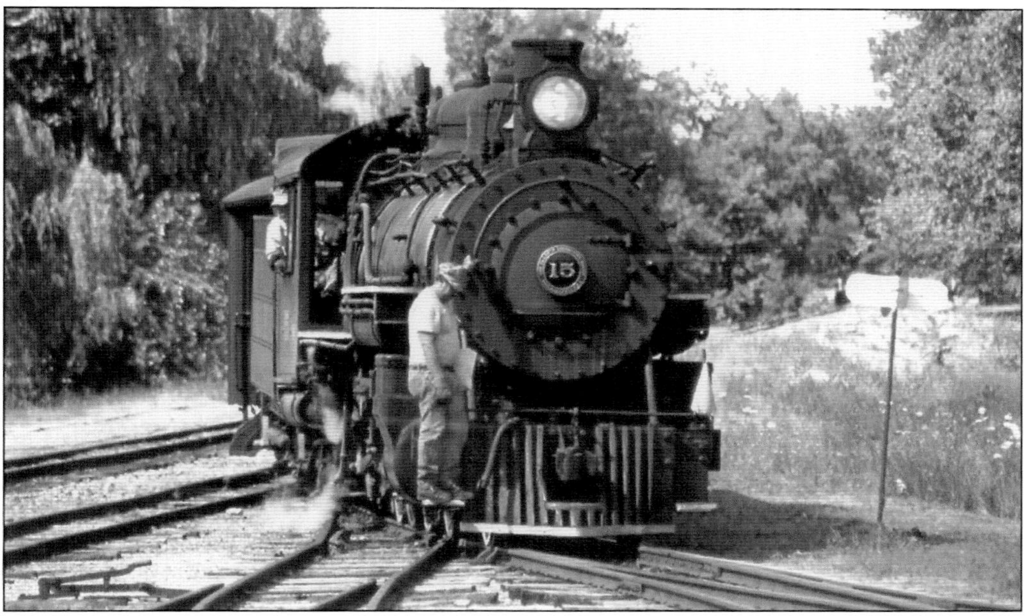

The last train of the day finds locomotive No. 15 ready to cross Meadow Street and enter the Rockhill Furnace yard on July 21, 2007. This yard was built in 1873 and includes maintenance shops, a roundhouse, and company offices. The shops were able to supply the parts and also had the capability to build rolling stock and maintain locomotives. (Photograph by Kenneth C. Springirth.)

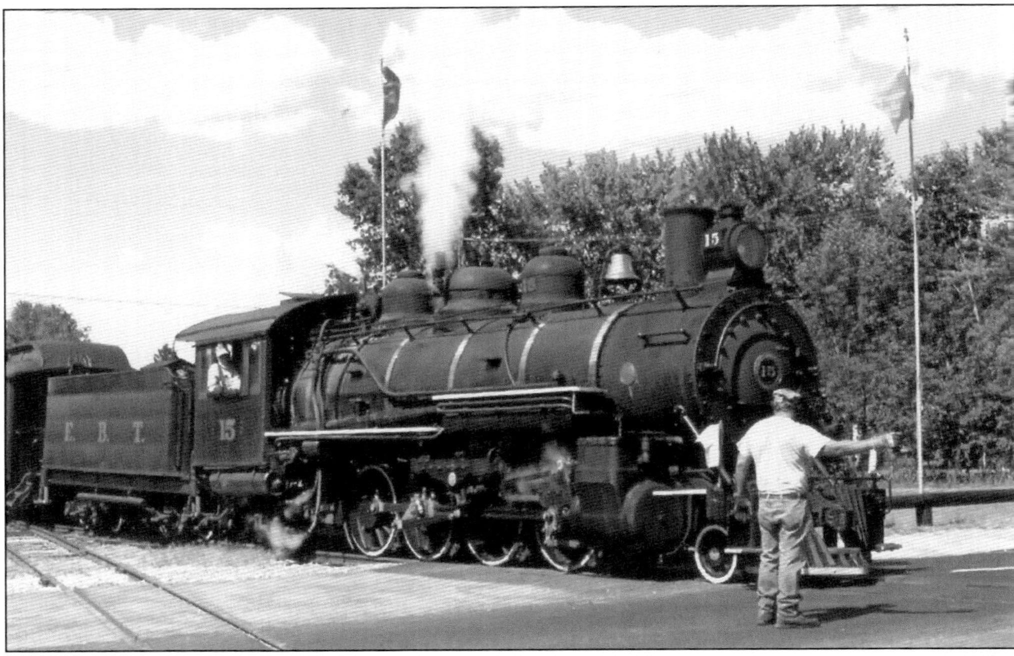

With engineer Thomas Holder in the locomotive cab, fireman Roy Miller is at the Meadow Street crossing in the borough of Rockhill Furnace making sure motorists are a safe distance away to allow safe passage for the East Broad Top Railroad train headed by locomotive No. 15 on July 21, 2007. (Photograph by Kenneth C. Springirth.)

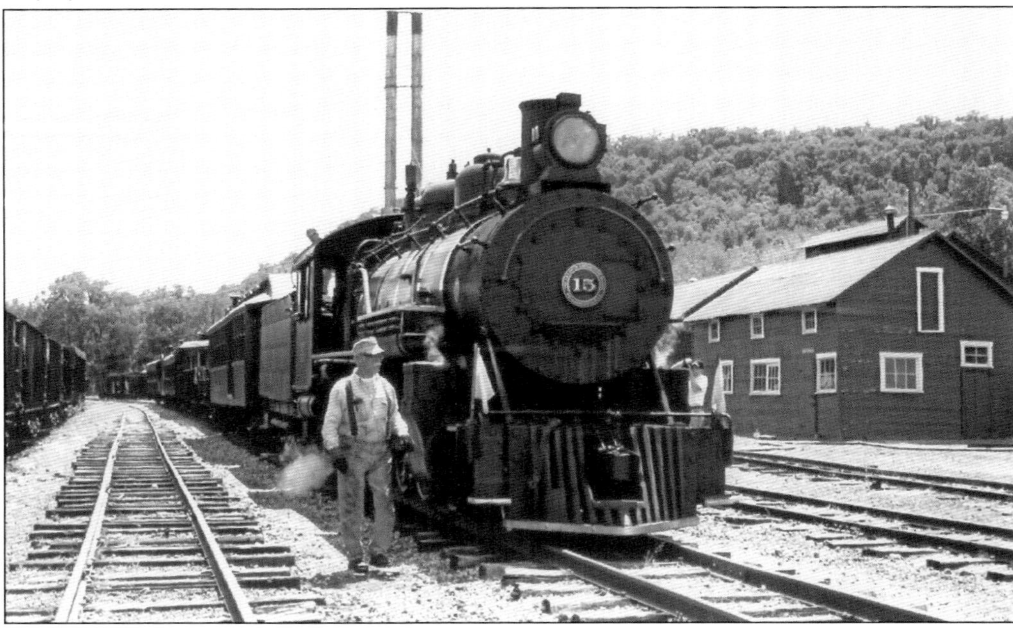

Engineer Thomas Holder is doing a walk-around review of East Broad Top Railroad locomotive No. 15 on July 21, 2007, at the Rockhill Furnace yard. A lineup of restored hopper cars can be noted on the left side of the photograph, and a portion of the shop complex is on the right side of the photograph. (Photograph by Kenneth C. Springirth.)

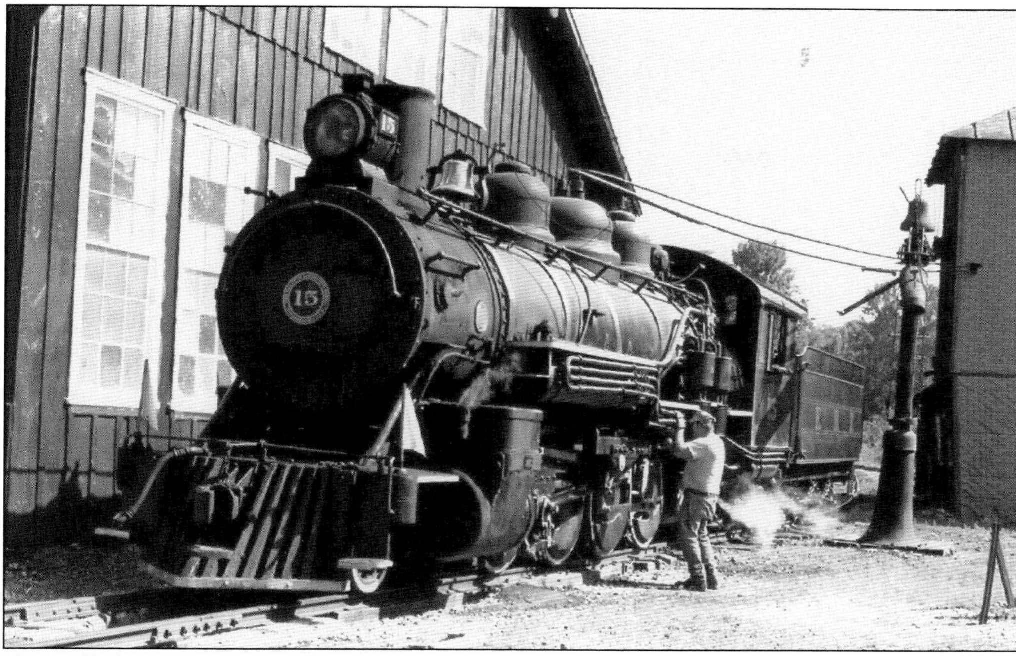

With all the train trips of the day completed, fireman Roy Miller is inspecting the external running gear of East Broad Top Railroad locomotive No. 15 at the Rockhill Furnace yard on July 21, 2007. Before the locomotive can be placed in the roundhouse, a considerable amount of inspection time is involved. (Photograph by Kenneth C. Springirth.)

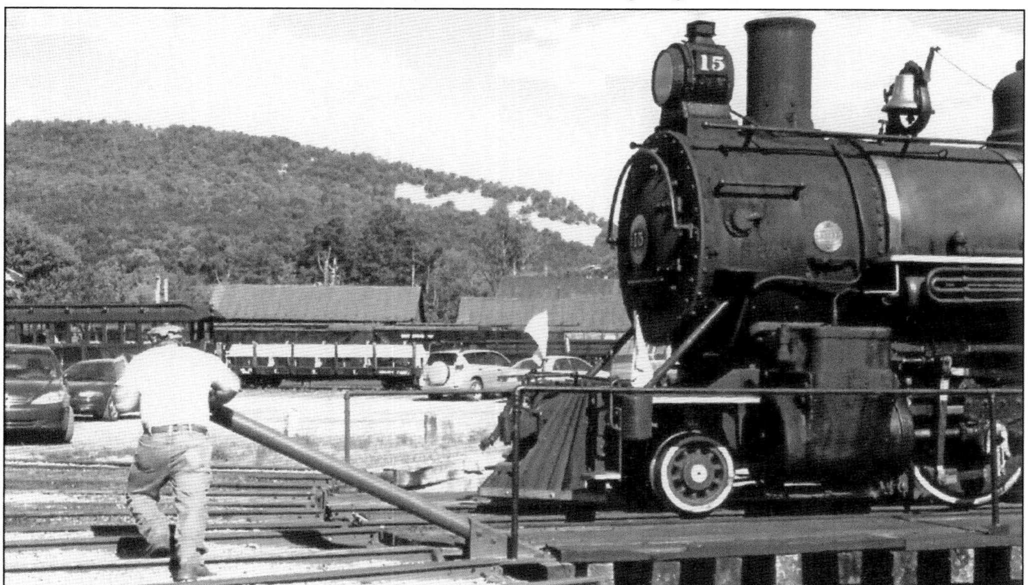

Baldwin Locomotive Works boiler No. 41,196 dated February 1914 is in sight below the smokestack near the front of East Broad Top Railroad locomotive No. 15 as fireman Roy Miller moves the turntable by hand to the appropriate track for the proper roundhouse stall. In 2007, all six of the Mikado-type steam locomotives were housed at the Rockhill Furnace roundhouse. (Photograph by Kenneth C. Springirth.)

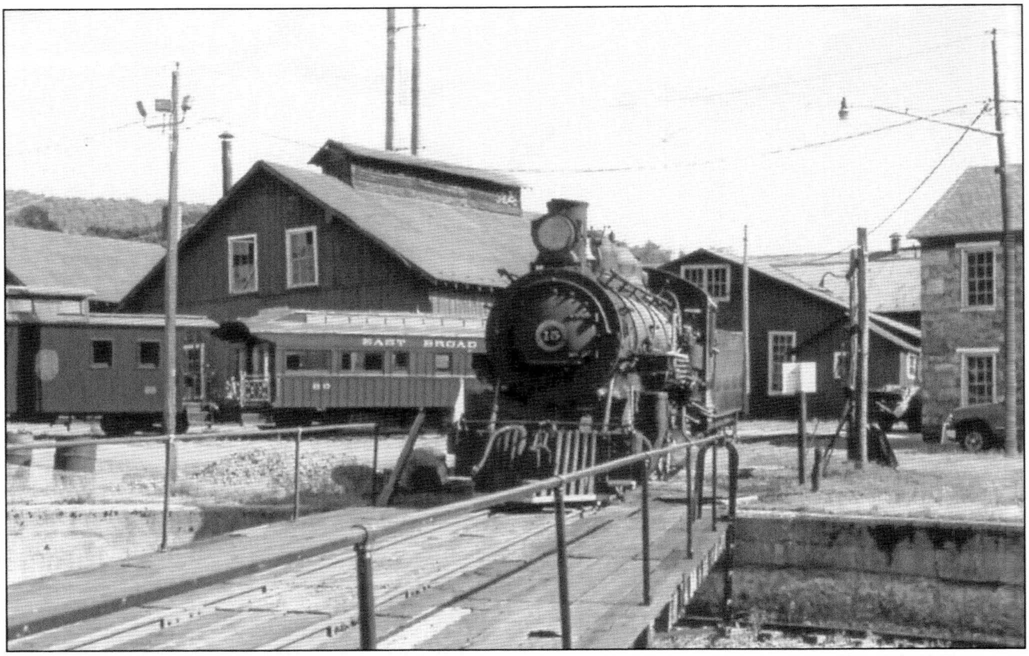

On July 21, 2007, East Broad Top Railroad locomotive No. 15 is coming on the Rockhill Furnace turntable. This deck steel plate girder construction turntable was purchased secondhand from the New York Central Railroad in 1914. In the background are caboose No. 28 and parlor car No. 20. (Photograph by Kenneth C. Springirth.)

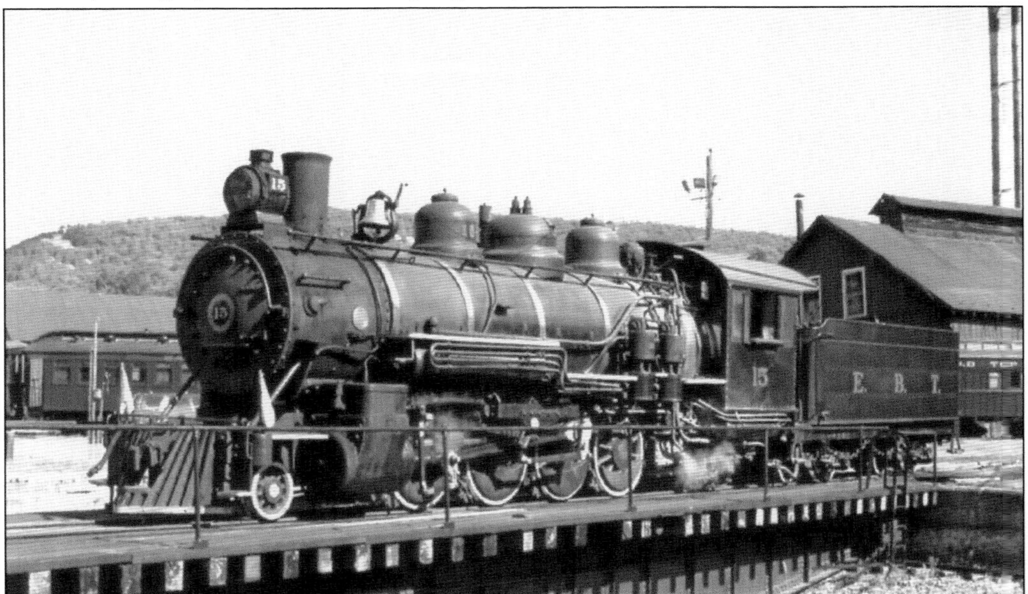

Locomotive No. 15 is being carefully positioned on the Rockhill Furnace turntable on July 21, 2007. When the locomotive is centered on the turntable, the fireman will be able to move the turntable by hand to the proper track for placement of the locomotive in the roundhouse. (Photograph by Kenneth C. Springirth.)

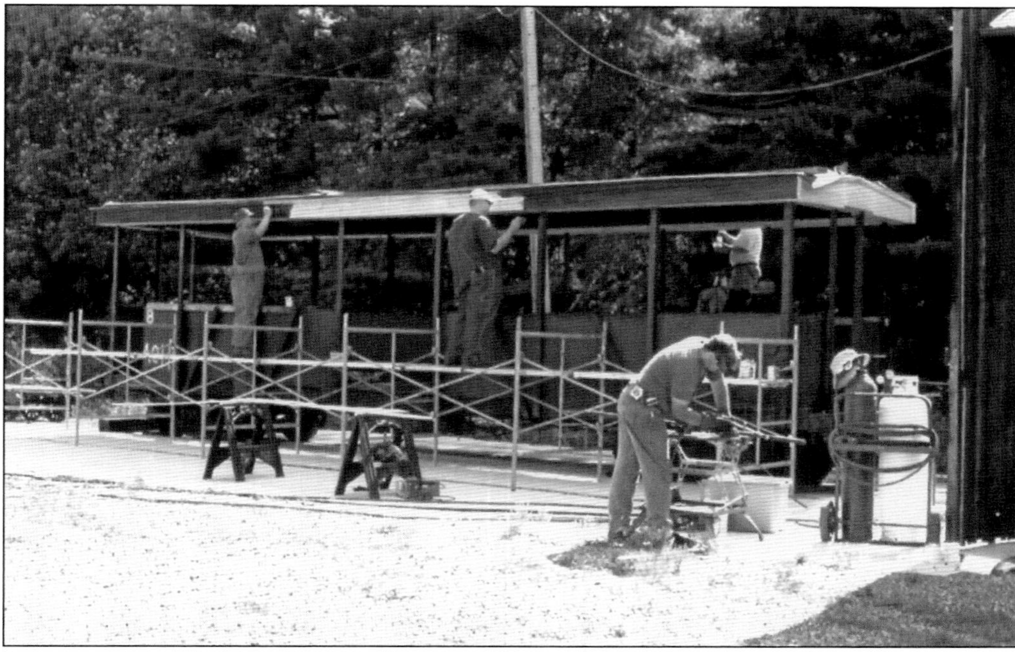

Volunteers from the Friends of the East Broad Top, which is dedicated to the preservation and restoration of the East Broad Top Railroad, are painting the former East Broad Top Railroad boxcar No. 168, which is being converted for passenger service. The 60,000-pound-capacity boxcar was built by the East Broad Top Railroad in 1920. (Photograph by Kenneth C. Springirth.)

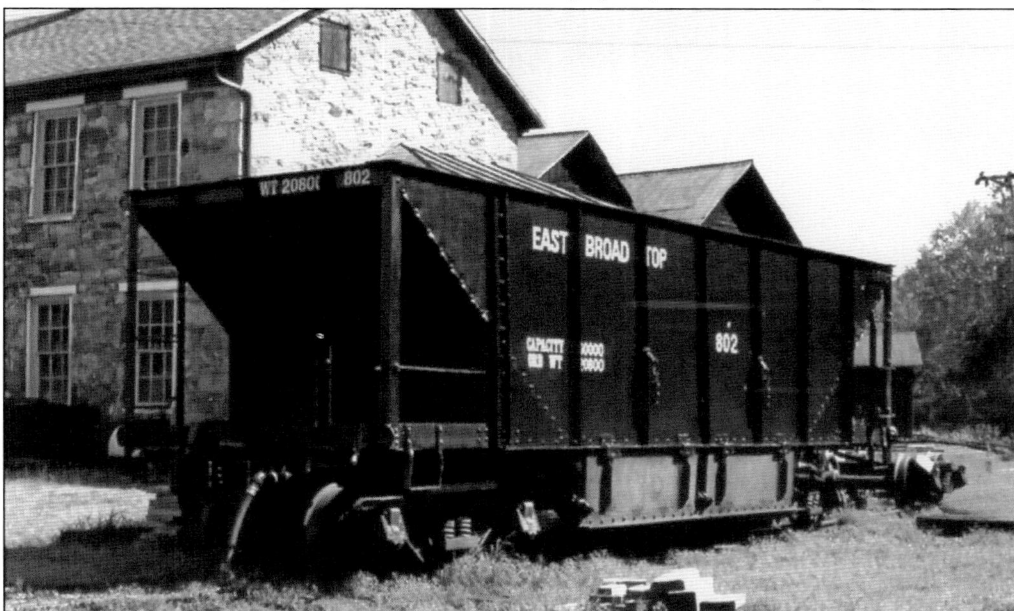

Volunteers of the Friends of the East Broad Top are rebuilding East Broad Top Railroad side-dump steel hopper car No. 802 as viewed on July 21, 2007, at the Rockhill Furnace yard with work progressing on repairs to the second truck. This was one of 10 steel hopper cars built by Pressed Steel Car Company in 1913. (Photograph by Kenneth C. Springirth.)

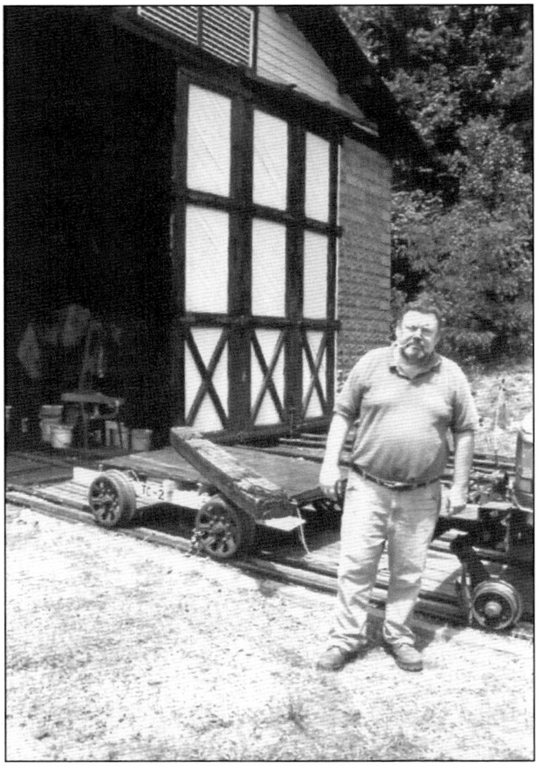

Allen Levin, president of the Mount Union Connecting Railroad, is shown in front of the East Broad Top Railroad engine house in Mount Union on July 7, 2007. The Mount Union Connecting Railroad has cleared the East Broad Top Railroad line from the Mount Union yard south to Pennsylvania State Highway 103 and has rehabilitated the engine house. (Photograph by Kenneth C. Springirth.)

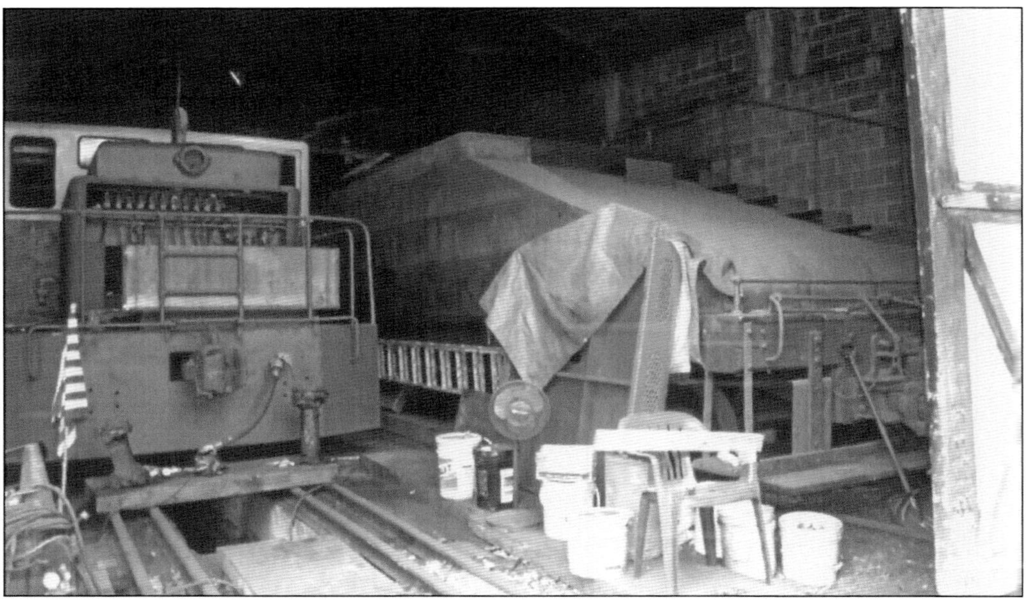

At the Mount Union engine house is Plymouth Locomotive Works diesel locomotive model CR-4, built in 1964 for the Benson Mines at Star Lake, New York. It was acquired by the Mohawk Adirondack and Northern Railroad and sold to the Mount Union Connecting Railroad. Seen is the tender of East Broad Top Railroad standard-gauge locomotive No. 3, which was built in March 1923 by Baldwin Locomotive Works. (Photograph by Kenneth C. Springirth.)

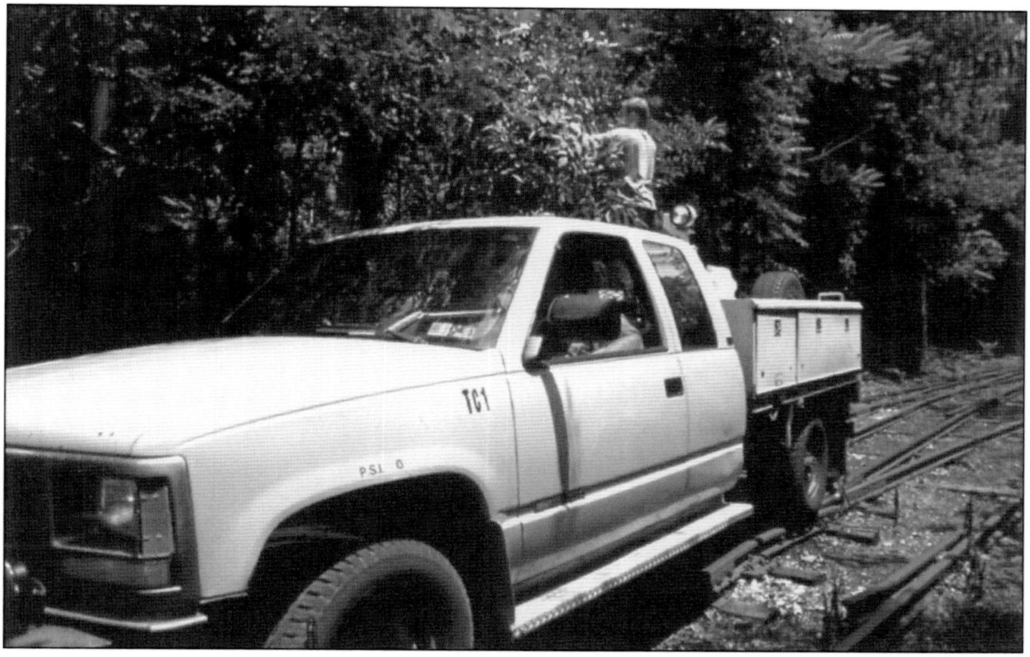

Mount Union Connecting Railroad GMC high-rail truck TC1 is on the cleared trackage east of the East Broad Top Railroad engine house in Mount Union as Nathan Hetrick prunes the trees along the line on July 7, 2007. In addition to track clearing, many new ties have been installed. (Photograph by Kenneth C. Springirth.)

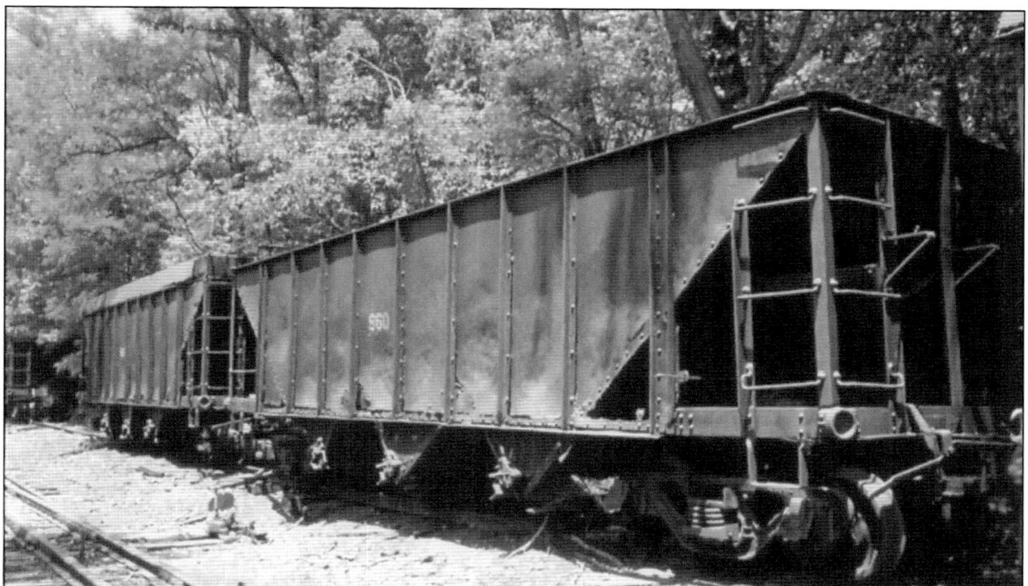

East of the East Broad Top Railroad engine house in the borough of Mount Union, a large number of East Broad Top Railroad hopper cars, inundated with dense vegetation, are in view on July 7, 2007, from the track cleared by the Mount Union Connecting Railroad. These hopper cars have not moved since the East Broad Top Railroad closed in 1956. (Photograph by Kenneth C. Springirth.)

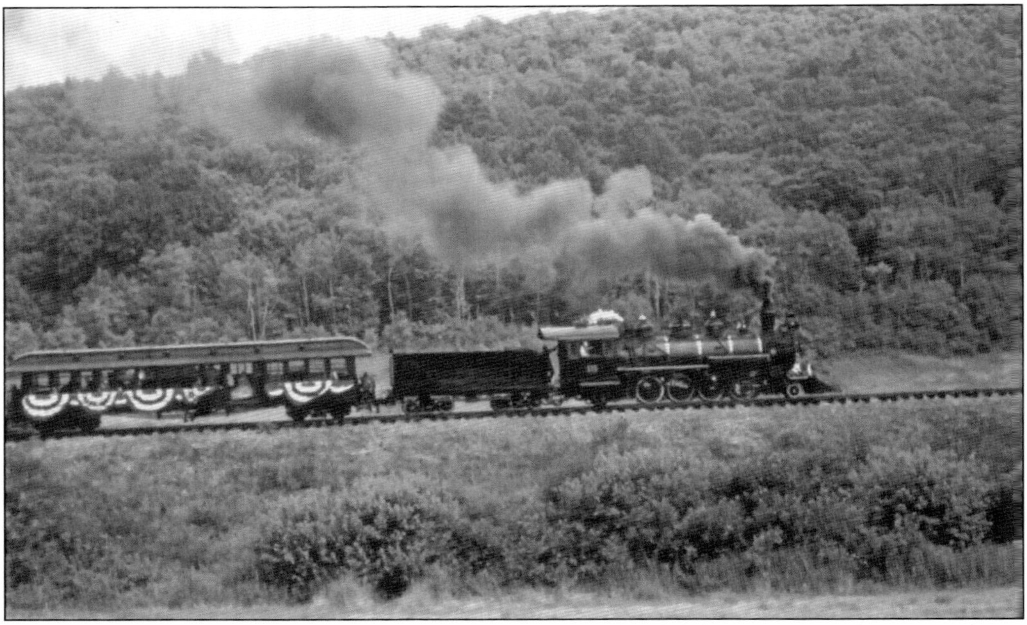

In the picturesque Aughwick Valley, a special train headed by East Broad Top Railroad locomotive No. 15 is south of the Runk Road Bridge and is heading south on July 24, 2007, for the filming of *Abraham Lincoln: The Speech That Saved America.* A balloon-style smokestack and temporary cowcatcher were installed on the locomotive and EBT was blanked out on the tender. (Photograph by Kenneth C. Springirth.)

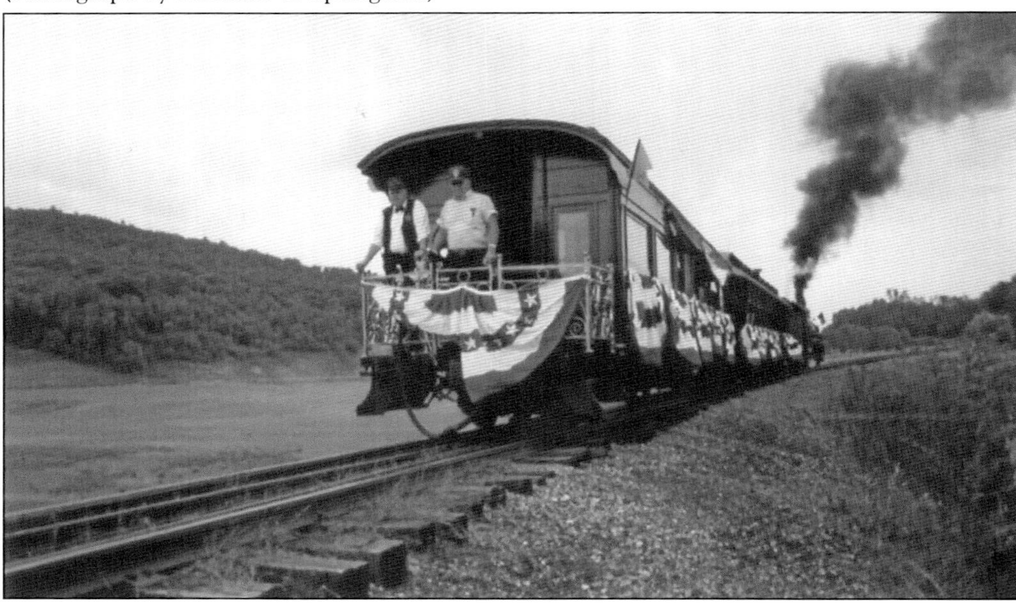

This special two-car train is south of the Runk Road Bridge on July 24, 2007. Locomotive No. 15 is pulling two passenger cars decorated with red, white, and blue bunting. East Broad Top Railroad general manager Stanley G. Hall is in the center of the observation platform of parlor car No. 20 handling details with the film crew for *Abraham Lincoln: The Speech That Saved America.* (Photograph by Kenneth C. Springirth.)

Four

TRAIN MEETS TROLLEY

Adjacent to the East Broad Top Railroad in the borough of Rockhill Furnace is the nonprofit Rockhill Trolley Museum operated by Railways to Yesterday, Inc., incorporated on August 14, 1962. Trolley operation began in August 1962 using a long cord attached to the trolley pole on Johnstown Traction Company car No. 311 and the other end of the cord attached to the motor generator set producing the 600-volt direct current. Standard-gauge track was constructed on the narrow-gauge roadbed. Overhead wire was erected by October 1962, permitting operation of car No. 311 over a portion of the Shade Gap branch of the East Broad Top Railroad. Official opening of the trolley line was on July 6, 1963. During 2001, the museum began a 2,844-foot extension over the Shade Gap branch toward Blacklog Narrows. A two-track terminal was constructed at Blacklog Narrows near United States Highway 522. The Kovalchick Corporation provided the steel track materials. Museum volunteers gathered over 380 rail joint bars (used to hold the rail lengths together) plus sorted and cleaned over 2,000 tie plates (which support the rails on the wooden crossties). The museum contracted out the major portions of the $160,000 construction project with K. W. Reese of Mercersburg constructing the track and other local contractors performing right-of-way clearing, tree removal, grading, and pole installation. Museum volunteers installed the overhead trolley wire plus constructed the second track at Blacklog Narrows and the concrete platform. The entire project was dedicated on August 9, 2003. The museum collection includes 21 trolleys from Johnstown; York; Scranton; Philadelphia; Harrisburg; Chicago, Illinois; Rio de Janeiro, Brazil; and Oporto, Portugal. As of August 2007, 15 trolleys are operable. The latest restoration project, Johnstown Traction Company car No. 355, was dedicated on June 9, 2007. This trolley car, last used on June 11, 1960, was completely restored and is featured on the front cover of *Johnstown Trolleys and Incline*. Trolleys at the Rockhill Trolley Museum meet each returning train of the East Broad Top Railroad. The Web site for the East Broad Top Railroad is www.ebtrr.com, and www.rockhilltrolley.org covers the Rockhill Trolley Museum. The trolley museum is staffed entirely with volunteers who donate their time and talents (and in many cases travel one to five hours, one way) for the operation and development of the museum.

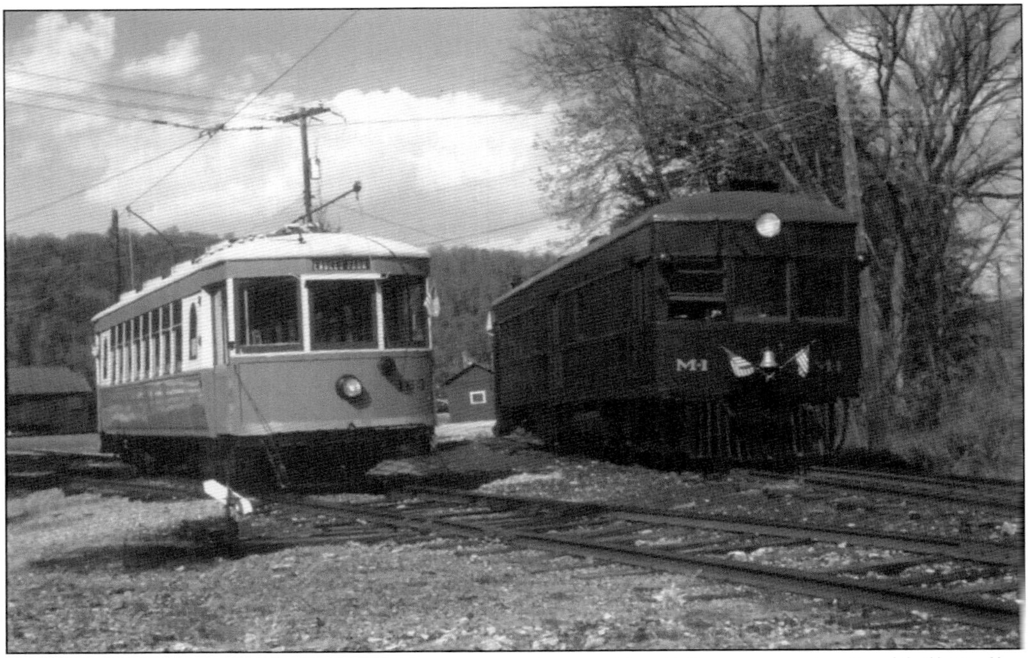

Magnificently restored former York Railways trolley car No. 163 poses at the Rockhill Trolley Museum with East Broad Top Railroad gas-electric motor car M-1 at the Rockhill Furnace wye on October 20, 2001. Both the railroad and the trolley museum have provided a unique learning experience for students of transportation. (Photograph by Joel Salomon.)

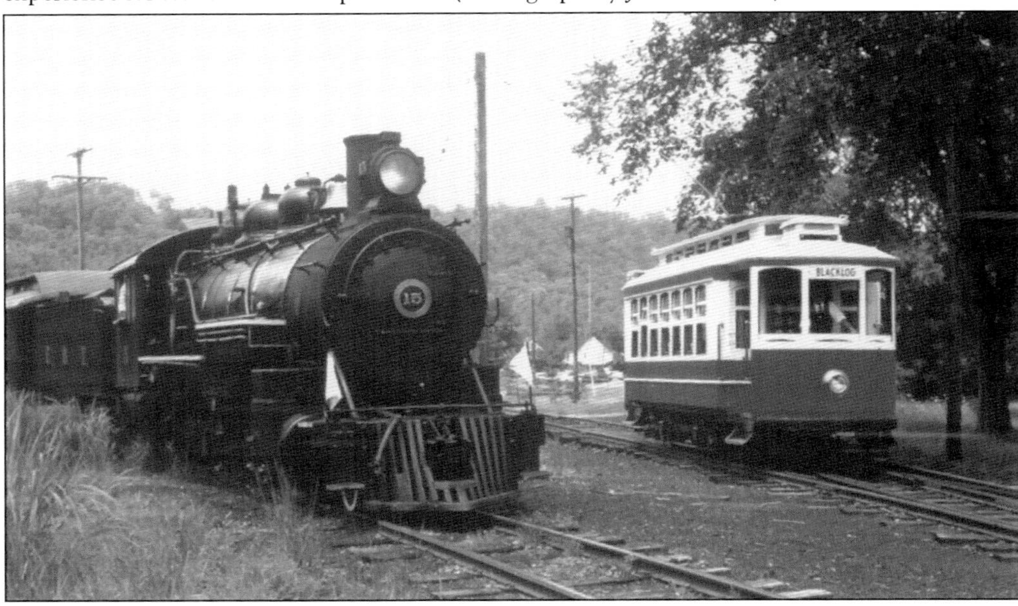

It is the classic train-meets-trolley with East Broad Top Railroad locomotive No. 15 and Rockhill Trolley Museum former Oporto, Portugal, trolley car No. 172 at the borough of Rockhill Furnace on July 11, 1987. This was Pennsylvania's first operating trolley museum. Years of dedicated hard work have made this museum an outstanding tourist and educational experience. (Photograph by Joel Salomon.)

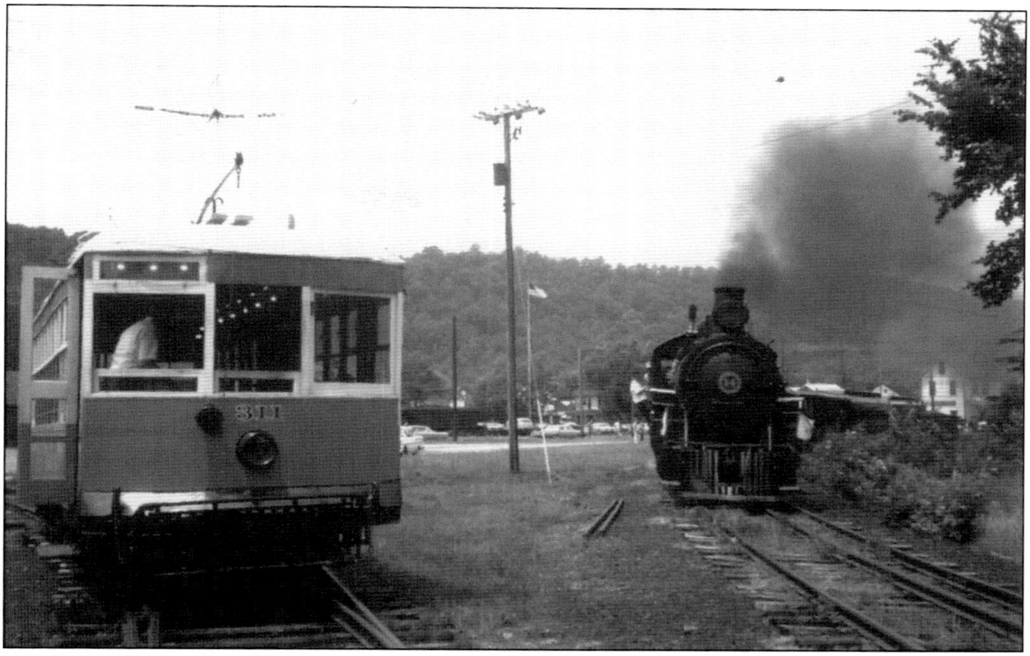

East Broad Top Railroad locomotive No. 14 is on the wye passing Rockhill Trolley Museum trolley car No. 311 on July 2, 1972. Built in 1922 by Wason Manufacturing Company of Springfield, Massachusetts, as car No. 14 for the Bangor Railway and Electric Company of Bangor, Maine, it was sold to Johnstown Traction Company in 1941 and renumbered as 311. (Photograph by Kenneth C. Springirth.)

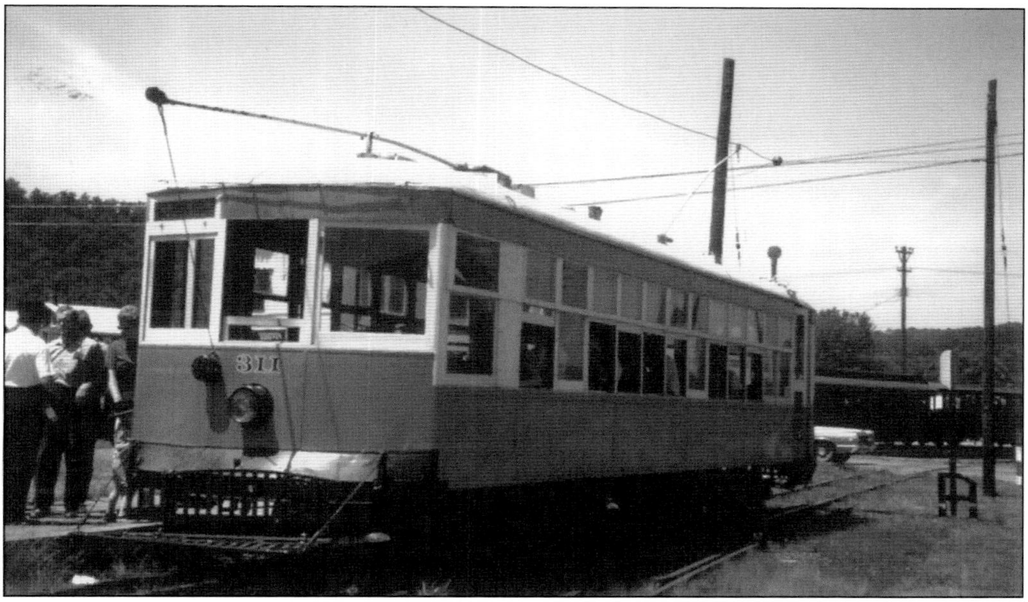

Trolley car No. 311 is at the Rockhill Trolley Museum on July 5, 1971. Operating in Johnstown from 1941 to the end of trolley car service on June 11, 1960, car No. 311 at that time was the last Birney-type trolley car operating in a United States city in regular public transit service. This was the first trolley car acquired by the museum. (Photograph by Kenneth C. Springirth.)

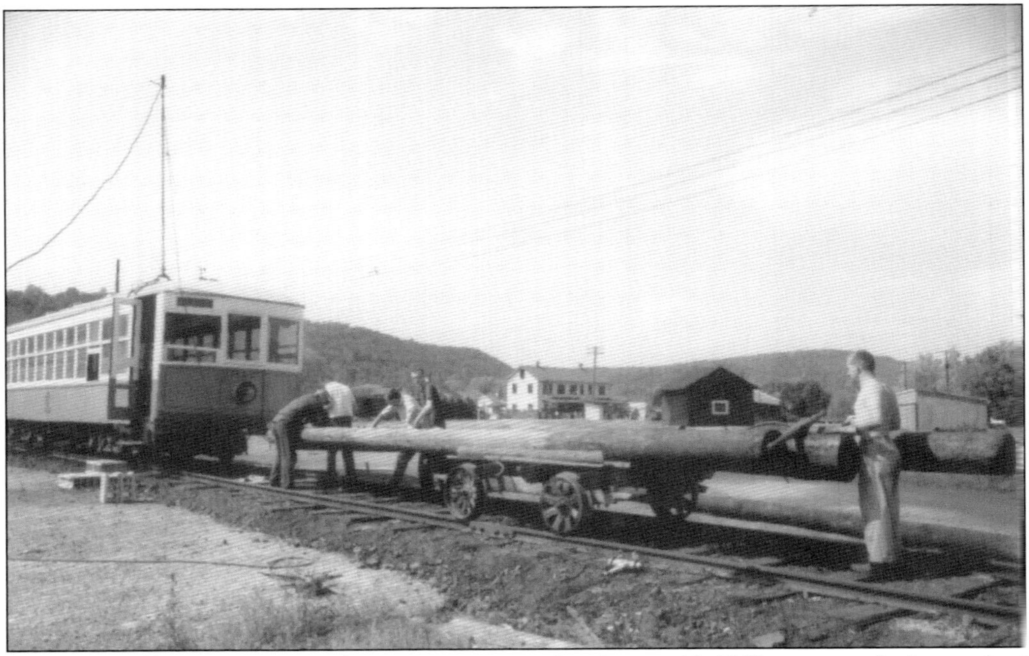

Rockhill Trolley Museum is under construction in this August 19, 1962, scene at the borough of Rockhill Furnace. Former Johnstown Traction Company car No. 311 is shown with a work crew preparing to set up poles to support the overhead wire that will supply electric power to run the trolley cars. (Photograph by Louis J. G. Buehler, Rockhill Trolley Museum collection.)

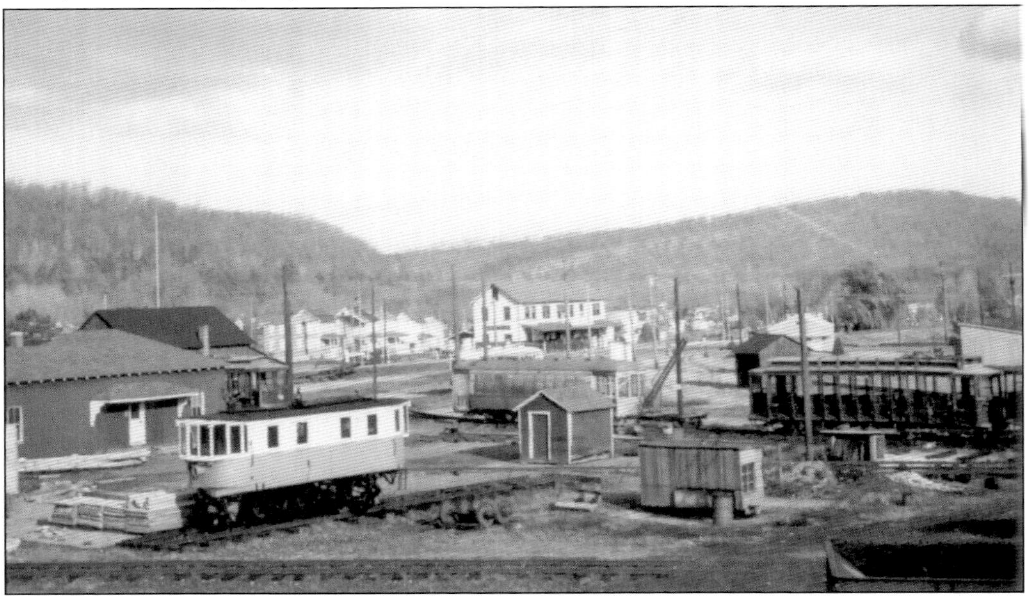

This November 6, 1965, view shows, from left to right, Washington, D.C., sweeper No. 09; behind it an open car from Rio de Janeiro, Brazil; in the center Johnstown Traction Company car No. 362; and on the right another open car from Rio de Janeiro, Brazil. The Orbisonia station of the East Broad Top Railroad is in the center of the picture. (Photograph by Louis J. G. Buehler, Rockhill Trolley Museum collection.)

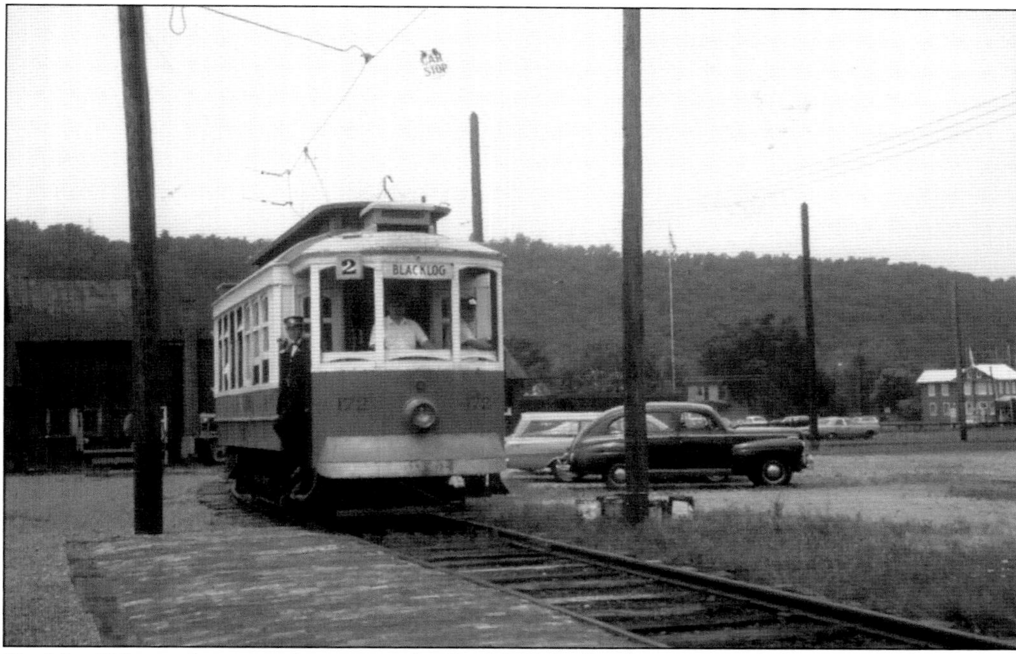

Car No. 172 is making another trip at the Rockhill Trolley Museum on July 2, 1972. This car was built in Oporto, Portugal, in 1929 based on a J. G. Brill Car Company design and featured an attractive interior with ornate carved wooden trim, brass fittings, and sliding end doors. It was a semi-convertible design where the windows could be raised into roof pockets. (Photograph by Kenneth C. Springirth.)

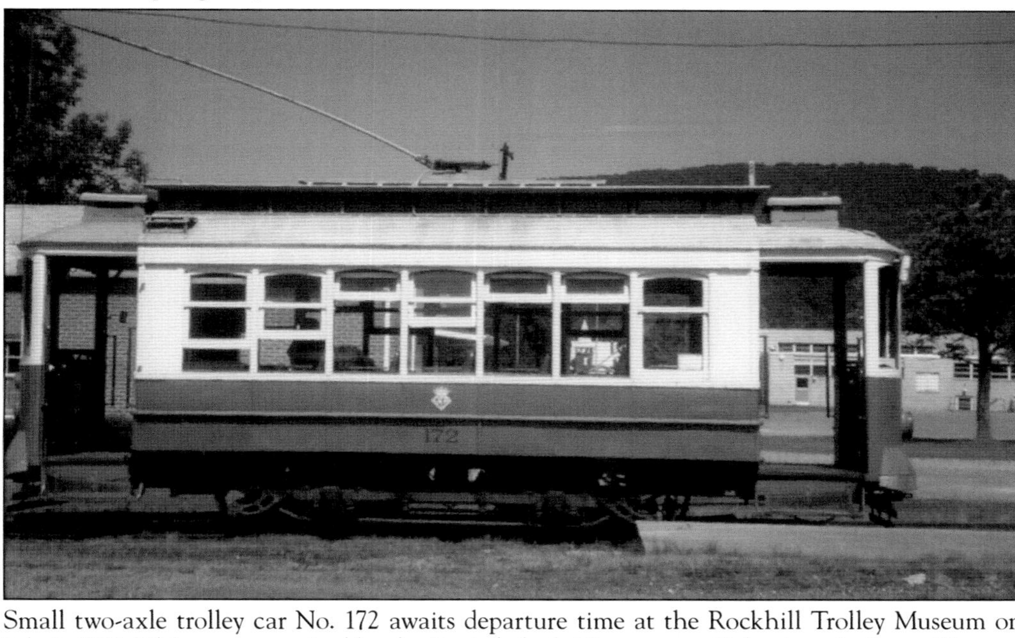

Small two-axle trolley car No. 172 awaits departure time at the Rockhill Trolley Museum on July 5, 1971. This car was retired by the Sociedade de Transportes Colectivos do Porto (Oporto, Portugal) and was acquired by the museum in 1967. In 1998, this car received major mechanical work and motor repair. (Photograph by Kenneth C. Springirth.)

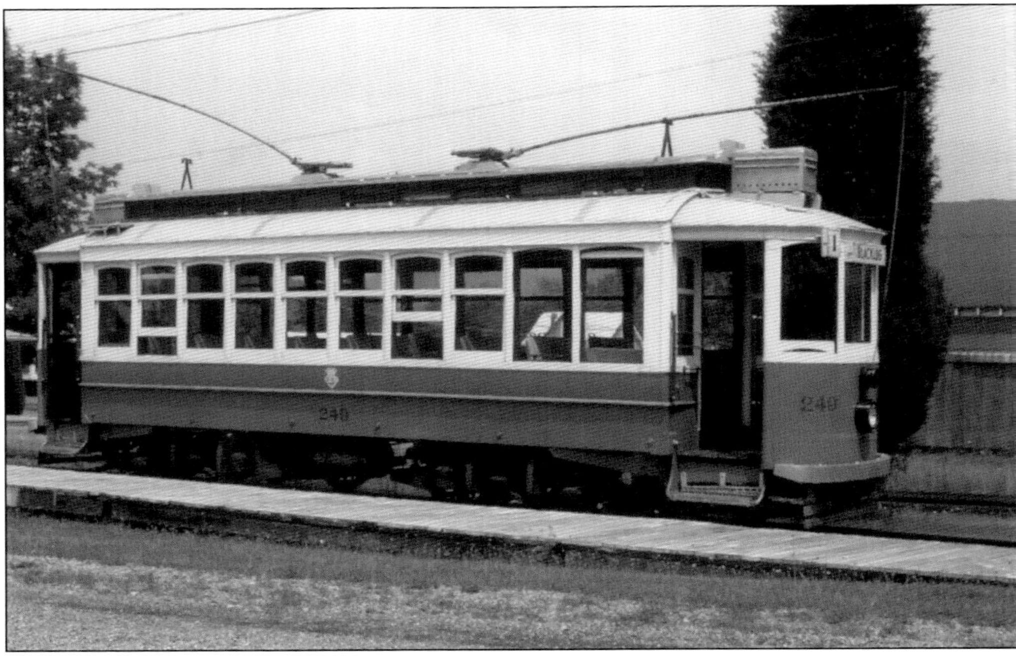

Car No. 249 meets the train at the Rockhill Trolley Museum on August 5, 1984. J. G. Brill Car Company built this car in 1904 for Oporto, Portugal. It was known as a semi-convertible car with windows that could be raised to the roof. The Sociedade de Transportes Colectivos do Porto retired this car in 1972. The museum acquired the car in October 1972. (Photograph by Kenneth C. Springirth.)

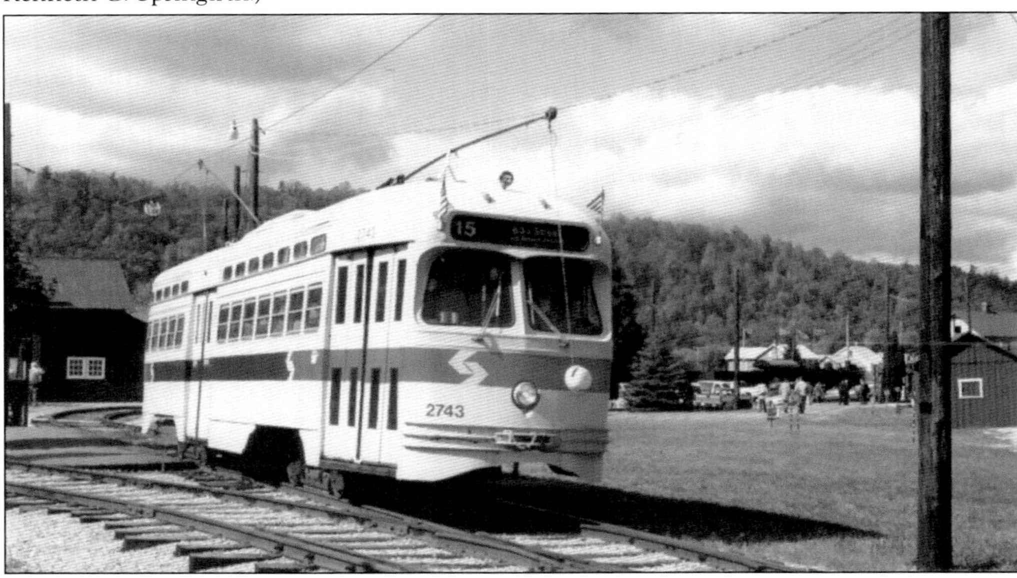

Presidents' Conference Committee car No. 2743 is at the Rockhill Trolley Museum on October 6, 2001. Built by St. Louis Car Company in 1947, this car operated in Philadelphia until 1993 and was acquired by the museum in 1994. Since Philadelphia trolleys use a track gauge of five feet two and a quarter inches, museum volunteers gauged the car to the museum track gauge of four feet eight and a half inches. (Photograph by Kenneth C. Springirth.)

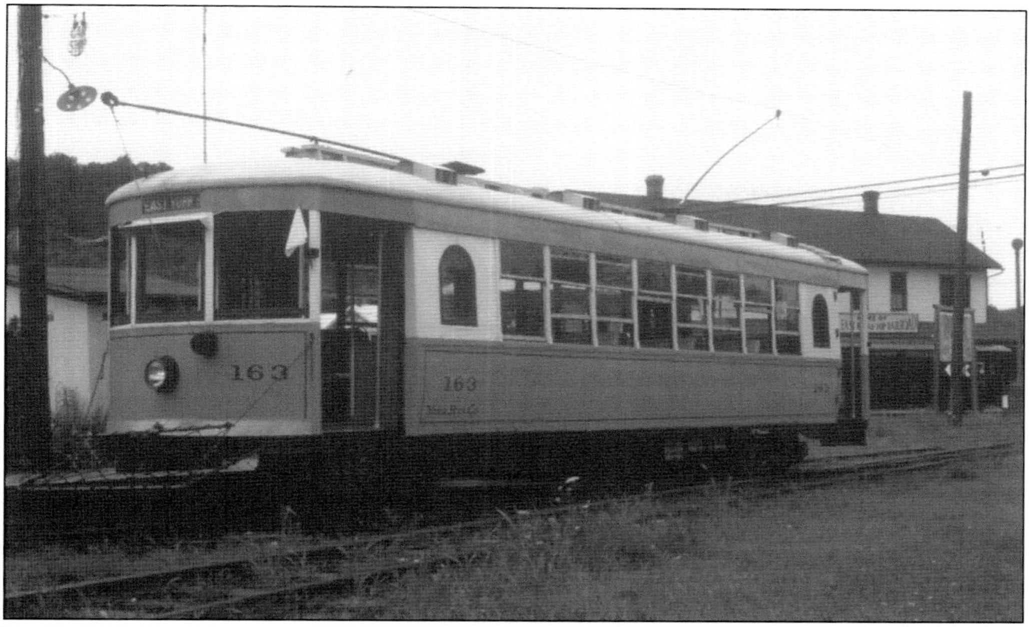

Rockhill Trolley Museum car No. 163 is awaiting the next train on August 6, 1995, with the Orbisonia train station in the background. Car No. 163 was built in 1924 by J. G. Brill Car Company for York Railways and was used until trolley car service ended in York on February 4, 1939. This car became a summer home along Conewago Creek north of York. (Photograph by Kenneth C. Springirth.)

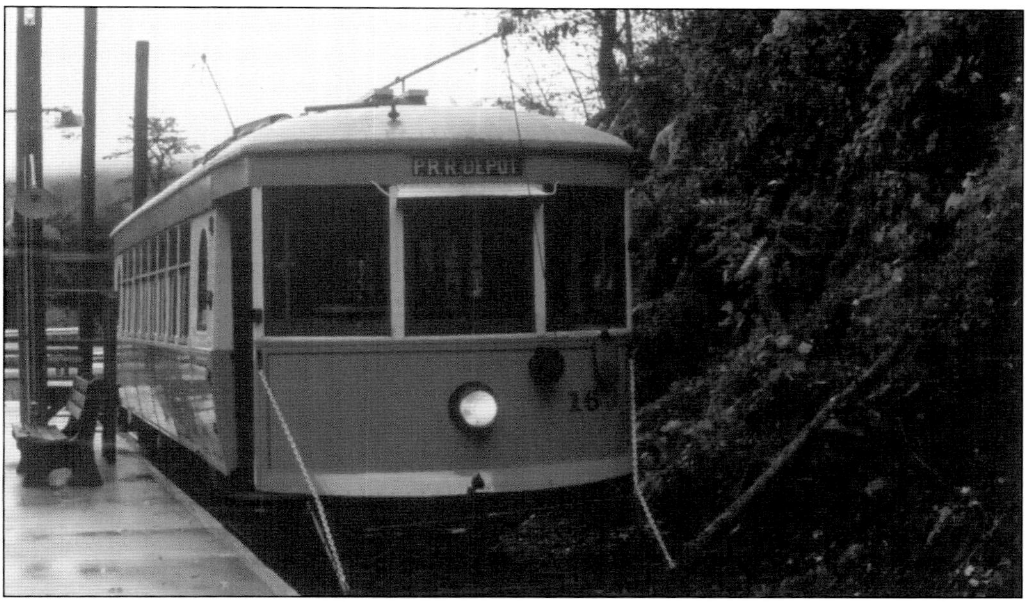

Curved side car No. 163 sparkles in the autumn rain at the Rockhill Trolley Museum on October 8, 2005. As a result of Hurricane Agnes in 1972, the former York Railways car body was knocked off its foundation, and the owners donated it to the Rockhill Trolley Museum. Following a 17-year worldwide search for the proper parts, museum volunteers painstakingly put this car back together. (Photograph by Kenneth C. Springirth.)

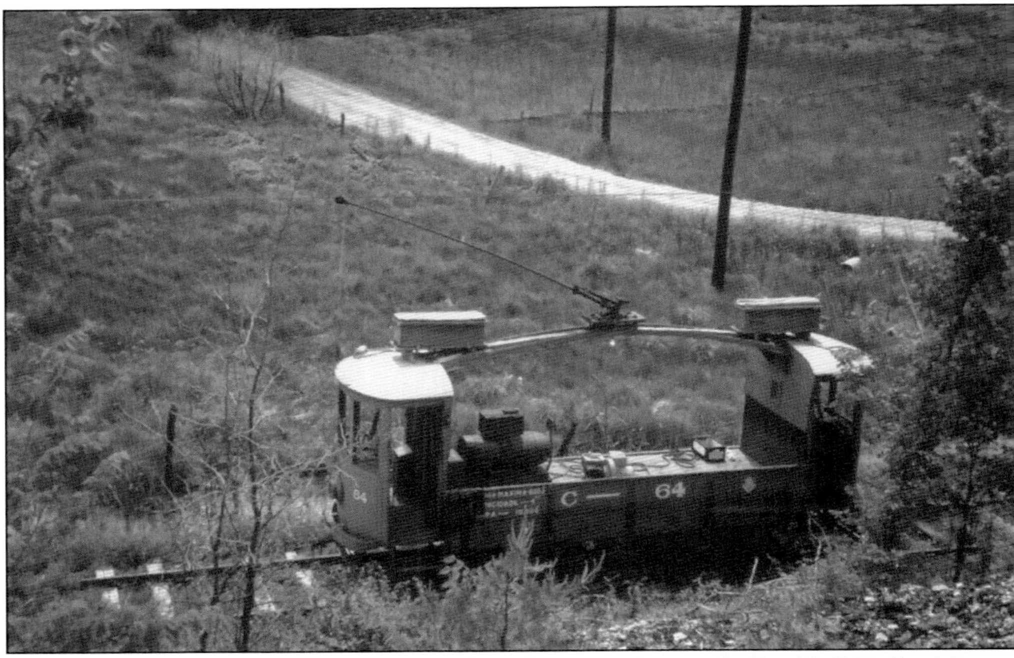

Looking down from the hillside, single-truck work car No. 64 is at the Rockhill Trolley Museum on June 2, 1968. This car was built by Sociedade de Transportes Colectivos do Porto during 1933 in Oporto, Portugal. Cars of this type were used to deliver coal to the company's electric power plant, haul ash from the power plant, and haul fish from the port to the markets. (Photograph by Kenneth C. Springirth.)

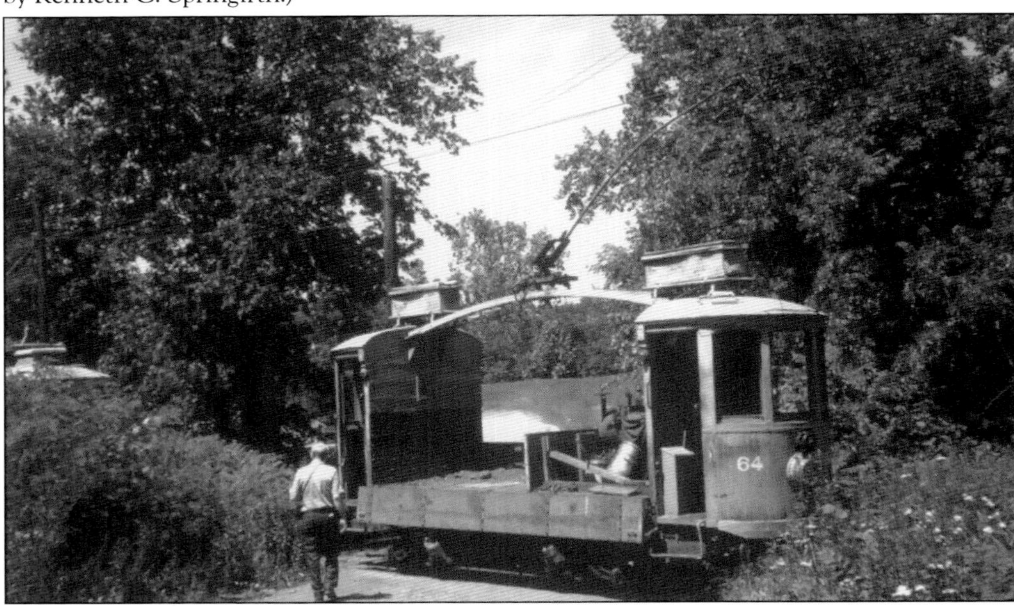

Car No. 64 is involved in a right-of-way project in this July 5, 1971, scene. The museum acquired this car during 1967, and it has been used to maintain track and overhead wire. Museum volunteers have installed on this work car an electric arc welder, acetylene cutting torch, air compressor, generator, and various tools. (Photograph by Kenneth C. Springirth.)

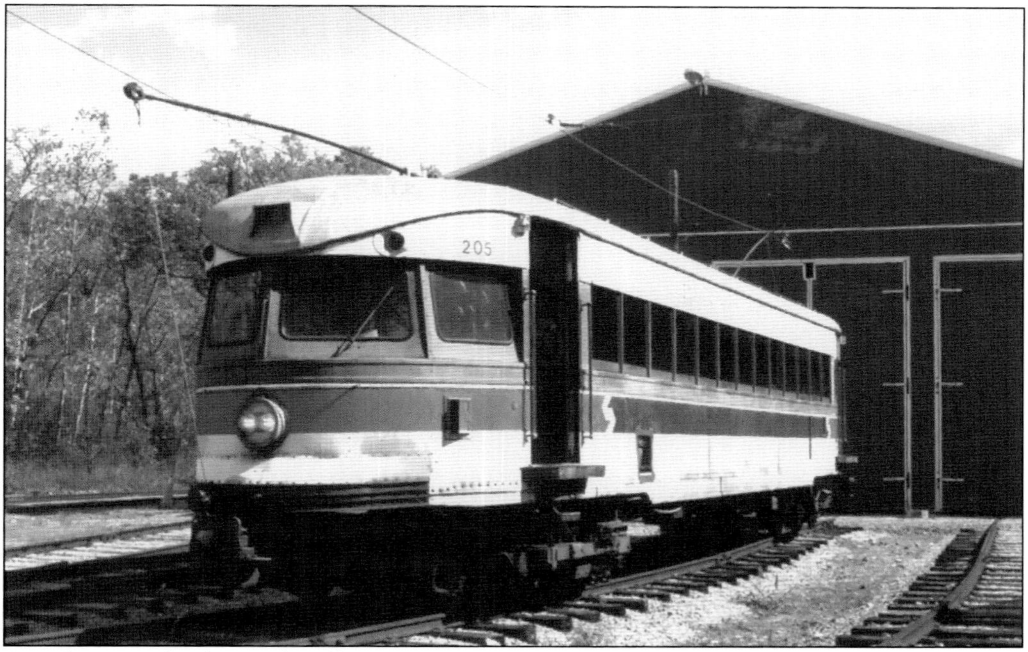

Aerodynamically designed Bullet car No. 205 is parked at the carbarn at the Rockhill Trolley Museum on October 6, 2001, for the next assignment. This car was one of 10 cars built for the Philadelphia and Western Railway's Norristown line by J. G. Brill Car Company each costing $31,000 in 1931. (Photograph by Kenneth C. Springirth.)

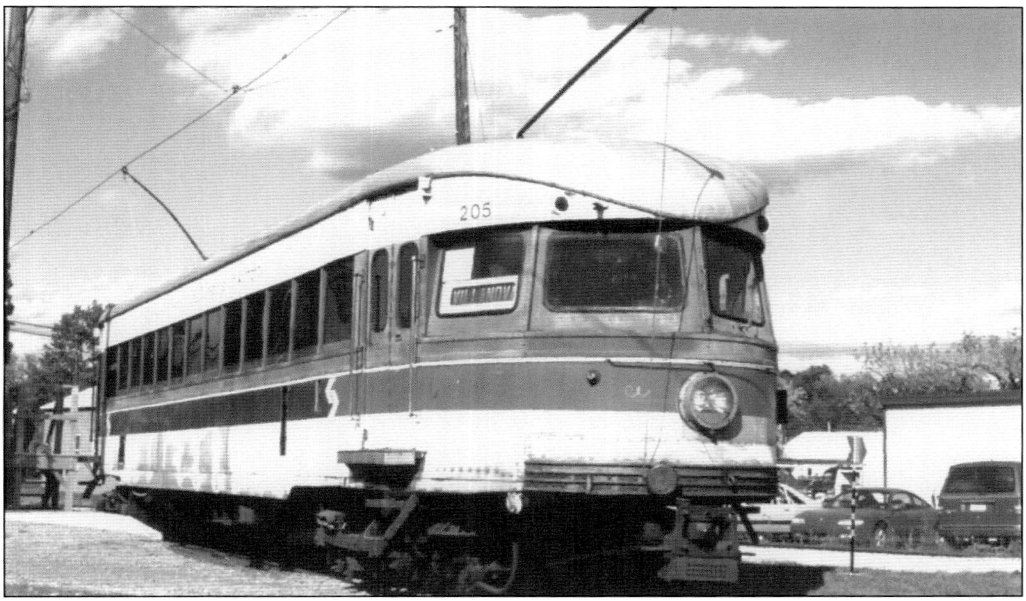

Lightweight aluminum body–designed car No. 205 is at the Rockhill Trolley Museum on October 6, 2001. The museum acquired this car from the Southeastern Pennsylvania Transportation Company in 1990, following 59 years of service. This car was originally built without trolley poles and received power from an electrified third rail. Museum volunteers designed and built the roof supports for the trolley poles. (Photograph by Kenneth C. Springirth.)

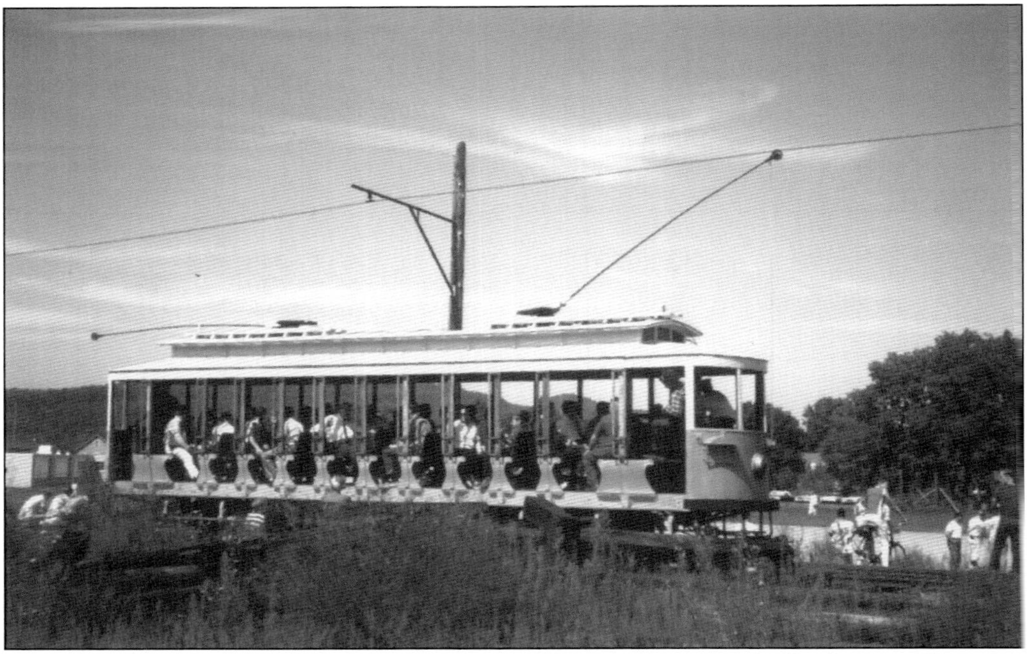

On September 4, 1967, open summer car No. 1875 is operating on the Railways to Yesterday Trolley Museum (Rockhill Trolley Museum today). This car was built in 1912 for Companhia de Transportes Colectivos of Rio de Janeiro, Brazil. It was acquired in 1965 and shipped by boat to New York City, where it went by railroad and truck to the museum. (Photograph by Kenneth C. Springirth.)

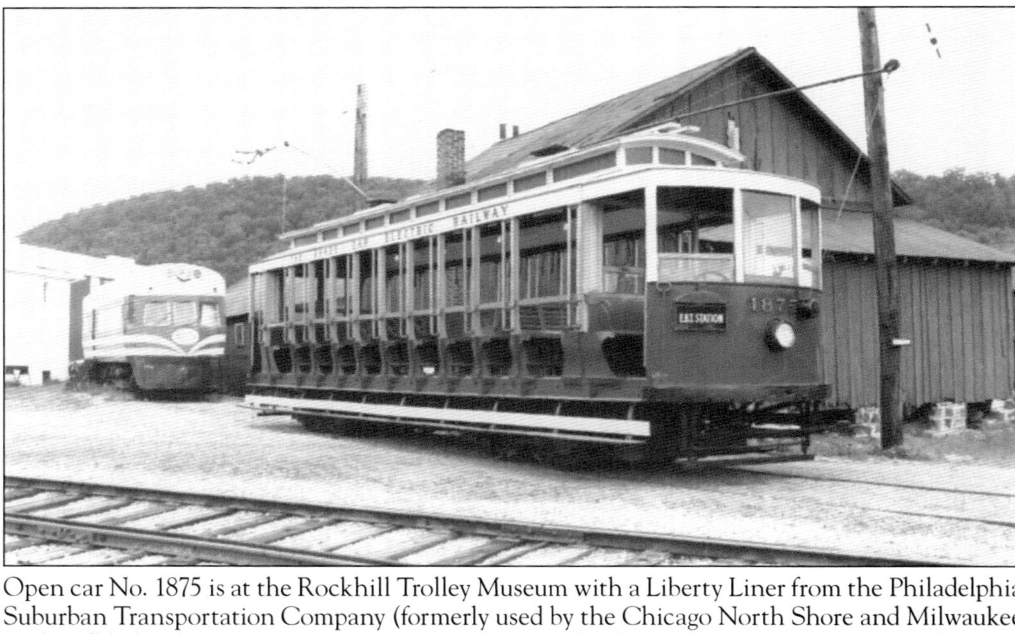

Open car No. 1875 is at the Rockhill Trolley Museum with a Liberty Liner from the Philadelphia Suburban Transportation Company (formerly used by the Chicago North Shore and Milwaukee Railroad) behind it on August 6, 1995. Car No. 1875 was built in 1912 to United States specifications but was assembled in Rio de Janeiro using Brazilian wood. A motorman to operate and conductor to collect the fares were needed for this car. (Photograph by Kenneth C. Springirth.)

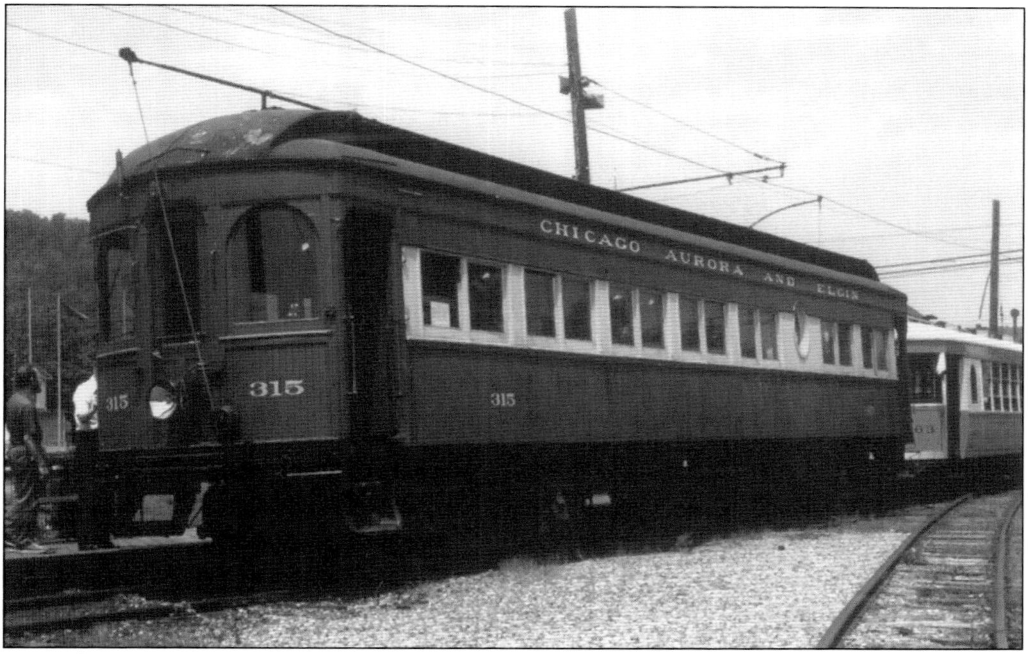

Interurban car No. 315 is shown at the Rockhill Trolley Museum on June 22, 1996. It was built in 1909 by the Kuhlman Car Company for the Aurora, Elgin and Chicago Railroad (which later became the Chicago, Aurora and Elgin Railroad) and was the lead car of the last train operated by that system on July 3, 1957. The Rockhill Trolley Museum acquired this car in 1961. (Photograph by Kenneth C. Springirth.)

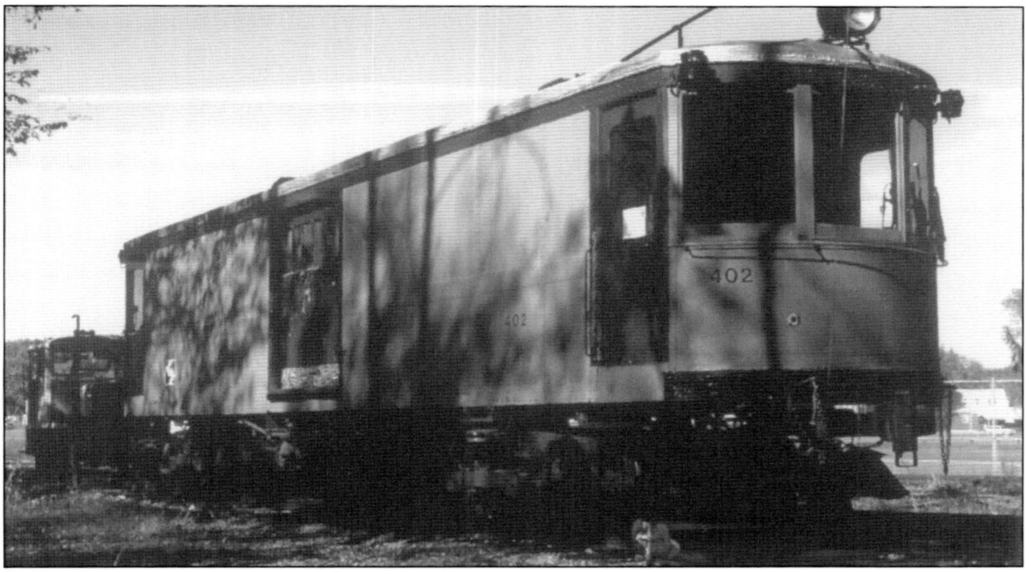

All-steel freight motor car No. 402 is shown at the Rockhill Trolley Museum on October 12, 1996. This single-end car had been used in eastern Michigan. The Philadelphia and Western Railway purchased it in 1943 and converted it to double-end operation for track and right-of-way maintenance, plus retrieving disabled railcars on the line. (Photograph by Kenneth C. Springirth.)

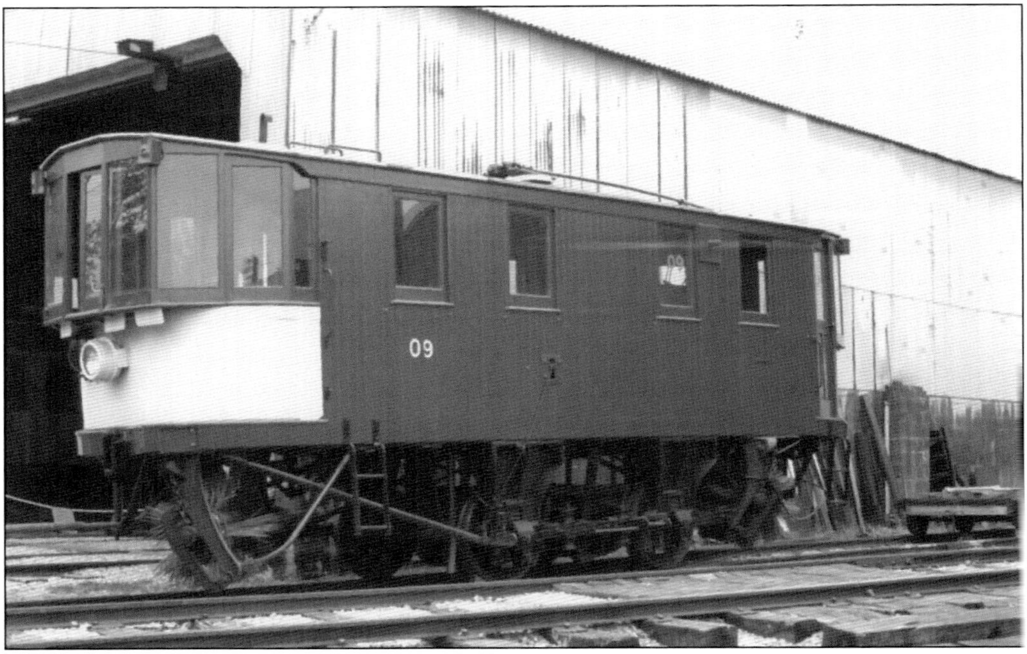

Snow sweeper No. 09 is on the siding at the Rockhill Trolley Museum on October 5, 2006. Built by the McGuire Cummings Manufacturing Company in 1898, this car cleared snow from trolley tracks in Washington, D.C. Following the end of DC Transit trolley car service in Washington, D.C., on January 28, 1962, the Rockhill Trolley Museum purchased this car. (Photograph by Kenneth C. Springirth.)

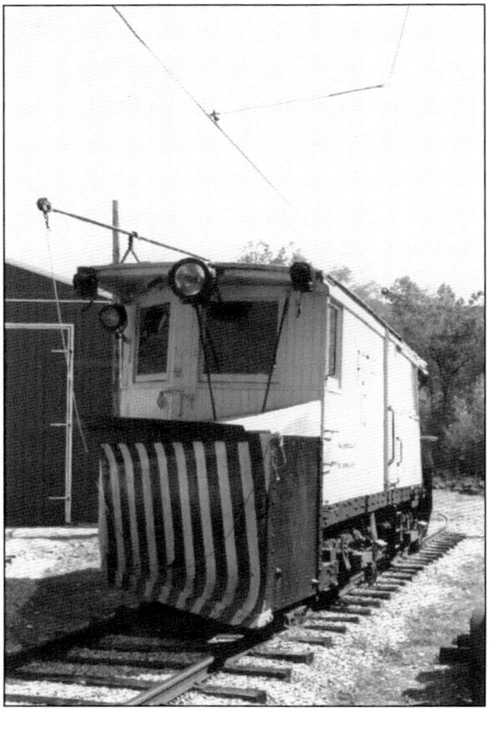

Snowplow No. 10 is basking in the sunshine at the Rockhill Trolley Museum on October 6, 2001. Built by Wason Manufacturing Company of Springfield, Massachusetts, in 1915 for the Philadelphia and Western Railway, this shear-type plow pushed snow to the right side of the track. The museum acquired this car from the Southeastern Pennsylvania Transportation Authority in 1988. (Photograph by Kenneth C. Springirth.)

Snow sweeper No. 107 is shown at the Rockhill Trolley Museum waiting for the next assignment on October 6, 2001. The master mechanic of the Chicago and Joliet Electric Railway built this steeple cab–designed car in 1910. When operations ended in 1933, it was sold to Scranton Railways, which became Scranton Transit on July 27, 1934, and was used until trolley service ended on December 18, 1954. (Photograph by Kenneth C. Springirth.)

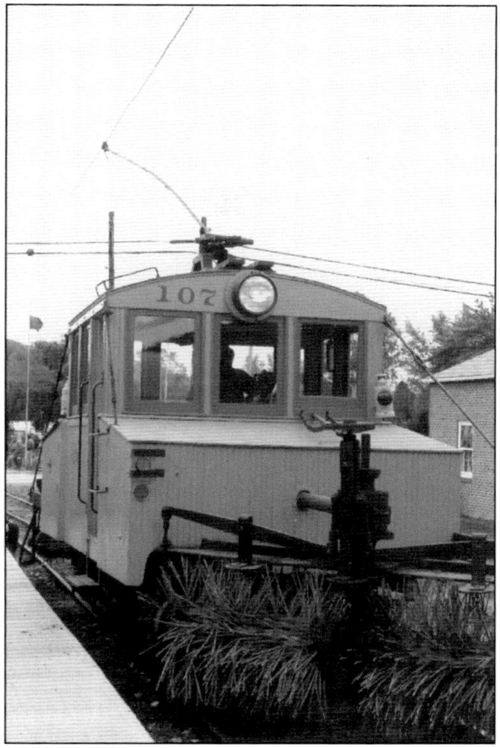

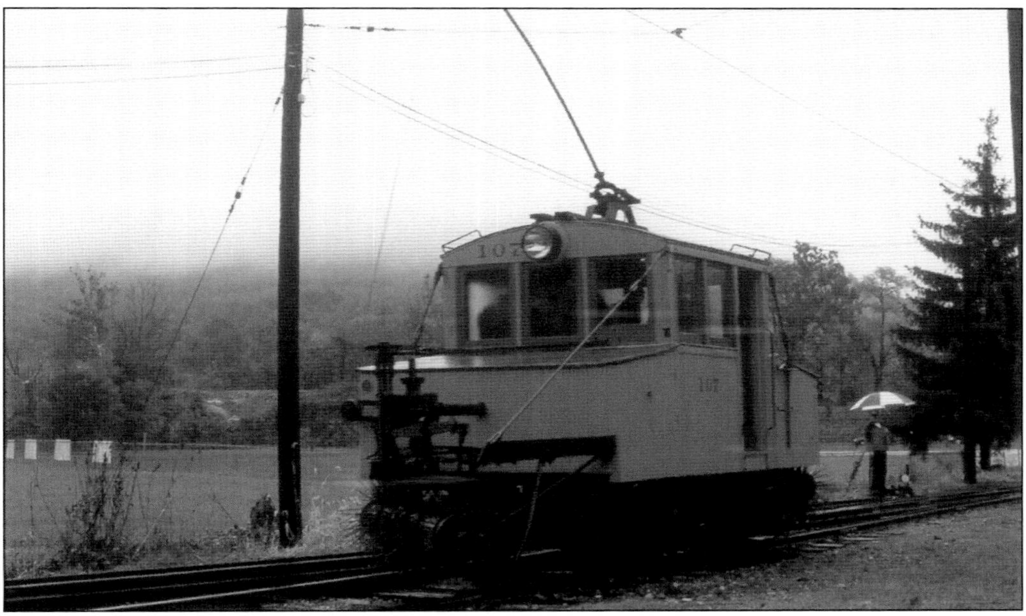

The rain of October 8, 2005, provides the setting for snow sweeper No. 107 at the Rockhill Trolley Museum. Following closure of the Scranton trolley system, the snow sweeper went to the Rail City Museum at Sandy Pond, New York, and later to the Magee Transportation Museum at Bloomsburg, Pennsylvania, until the 1972 Hurricane Agnes flood, which closed the museum. The Rockhill Trolley Museum acquired the car in 1973. (Photograph by Kenneth C. Springirth.)

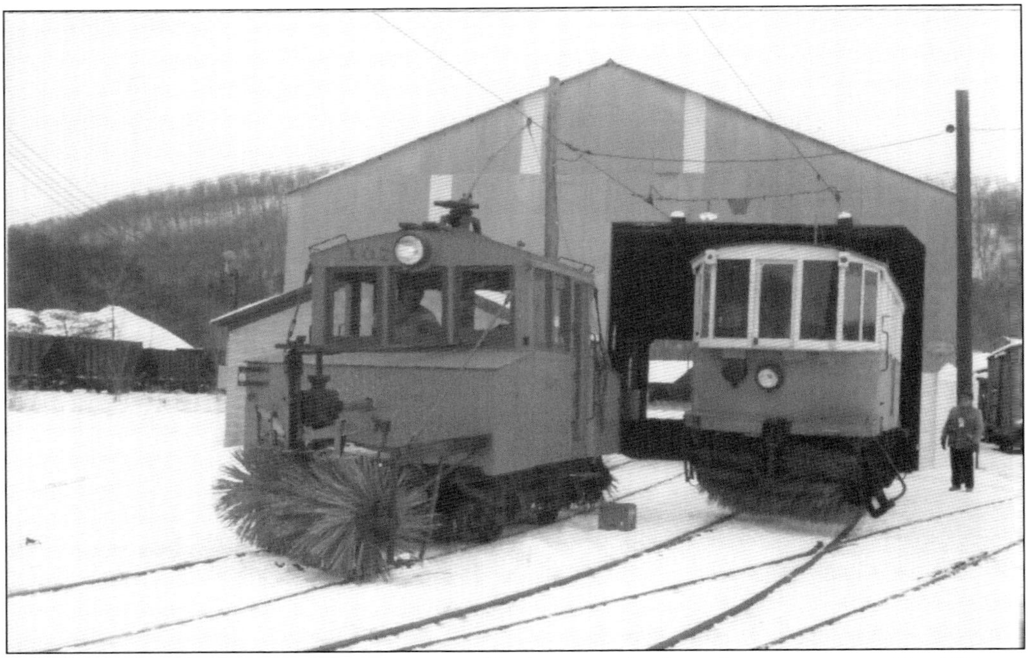

From left to right, Scranton Transit (originally Scranton Railways) snow sweeper No. 107 and DC Transit snow sweeper No. 09 are ready for duty to handle the snow at the Rockhill Trolley Museum for the February 1979 Winter Spectacular. It was quite a sight to view both snow sweepers with their rotating brooms in action. (Photograph by James A. Gillin.)

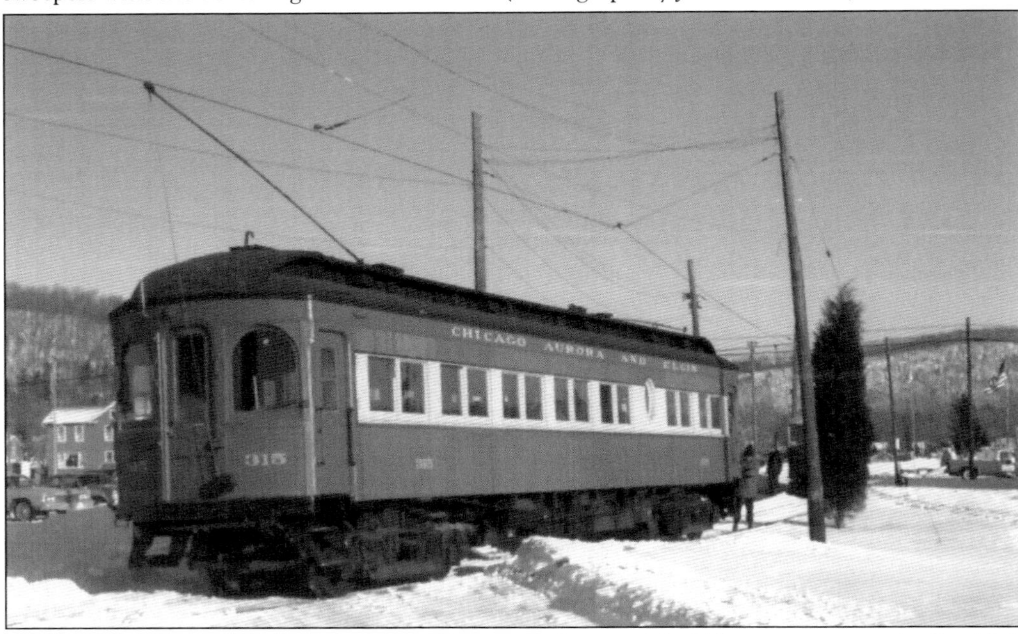

Chicago, Aurora and Elgin Railroad wooden interurban car No. 315 is in service at the Rockhill Trolley Museum for the February 1979 Winter Spectacular. This ornate car has provided an example of the splendor of the interurban era where the trolley car connected cities and provided dependable all-weather transportation. (Photograph by James A. Gillin.)

Emily Wills, Miss Pennsylvania, breaks the ceremonial bottle of champagne on the bumper of car No. 355 on June 9, 2007, during the dedication of this completely rebuilt trolley car at the Rockhill Trolley Museum. Lyons Industries of Ebensburg did the major restoration work with museum volunteers installing the trolley poles and air system and completing electrical work. (Photograph by Kenneth C. Springirth.)

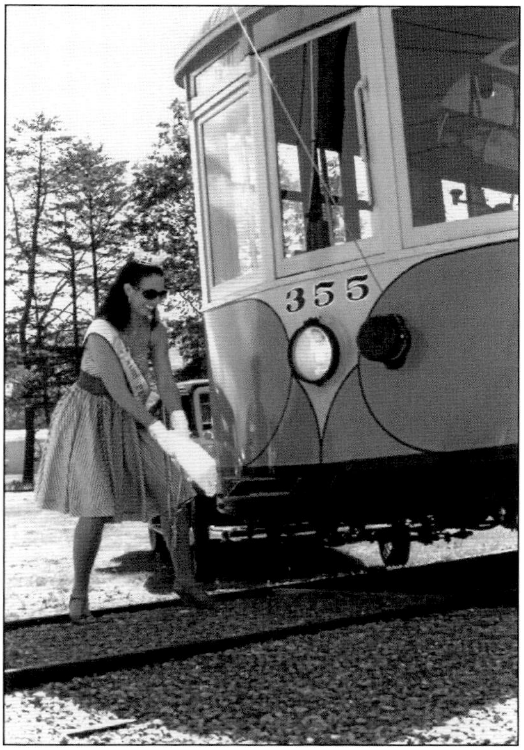

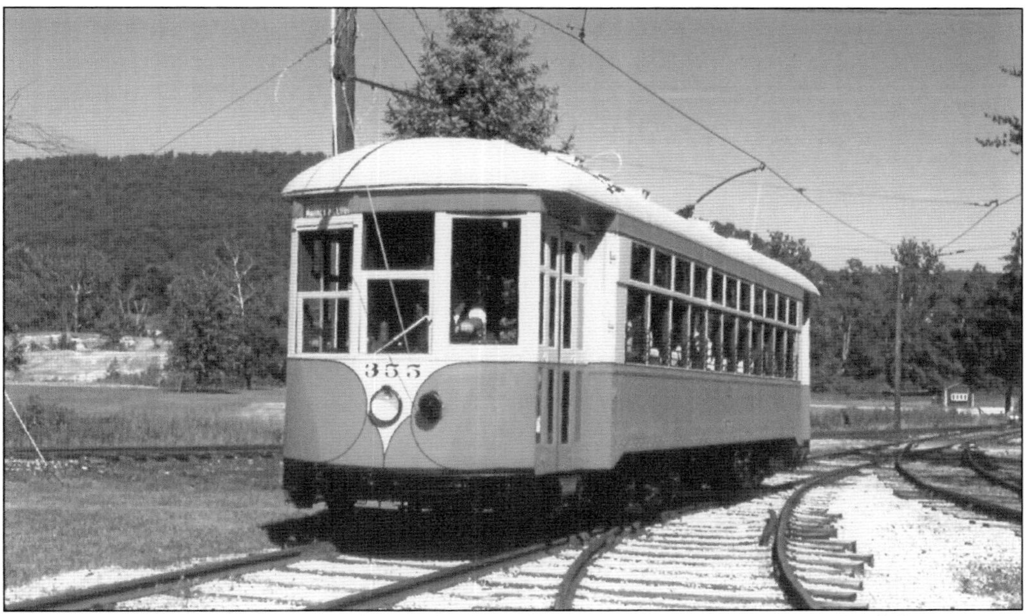

Trolley car No. 355 is pictured at the Rockhill Trolley Museum on June 9, 2007. Built by St. Louis Car Company in 1925 for Johnstown Traction Company as a single-end car and later modified for double-end operation, this car operated on the last day of trolley car service in Johnstown on June 11, 1960, and was acquired by the Rockhill Trolley Museum during 1970. (Photograph by Kenneth C. Springirth.)

Consistent with our mission to preserve history on a local level, this book was printed in South Carolina on American-made paper and manufactured entirely in the United States. Products carrying the accredited Forest Stewardship Council (FSC) label are printed on 100 percent FSC-certified paper.

MADE IN THE USA